The American Crisis Series

Books on the Civil War Era

Steven E. Woodworth, Assistant Professor of History,
Texas Christian University
SERIES EDITOR

∼ The Civil War was the crisis of the Republic's first century
—the test, in Abraham Lincoln's words, of whether any free government could long endure. It touched with fire the hearts of a generation, and its story has fired the imaginations of every generation since.
This series offers to students of the Civil War, either those continu-
ing or those just beginning their exciting journey into the past, con-
cise overviews of important persons, events, and themes in that
remarkable period of America's history.

Volumes Published

James L. Abrahamson. *The Men of Secession and Civil War, 1859–1861*
(2000). Cloth ISBN 0-8420-2818-8 Paper ISBN 0-8420-2819-6

Robert G. Tanner. *Retreat to Victory? Confederate Strategy Reconsidered*
(2001). Cloth ISBN 0-8420-2881-1 Paper ISBN 0-8420-2882-X

Stephen Davis. *Atlanta Will Fall: Sherman, Joe Johnston, and the
Yankee Heavy Battalions* (2001). Cloth ISBN 0-8420-2787-4
Paper ISBN 0-8420-2788-2

Paul Ashdown and Edward Caudill. *The Mosby Myth: A Confederate
Hero in Life and Legend* (2002). Cloth ISBN 0-8420-2928-1
Paper ISBN 0-8420-2929-X

Atlanta Will Fall

Atlanta Will Fall

Sherman, Joe Johnston, and the Yankee Heavy Battalions

The American Crisis Series

BOOKS ON THE CIVIL WAR ERA

NO. 3

Stephen Davis

A Scholarly Resources Inc. Imprint
Wilmington, Delaware

Scholarly Resources Inc.
104 Greenhill Avenue
Wilmington, DE 19805-1897
www.scholarly.com

Library of Congress Cataloging-in-Publication Data

Davis, Stephen, 1948–
   Atlanta will fall : Sherman, Joe Johnston, and the Yankee
heavy battalions / Stephen Davis.
      p.   cm. — (American crisis series ; no. 3)
   Includes bibliographical references (p.) and index.
   ISBN 0-8420-2787-4 (alk. paper) — ISBN 0-8420-2788-2 (pbk. :
alk. paper)
   1. Atlanta Campaign, 1864.   2. United States—History—
Civil War, 1861–1865—Artillery operations.   3. Sherman,
William T. (William Tecumseh), 1820–1891.   4. Johnston,
Joseph E. (Joseph Eggleston), 1807–1891.   5. Hood, John Bell,
1831–1879.   I. Title.   II. Series.

E476.7 .D38 2001
973.7'371–dc21   00-066108

For my great sons, Lawrence and Paul

y'all swell

Author's Foreword

A word about the theme of this book, its organization, and my entitling of it. I happen to think that by the time General J. B. Hood took command of the Confederate army defending Atlanta, on the morning of July 18, 1864—when enemy forces were just five miles from the city suburbs, when his 50,000 outnumbered troops faced 80,000 Yankees—he was without realistic strategic options. He explored every tactical opportunity he could and achieved some measure of success in just holding out as long as he did. But we must conclude that when Hood took command, the fall of Atlanta was foregone. Hood's predecessor, General Joseph E. Johnston, had allowed General William T. Sherman's armies to advance a hundred miles into Georgia across three major river barriers and had fought no major engagement to stop them. If the South had any realistic chance of saving Atlanta, it belonged to Joe Johnston, and he had squandered it. Thus, I place the responsibility for the fall of Atlanta not with Hood (he just happened to be on watch) but with Joe Johnston.

Yet the responsibility was not with Johnston alone. Throughout the campaign Sherman possessed such numerical strength, such sharp strategic thinking, such confidence, logistical mastery, and aggressive determination, that the combination of these advantages against Johnston's passivity combined to determine the outcome of the campaign. This inevitability—I use the word despite historians' almost universal reluctance to term any event "inevitable"—had been seen as early as late May, when the Southern newspaper correspondent Henry Watterson, writing as "Shadow" from Atlanta, predicted, "Atlanta will fall." He gave three reasons: Sherman's superb generalship, the Yankees' numerical superiority, and (though he skirted the words) a supine, even timid Confederate army leadership. Hence, my title "Atlanta Will Fall: Sherman, Joe Johnston, and the Yankee Heavy Battalions."

What, then, was there left for Hood to do? The second part of my study takes on a slightly different form from the first, which is a more conventional narrative of how Johnston came to give up his chances for success. Because I believe Hood assumed command without any real chance of success, I have given Part Two the style of an extended essay about why I think John Bell Hood has been handed essentially a bum rap for the fall of Atlanta. Faced with impossible odds, he manfully did all he could to prevent the inevitable outcome. At the very least, Hood accomplished what his government and country expected of him: simply, as President Jefferson Davis put it, not to give up Atlanta without a fight. More, Hood actually achieved a measure of tactical success in his first six weeks of command, leading some Southerners (and Yankees) to think that maybe Atlanta *could* hold out till after the North's election day. Indeed, by mid-1864, the South's hope for any measure of victory lay in denying the Republicans a big military success, without which they could not justify prolonging the war. But when Sherman's smart, aggressive strategy and his superior numbers combined to force the Confederates to abandon the city, and the North's President Abraham Lincoln won election two months later and ... well, we all know the end of the story.

CONTENTS

JOHNSTON'S RETREAT TO ATLANTA; OR, A SMART AND SCRAPPY SHERMAN USES HIS STRENGTH TO COW AND BLUDGEON AN OUTNUMBERED, LESS RESOLUTE OPPONENT

CHAPTER ONE

Introduction: The Sherman-Johnston Match-up in Mississippi, July 1863, as Omen of Atlanta's Fall

I observe my own feeling on the subject, and I think
Atlanta will fall.
—"Shadow" [Henry Watterson], "Letter from Atlanta,"
   May 24, 1864

EVEN A NONCOMBATANT could see it coming. Three weeks into Major General William Tecumseh Sherman's campaign against General Joseph E. Johnston, the ardently pro-Southern veteran journalist Henry Watterson, writing as "Shadow" for a Mobile, Alabama, newspaper in May 1864, predicted the fall of Atlanta.

> You want to know, I suspect, my candid opinion of the real situation of Atlanta. I will tell you frankly. I do regard the city as in imminent danger. . . . I observe my own feeling on the subject, and I think Atlanta will fall. But, on the other hand, there is a chance for a battle upon the Chattahoochie, and if we fight there, our show for victory is excellent. We may repel every effort to flank us, and we may win a decisive action. Then are we safe. Still it appears to be very much the other way, when we consider that Sherman has succeeded in a series of flank movements from Dalton down. What, we very naturally inquire, is to prevent a continuance of the same?—As yet the matter is undeveloped, and while there is life there is hope. The enemy's strength is one hundred thousand. They are well handled. I know nothing at all of our strength, but I should estimate it at a lower figure. The next ten days will decide everything.[1]

Although Watterson did not report Johnston's strength, he knew the Yankees enjoyed numerical superiority and that Sherman's forces were "well handled"—the enemy commander was capable and not prone to blunder. And though he said nothing about the Confederate leadership, he expressed some doubt about Johnston's talent as an army commander. Thus Watterson identified the three reasons Atlanta would indeed fall: Sherman's talent, Johnston's passivity, and the Northerners' numerical strength.

Even before the spring of 1864, the war had already pitched Sherman, Johnston, and the Yankees' heavy battalions together in a confrontation that reinforced Watterson's prediction. It had occurred in mid-1863 in Mississippi when Sherman commanded one of three corps in General Ulysses S. Grant's army, just after Grant's capture of Vicksburg, the key Mississippi River fortress. A West Pointer with thirteen years' army service, Cump, as Sherman was known, had blossomed under Grant's friendship and guidance. Sherman's first year in the war, however, had been mediocre—worse than mediocre, given his relief from command in Kentucky, November 1861, for a well-publicized collapse of self-confidence that was described at the time as a nervous breakdown. Returned to duty three months later and thrown into association with General Grant, Sherman did well, serving first in the bruising battle of Shiloh, Tennessee. In summer 1862, as military governor of Memphis, he developed his now famous views on "hard war"—the need to push to Union victory by considering the entire Southern populace as an extension of the Rebel armies. His resolve grew stronger when he served as corps commander under Grant, as the latter began his long campaign to capture Vicksburg, the key Rebel fortress on the Mississippi. Once the Federal forces had pressed in, in mid-May 1863, and ringed the river city in siege lines, Sherman's main task was to guard against any approach of Rebel reinforcements from the east. A small Confederate army Johnston had assembled in the center of the state was hovering well east of Vicksburg at the time of the surrender. Grant ordered Sherman to march east, push Johnston back, and rip up the railroads around Jackson, the state capital.

Sherman fulfilled this order in a two-week campaign that previewed the Sherman-Johnston match-up in north Georgia ten months later. Reinforced and leading an army of 46,000, Sherman started marching on July 4, the very day Grant received Vicksburg's surrender. Johnston, commanding about 23,000 men and thus outnumbered 2 to 1, had no intention of seriously opposing the Federal advance. He marched his troops straight back to Jackson, where they dug in and awaited the enemy. What were Johnston's plans? In a message to his troops July 9, he spoke of sustaining a "pledge" and staying with his men "unto the end," but beyond that the general's message was vagueness itself—very telling.

Arriving outside Jackson, Sherman began deploying his forces in semi-siege lines on July 10. Refusing to attack the Rebels in their works, he ordered his commanders to press the enemy constantly, gaining ground in little sorties wherever opportunity allowed. Union artillery also pounded the Confederate lines and the city of Jackson itself. Meanwhile Sherman ordered cavalry detachments to both the south and the north in order to cut the railroads emanating from Jackson. If the siege dragged on Sherman could hope that shortage of supplies might compel Johnston to evacuate and retreat.

Committed to his passive defense but fearing failure, General Johnston fretted, and in daily letters to President Jefferson Davis, he vented freely. A Federal bombardment on July 12 demonstrated the "weakness" of his position and its "untenableness against a powerful artillery." "If the position and works were not bad," he wrote the next day, "want of stores (which could not be collected) would make it impossible to stand a siege." Then, if weak position or scanty stores did not do him in, he could be flanked. An enemy column reportedly marching against his right, he informed the president on the 14th, "will compel us to abandon Jackson." "If the enemy will not attack, we must, or at the last moment withdraw." Significantly, however, he added, "We cannot attack seriously without risking the army." This message of the 13th was reinforced two days later: "The enemy will not attack but has intrenched [and] is evidently making a siege which we cannot resist. It would be madness to attack him."[2]

To Johnston's credit, when he heard on July 14 that a Union wagon train from Vicksburg was bringing artillery ammunition to Sherman's army, he dispatched cavalry behind Union lines to attack it. The Federals, however, were forewarned. Grant sent a strong escort with the train, and Sherman sent reinforcements back to join a garrison he had left along the wagon route. As a result, the Southerners approached the train, but feeling unable to attack it, they withdrew.

In this game of nerves between the two leaders, Sherman was enforcing his will and Johnston was buckling. While the Confederate leader passively awaited his fate, Sherman persisted in putting together a winning combination of tactics. If infantry pressure or cavalry raids would not shake the Rebels out of Jackson, then, he reasoned, continued artillery bombardment might at least provoke them into making a foolhardy attack. He therefore gave orders on July 14 for a general "artillery practice," a "steady, unceasing crossfire" of rifled cannon aimed at the town and the Pearl River bridge while smoothbore Napoleons pounded the enemy works—shots every five minutes, around the clock. In directing fire against the town itself, as well as the enemy forts or troops, Sherman intended to force Johnston out of Jackson. He wrote to Grant on July 14 that with enough artillery ammunition, "I can make the town too hot to hold him."[3]

Sherman's plan worked. The Union artillery fired as ordered on the 15th. The next day Johnston learned that the Yankees would be receiving their big ammunition train and therefore would likely step up their bombardment. When he also learned that day that the enemy had crossed the Pearl River beyond his right, Johnston felt more vulnerable than ever and announced that the time had come to evacuate Jackson. The Confederates withdrew on the night of July 16–17 eastward toward Brandon.

A comparison of Johnston's and Sherman's conduct of their operations in the Jackson Campaign of July 4–17, 1863, shows General Johnston to be the weaker, less resourceful of the two. Faced with superior enemy numbers, Johnston fell back quickly to Jackson when he discerned no strong defensive position at which to fortify and offer battle. At that point, he held his army inertly in the state capital's defenses, hoping the Federals would attack. When they did not, the Confederate commander had to decide between two courses of action: launch an attack himself or abandon the city. In the end, outnumbered and fearing that Sherman would use his superior strength to outflank him or cut off his supplies, Johnston caved in. In retrospect his conduct boded ill for the Confederacy as the two leaders moved toward their next confrontation in northern Georgia.

The Jackson Campaign, in contrast, shows Sherman to be smart, scrappy, and skilled in his use of his superior numbers. Though by temperament an energetic, impatient man, he was not rash. Faced with an enemy, even an outnumbered one, behind defensive works, he avoided costly, fruitless assaults. Instead, he chose to pressure his foe with lines pushed constantly closer, daily skirmishes, occasional reconnaissances-in-force, and a sustained artillery bombardment. Sherman also sent his available horsemen off from both flanks to break the rail lines entering Jackson from north and south. Clearly, logistical considerations were a top priority in Sherman's strategy. Furthermore, he took steps to ensure that the Rebels could not do to him what he wanted to do to them. Johnston's half-hearted effort to intercept the Union ammunition train with a small cavalry raid, July 14–16, failed mainly because Sherman kept or detached sufficient forces in his rear to thwart the Rebel raiders. Finally, all along the way, General Sherman radiated confidence in his ability to win. While Johnston throughout the semi-siege lamented his troubles and weakness, Sherman sent back to Grant at Vicksburg a series of self-assured, even cocky messages: "All is well with me now" (July 12); "All well with us" (July 13); "All is well with us" (July 14).[4]

Underpinning this confidence was Sherman's knowledge that he could use his superior numbers to flank Johnston's stronghold, threaten his communications, and force the issue. He even began to predict the Rebels' retreat. "If Johnston is going to make a retrograde movement," Sherman wrote on the night of July 15, "I hope to detect it promptly." When he did so, Sherman was not surprised. "General Johnston evacuated Jackson last night" was Sherman's laconic telegram to Grant at dawn of the 17th. The campaign was over; of its outcome the Union commanding general seemingly had had no doubt all along.[5]

Chapter Two

How Joe Johnston Earned His Reputation for Retreating

To FIND FURTHER OMENS of the outcome of the Atlanta Campaign, one need only survey General Joseph E. Johnston's prior performance as a Confederate army commander, especially in Virginia during 1861–62. There he established an unfortunate reputation for strategic and tactical hypercautiousness, incommunicativeness, and cantankerousness toward his commander in chief, as well as a predisposition to the retrograde—so much so that well before the Atlanta Campaign, Johnston had developed a reputation for retreating. Here is how he earned it.

For his long service in the old army, Johnston received a brigadier general's commission in the Confederate army in mid-May 1861. With the commission came a field command, the second most important one in Virginia: the Confederate force at Harpers Ferry, guarding the lower entrance to the vital Shenandoah Valley. Arriving at Harpers Ferry in late May, Johnston quickly and rightly discerned that the place could not be held against enemy crossings of the Potomac River upstream or down. He therefore held the town as long as he could, three weeks, before movements of the larger Federal force across the river compelled him to withdraw. During those weeks, however, Johnston seemed insistent, to an extent not altogether flattering to himself, that he not be held accountable for ordering any retreat. He sent a series of messages to headquarters in Richmond, explaining his difficulties and asking for instructions. Finally, Adjutant General Samuel Cooper came to the point: "As you seem to desire . . . that the responsibility of your retirement should be assumed here, . . . you will consider yourself authorized, whenever the position of the enemy shall convince you that he is about to turn your position . . . to destroy everything at Harper's Ferry . . . and retire upon the railroad towards Winchester."[6]

Thus, the war was barely a month old, and already Johnston was demonstrating what may be seen as a weakness of character: an apparent predisposition to retreat, coupled with reluctance to be blamed for his actions. Quite soon, however, he was able to bask in the glow of the first great Confederate victory of the war, the battle of Manassas. After withdrawing his forces (five brigades, 9,000 men) from the Valley, he joined General P. G. T. Beauregard's army at Manassas. Although Johnston was the senior officer, he allowed Beauregard to assume tactical field command when the Yankees attacked the next day, July 21. Johnston himself played a key role directing troops to the fighting on the Confederate left, which he rightly recognized was the decisive part of the field.

After the Southern victory, however, Johnston lapsed into an unseemly pettiness in his quest for verification of seniority with other officers. Based on Confederate legislation passed that spring, Johnston had reason to believe that he was the senior ranking general in the Confederate army, second only to the commander in chief himself, President Jefferson Davis. When Davis submitted to the Senate in late August his five nominations for general's commission, he dated their seniority in such a way that Johnston, instead of being first, came out fourth in line. Surprised, embarrassed, and angry, Johnston expressed his indignation in a letter of September 12 to the president, who replied with a short, sharp letter of his own. This letter ended the correspondence over Johnston's rank; but the disagreement and verbal firefight between Johnston and Davis of September 1861 also ended their previously cordial, even warm relationship. Thereafter, in their dealings with each other, both men were increasingly distrustful and distant.

The enmity was slow to build, however, and Davis, for a while, maintained confidence in Johnston. He transferred Beauregard to the western theater and gave Johnston command of the "Army of the Potomac," 40,000 strong, the main Confederate force in Virginia. Throughout the summer Johnston's army held lines near Centreville. Then, by order dated October 22, 1861, the administration put Johnston in command of the new, larger Department of Northern Virginia. To Johnston's Army and District of the Potomac were added those forces under General Thomas J. (Stonewall) Jackson in the lower Shenandoah Valley and Major General Theophilus Holmes north of Fredericksburg.

Charged with holding northern Virginia, Johnston knew it would be only a matter of time before his forces must retreat before General George B. McClellan's Union Army of the Potomac around Washington, 100,000 strong. In fact, on February 19, 1862, Johnston met with Davis and his Cabinet to discuss the timing of the army's prospective retreat. When it did pull back, March 8–9, to behind the Rappahannock River, the movement seems to have caught Davis off guard. Johnston waited till March 13, after the retreat was completed, to write to the president, who rather icily acknowledged receipt of the letter as "the first information of your retrograde movement." Just as galling was the large loss of property resulting from Johnston's retreat, which could not be removed by rail or road: heavy artillery, thousands of pounds of cured meat, and much baggage belonging to the officers and men. Loss of personal belongings caused much grumbling against Johnston; some of the complaints reached Davis. But the president's main criticism was that his general had left him uninformed. "Before the receipt of yours of the 13th I was as much in the dark as to your purposes, condition and necessities as at the time of our conversation on the subject about a month since," Davis wrote, referring to the Cabinet meeting of February 19. His import was unmistakable: the president suspected that his chief field general in Virginia, leading the army that was guarding the Confederate capital, was keeping his plans secret or selectively hidden, especially when they involved a retreat. In the face of these developments, Johnston should not have been surprised to learn that effective March 13, General Robert E. Lee was henceforth "under the direction of the President, charged with the conduct of military operations in the armies of the Confederacy." Actually, the timing of this order was coincidental, reflecting Davis's efforts to quiet his critics in the Confederate Congress, who wanted a general of Lee's experience to assist the president in formulating Confederate strategy. But as a longtime friend of "Old Joe," Lee would also help the president communicate with the sometimes peculiarly uncommunicative Johnston.[7]

Even Lee and Johnston, as it turned out, were not able to agree on how to respond to the impending advance of the enemy forces. On March 17 McClellan began moving his Army of the Potomac from the vicinity of Washington down the Chesapeake Bay to landings near Fort Monroe, at the tip of the Peninsula, which was formed by the James and York Rivers. As McClellan's intentions to advance up the Peninsula with his whole army became clear, Johnston's command was enlarged to include the Peninsula, and Confederate forces began concentrating there. To form strategy, Johnston met with Davis and Lee on April 14 in Richmond. At the meeting, Johnston advocated abandoning the lower Peninsula in favor of concentrating in front of Richmond, with troops brought from the Shenandoah Valley and as far away as the Carolinas. Only then, after McClellan had been drawn as far as possible from his base, did Johnston believe the campaign should be decided in a pitched battle before the capital. Such was Johnston's strategic outlook: when faced by a numerically superior enemy, withdraw to the main objective, concentrate all available forces, and fight the decisive battle where the enemy would be as far removed from his source of supplies and reinforcements as possible. In spring 1862 that strategy meant right outside the nation's capital; but Johnston seemed oblivious to the anxieties such proximity would create in President Davis. At least partly for this reason, Lee argued against the plan, stressing that the enemy should be held as long as possible on the lower Peninsula and that other parts of the Confederacy could not be left defenseless. The president sided with Lee.

So ordered, Johnston held his lines near Yorktown another three weeks, aided immensely by McClellan's commitment to a formal siege and preparation for a huge artillery bombardment. During this period, in late April, Johnston reminded Lee repeatedly of his intent to fall back on Richmond. Hints of pessimism, even defeatism, tinged these messages, such as one on April 29 when Johnston warned that McClellan's impending barrage would begin a fight "which we cannot win. The result is certain; the time only doubtful." Worse, if the Yankees used their naval strength to advance up the James River, "the fall of Richmond would be inevitable, unless we anticipate it." With McClellan's siege artillery about to open fire in the first week of May, Johnston cagily planned his withdrawal, informing the president on May 1: "We can do nothing here. . . . The enemy will give us no chance to win. We *must* lose. By delay we may insure the loss of Richmond too."[8]

When Johnston evacuated his lines at Yorktown, May 3–4, he did so skillfully and stealthily. Thereafter, he moved his army as fast as he could up the Peninsula toward Richmond, fearing the Federals' use of river transport to lodge troops on his flanks. By May 9, Johnston had taken his army to a line within twenty miles of the Confederate capital. McClellan and his 100,000 men were marching slowly but inexorably toward Richmond. Justifiably concerned, President Davis and General Lee visited Johnston at his headquarters on the 12th to hear his plans. Johnston, however, gave them nothing more specific than his intent to await McClellan's approach and look for an opportunity to give battle.

On May 15, Johnston ordered his forces back across the Chickahominy. The Confederates burned the river bridges and in the next several days moved almost to the outskirts of Richmond. (General McClellan himself was surprised that the Rebels did not attempt a defense of the river. Unless Johnston "has some deep laid scheme that I do not fathom," McClellan wrote on May 22, "he is giving up a great advantage in not opposing me on the line of the Chickahominy.") With the enemy drawing nearer daily, the president grew

ever more anxious to know his field commander's plans. Both he and
Lee wrote to Johnston on the 17th, the president sending his letter by
courier. Johnston, unfortunately, chose not to reply. Only on May 18
did Davis learn that, far from contesting McClellan's crossing of the
Chickahominy (the president's hope and expectation), Johnston had
given up his position near the river and some of his troops were now
camped in the virtual suburbs of the capital. Surprised and distressed, Davis rode to army headquarters on the 18th and asked
Johnston bluntly whether he planned to give up Richmond without
a fight. The general's answer was hedged with contingencies. Later
that day Davis asked Lee to write, asking Johnston to come into the
city and explain his plans. The general, in an almost insubordinate
show of determination, did not, instead sending to headquarters on
May 19–20 two missives that did not at all disclose his intentions.
Finally, on the 21st, Davis again had Lee write, this time more
directly: "The President desires to know . . . the programme of operations which you propose. . . . Your plan of operations dependent
upon circumstances perhaps yet to be developed, may not be so
easily explained, nor may it be prudent to commit to paper. I would
therefore respectfully suggest that you communicate your views on
this subject directly to the President." Even to this Johnston chose
not to reply directly, sending a letter to Lee on May 22 that revealed
nothing of how he planned to drive McClellan back. This time Davis
himself wrote to Johnston, on the 23d, hinting his belief that Confederate dispositions were in disarray or at least were without obvious purpose; he based his insinuations on a horseback ride he had
conducted personally along part of the Confederate lines.[9]

On the 23d, Johnston finally met with Lee and disclosed that he
had begun to plan an attack. The next day, in a meeting in Richmond,
Johnston announced to the president himself his intentions, based
upon the enemy's recent dispositions. McClellan had brought his
army to within just ten miles of Richmond, positioning it on both
sides of the Chickahominy—three corps on the north bank, two on
the south. This split gave Johnston's forces, now reinforced to 75,000,
an opportunity to assault part of the Yankee army while the rest of
it stood by, unable to assist. But for several days Johnston wrestled
with the question of which part to attack, and when he met with Lee
on the 26th he was still undecided. (Obligingly, General McClellan
gave Johnston all the time he needed. The Federal commander's

plan was to bring up his heavy artillery, as he had prepared to do at Yorktown, and bombard the Rebels from siege lines.) After finally setting the date for the battle (Thursday, May 29), Johnston decided that rather than attack on the north bank, he would assail the smaller enemy force near Seven Pines, a crossroads on the south side of the river. Because of this shift in objective, Johnston launched his attack not on the 29th but on the 31st.

The resulting battle of Seven Pines (called Fair Oaks by Northerners, after a nearby rail station) failed to meet Johnston's hopes. Sound in concept, his plan called for up to 21 Confederate brigades to crush a single Union corps. As it happened, though, the assault columns became jumbled and most of Johnston's force never saw action. The Confederate attack achieved some initial success, driving the enemy back, but then it lost momentum. Toward the end of the day Johnston realized that the battle would have to be renewed on the morrow, despite the fact that McClellan could by then feed reinforcements from north of the Chickahominy. But Johnston would not oversee the second day's fighting. Riding to the battlefront about 6:00 P.M. on the 31st, he received a musket-ball flesh wound in his right shoulder, then was struck more seriously by shell fragments in the chest and thigh. The general was borne from the field on a stretcher, treated, and carried into Richmond. In his absence, the next morning his second in command, Major General Gustavus W. Smith, resumed the fight with no decisive result; Robert E. Lee arrived to take command that afternoon and ordered the army back to its original positions.

By reviewing Johnston's management of the Peninsula Campaign, one can draw a number of inferences about his strategic and tactical sense. First, in the face of the enemy's numerical superiority, Johnston called for a concentration of all available troops in front of the strategic prize (at this point, the city of Richmond), and there the waging of the decisive battle. He had lost the debate with Lee in the important conference of April 14, when the latter argued for a delaying defense of the lower Peninsula to gain time (which Lee used, incidentally, to assemble reinforcements for Johnston's army). But then, after holding his Yorktown lines for three weeks, Johnston retreated rapidly up the Peninsula, without seeking an opportunity to give battle. Even the cautious McClellan was moved to remark on this lack of pugnacity, at least concerning Johnston's abandonment of the Chickahominy as a place to offer battle. In sum, from mid-April to late May, Johnston found ways to manage events to conform to his strategic concept—falling back before Richmond, and there looking for an advantageous fight. When events turned out as he had wished, Johnston could not resist rubbing it in to his superiors. "I have more than once," he reminded Lee in a letter of May 28, "suggested a concentration here of all available forces."[10]

Second, with regard to the strategic prize itself, the city of Richmond, General Johnston at times displayed a remarkable nonchalance that shows up in his communiqués to Lee and Davis in late April and early May in which he envisions scenarios for the fall of the nation's capital. In truth, the president, his Cabinet, and General Lee were forced at one point to discuss contingency plans for such a disaster, but it is noteworthy, as a commentary on the differences between Johnston and Lee, that the latter brought an abrupt end to such discussions with his tearful, angry exclamation, "Richmond must not be given up!" How great a contrast was the attitude of General Johnston in his letter to Lee of April 30, in which he confessed, "We are engaged in a species of warfare at which we can never win." Johnston went on to say that McClellan, as he had done at Yorktown, would "depend for success upon artillery and engineering. We can compete with him in neither." The dispirited general further forecast, "We can have no success while McClellan is allowed, as he is by our defensive, to choose his mode of warfare"; yet Johnston did that very thing—stayed on the defensive and let McClellan choose his mode of warfare.[11] Having predicted the fall of Richmond in his earlier letters, Johnston now seemed inclined to wish his prophecy to fulfillment—indeed, it could have been argued he almost wanted it to happen.

Just as Johnston seemed to overlook the disastrous psychological effect of the loss of Richmond upon the Confederate war effort, so too did he apparently fail to heed how his fifty-mile retrograde from Yorktown to Richmond might demoralize his troops and the Southern citizenry as a whole. The literature is filled with unhappy expressions from Johnston's soldiers, such as that of John Tucker, private in the Fifth Alabama Infantry, who recorded in his diary, after having marched through the town of Williamsburg, "All the eligible places in the buildings were crowded with men women & children all of whom wore a countenance of Sadness & deep regret.

They knew we were on the retreat and . . . [were] burning with a feeling of humiliation at the prospect of their quiet firesides soon being visited by a set of 'yankee Marauders' & made desolate."[12]

Perhaps most obvious was Johnston's damaging disposition to keep his commander in chief in the dark. After changing the plans for his attack, Johnston did not notify Davis, who on the originally designated day for the fight, May 29, was chagrined to find himself riding out to the field of a nonexistent battle. Even Johnston's sympathetic biographer, Craig L. Symonds, suggests that at this point, scarcely a year into the war, "perhaps . . . Johnston had come to distrust and dislike Davis so much that he simply avoided communication with him."[13] This kind of relationship did not bode well for Davis, for Johnston, or—most of all—for the infant Confederacy.

At the same time, however, we must credit Johnston with recognizing and acting on a great opportunity for an attacking battle. After the Confederates had retreated to the very doorsteps of the capital without engaging the enemy in a major fight, McClellan gave Johnston a gift, in Davis's words, for "which we can hardly hope": a river-divided Union army, so straddled as to negate its numerical superiority.[14] Even then, because of tactical considerations, Johnston vacillated almost a week before concluding on the battle plan that suited him. Here we are reminded of the story of Joe Johnston on the prewar hunt, of how he never fired because the birds were always too high or too low, even while his companions were filling their bags to the limit. Such indecisiveness could lead to overcaution, to lack of forceful action. Fortunately, McClellan's river straddling gave Johnston an opportunity for a bold stroke. Without this "gift," Johnston might well have allowed McClellan to launch his siege and bombardment, causing (as Johnston had despaired) a Confederate evacuation of Richmond.

Finally, one may conclude that Johnston's intention of deciding the entire campaign (and with it the possible loss of the Confederate capital) on one big battle fought just beyond the outskirts of Richmond was hugely risky and maybe even foolhardy, given McClellan's superior strength. Johnston's attack at Seven Pines, however, yielded one enormous benefit to the Confederacy, evident to us only in hindsight: Joe Johnston was put out of action, allowing Robert E. Lee to assume command of his army. One may speculate, though documentary evidence is absent, that Johnston felt great relief in handing over his very difficult predicament to a brother officer. General Lee went on to forge his historic record with the Army of Northern Virginia, beginning with his defeat of McClellan in the Seven Days' Battles. Johnston could only look on as he convalesced from his wound, on medical leave in Richmond from the first of June to mid-November 1862.

On November 12, Johnston reported himself to Secretary of War George W. Randolph as fit for duty. It was obvious to all that he would not resume his previous post—Johnston's old Army of the Potomac was now Robert E. Lee's Army of Northern Virginia. In fact, there was no army command available throughout the Confederacy. So President Davis, notwithstanding the bad feelings that had developed between the two men, assigned Johnston to a difficult, demanding role that recognized his talents as a professional soldier and strategist, as well as the army's third-ranking general. (Albert Sidney Johnston's death at Shiloh, April 6, 1862, had moved Johnston up a notch.) The administration created a huge super-department, stretching from the Appalachians to the Mississippi River, and gave Johnston authority to achieve strategic harmony among the three armies then operating within the region: Braxton Bragg's Army of Tennessee, some 40,000 strong at Murfreesboro; John C. Pemberton's army of 22,000 at Vicksburg; and Kirby Smith's 9,000 men in East Tennessee. Johnston was senior in rank to all three of these generals, but beyond that his actual authority over them remained vague. (The army commanders, for example, reported directly to President Davis, not to Johnston.) Nevertheless, Johnston accepted the assignment, even though he felt useless, "laid on the shelf." He asked Davis to be relieved, but the president declined. Thus, throughout the winter and into spring 1863, Johnston functioned as both strategic facilitator and supernumerary—an odd and obviously embarrassing admixture of responsibility and idleness.

The advance of General Ulysses S. Grant's Federal army against Vicksburg, and the alarming prospect of that bastion falling, compelled the War Department to bring Joe Johnston off the shelf. On May 9, 1863, he was instructed to go to Mississippi, take command of troops being assembled at the state capital, Jackson, and coordinate with Pemberton against Grant. But, arriving in Jackson on the 13th, Johnston judged immediately, "I am too late." Pemberton's army was thirty miles to the west, and Grant had positioned his forces between Pemberton and Johnston. When the Confederates could not achieve a junction, Grant drove Pemberton back to his defenses at Vicksburg and laid siege to the place. Although reinforced to over 20,000 men, Johnston in central Mississippi felt powerless. Apparently urged by Davis to attack Grant regardless of the odds in order to help Pemberton break out, Johnston seemed to be taking steps to do so when he learned of Pemberton's surrender, July 4.

Throughout the Vicksburg Campaign, General Johnston maintained a characteristically pessimistic outlook on his situation. "There are such odds against us here as Napoleon never won against," he confided to a friend on June 7. "The only imaginable hope is in the perpetration by Grant of some extravagant blunder and there is no grounds for such hope." A week later he advised Secretary of War James A. Seddon, "I consider saving Vicksburg hopeless." This defeatist attitude, regardless of how tactically merited, allowed many in the Confederate administration to view Johnston as unaggressive, even timid. A high-ranking Southern officer recalled Jefferson Davis later ascribing the fall of Vicksburg to "want of provisions of inside, and a general outside who wouldn't fight." Added to this were the president's recollections of how Johnston had failed to communicate with him when McClellan was closing in on Richmond the preceding spring. Four days after the surrender at Vicksburg, Davis telegraphed to Johnston in Mississippi, requesting, in a calculatedly chilling way, "such information . . . as the Government has a right to expect from one of its commanding Generals in the field." To Lee the president confided, "I can only learn from him of such vague purposes as were unfolded when he held his army before Richmond." A few days later, on July 25, Davis formally stripped Johnston of authority over the Department of the West and put him in charge of a smaller area, Mississippi and southern Alabama, whose focal point was the defense of Mobile.[15]

By the following fall, however, the thrust of the war was in Tennessee and north Georgia—where Braxton Bragg lost Chattanooga in early September, won the battle of Chickamauga two weeks later, then suffered disastrous defeat at Missionary Ridge two months after that. Bragg's subsequent removal from command created a vacancy for the leadership of the Army of Tennessee, which the president had to fill.

The executive decision, to no one's surprise, did not come easily. To be sure, Davis quickly accepted Bragg's request for relief from command, November 30. Lieutenant General William J. Hardee, second in seniority, took charge of the army, but he made clear he would do so only for an interim. Thus, the administration was left with the dilemma of whom to name. The president spent almost two weeks deliberating the issue, talking with Secretary of War Seddon, probably calling in his Cabinet, certainly consulting General Lee. Of the army's full generals, only two names were under serious consideration—P. G. T. Beauregard and Joseph E. Johnston. (If Lee was ever considered for transfer west, it was only momentarily; as Adjutant General Cooper expressed it to Hardee, "It is needless to name Lee, who is now indispensable where he is.")[16] The real decision seemed to be between Beauregard and Johnston. But Beauregard had impressed the administration too much as a textbook visionary to grasp the difficult realities of Confederate army command, whereas many men had written to the president recommending Johnston for the post, including Davis's good friend Lieutenant General Leonidas Polk. With all of these influences bearing upon him, Davis swallowed his doubts and his personal feelings about Johnston and bowed to the clamor among many for Johnston's return to army command as well as to the realization that the government had no one else to turn to. On December 16, 1863, the president named Johnston to lead the Army of Tennessee. Johnston immediately accepted, aware that he was advancing from a departmental backwater to field command of the Confederacy's second most important army. He took to this new post all the reputational baggage he had so carefully accumulated for himself.

CHAPTER THREE

SHERMAN PREPARES TO ADVANCE

TWO OF THE THREE key Union advantages in the north Georgia campaign—superior numbers and smart, scrappy leadership—came to bear through a major reorganization of Union forces in the western theater seven months before the campaign opened. By direction of President Abraham Lincoln, in October 1863 the military departments of the Cumberland, Tennessee, and Ohio, each of which had had its own army and separate commander, were now placed together in what was to be called the "Military Division of the Mississippi." Command of this three-army group went, not surprisingly, to the North's winningest general and recent captor of Vicksburg, Ulysses S. Grant. Grant's first order after taking charge named Major General William Tecumseh Sherman as his successor to lead the Army of the Tennessee. For the Army of the Cumberland, largest by far of the three, he fired Major General William S. Rosecrans, who had lost the battle of Chickamauga in north Georgia and was now cowering, under virtual siege, in Chattanooga. (Smallest of them was the "Army of the Ohio," really an army corps at Knoxville, which Major General John M. Schofield was eventually assigned to lead.) Grant replaced Rosecrans with Major General George H. Thomas. Thus Grant, Sherman, and Thomas fought together at Missionary Ridge, November 25, when Bragg's army was driven from the field. Later, Sherman's campaign across Mississippi, from Vicksburg to Meridian in February 1864, presaged his later March to the Sea in its purposeful destruction of crops, railroads, and other resources; his wrecking and burning of Meridian itself presaged the later, better-known burning of Atlanta.

In early March 1864, when Lincoln promoted Grant to lieutenant general, named him general in chief of all U.S. forces, and called him east to supervise operations in Virginia, Grant entrusted the military division leadership to his loyal and capable friend Sherman. Thus General Sherman on March 18 took over an extensive super-department, to which was added Arkansas for good measure so he could coordinate forces west of the Mississippi, too. Within days after Grant was promoted and Sherman succeeded him, the two friends met in Cincinnati and worked out their plan for simultaneous advances against Lee's and Johnston's armies—all Rebel armies, really, for Grant envisioned a coordinated offensive on all fronts from Virginia to Texas. Two weeks later, April 2, 1864, Grant crystallized his plan in a confidential letter to Sherman that laid out the latter's part in the grand operation clearly and simply:

> You I propose to move against Johnston's army, to break it up and to get into the interior of the enemy's country as far as you can, inflicting all the damage you can against their war resources.

I do not propose to lay down for you a plan of campaign, but simply to lay down the work it is desirable to have done, and leave you free to execute in your own way. Submit to me, however, as early as you can, your plan of operations.

Sherman understood perfectly and unfolded to Grant in a long let-ter of April 10 his plan for the campaign. In brief, he expected to push Johnston back to Atlanta, then proceed to cut the city's railroads, forcing the Rebels to give up the city and retreat farther. He boiled it down to this: "I will not let side issues draw me from your main plan, in which I am to knock Joe Johnston, and do as much damage to the resources of the enemy as possible."[17]

In the next month and a half Sherman toured his three armies: Thomas's Cumberland around Chattanooga, Schofield's Ohio at Knoxville, and his own Army of the Tennessee, now led by Major General James B. McPherson, scattered about northeast Alabama. Sherman also directed his reinforcement and supply. By the end of April he had in his "grand army," as he styled it, an effective strength of 110,000: 93,000 infantry, 12,500 cavalry, and 4,500 artillerymen serving some 250 guns. These formidable numbers did not include another 93,500 men "present for duty" scattered at posts through-out Tennessee, Kentucky, Alabama, and Mississippi, many of whom, especially around Nashville and Chattanooga, helped secure lines of communication. Less important garrisons were reduced, though, as Sherman beefed up his army. Two weeks before the campaign opened in early May 1864, he was hurrying forward two divisions from as far away as Cairo, Illinois. He also hoped to have another 10,000 reinforcements (Brigadier General A. J. Smith's corps) from Louisiana, but Federal defeat in the Red River Campaign (especially at the battle of Mansfield on April 8) meant that Sherman would begin without them.

Given this strength, representing by far the largest Union army ever assembled in the western theater, Sherman had every reason to feel confident. There was, however, the problem of keeping his troops fed and equipped, which Sherman all along felt was his biggest challenge. He assumed that a field army of 100,000 men would be as large a force as he could supply (and this count did not include the army's 45,000 horses and mules, which would have to be fed as well). To this task the commanding general applied him-self with characteristic determination and zeal. In fact, the way in which Sherman addressed his logistical problem and conquered it says much about his superior generalship.

In winter 1863–64, rations, forage, arms, ammunition, and equipment were brought to Sherman's forces by railroad from Louisville through Nashville to Chattanooga. This operation, Sherman judged in early April, was sufficient to meet the daily needs of his men and animals, but he wanted a surplus of stores close at hand, at Chattanooga and Decatur, Alabama, sufficient for seventy days, in case the rail lines to Nashville and Louisville were cut by Rebel cavalry. Thus, on April 2 in Nashville he met with his quartermaster and railroad chiefs to determine the steps necessary. It became a matter of mass, numbers, and movement. There were plenty of supplies at Nashville (24 million rations and grain for 50,000 animals for the rest of the year); the question was one of moving them forward. Sherman and his staff calculated that a soldier needed two pounds of food daily, and a horse twenty. Therefore, to build up the kind of stockpile Sherman wanted, 130 cars, each carrying ten tons, had to unload at Chattanooga every day. The railroaders pressed more locomotives and rolling stock into service, so that Sherman on April 24 could report with great satisfaction to Grant that he had increased the daily car-run serving his army from between 65 and 80 to anywhere from 130 to 190. The commanding general also issued strict orders for each train to carry the maximum freight: no civilian traffic; no private parcels; and troops and cattle must walk, not ride. Anticipating an outcry, especially from the charities and evangelical groups trying to serve the soldiers, Sherman developed a standard reply: "Show me that your presence at the front is more valuable than two hundred pounds of powder, bread, or oats."[18] By this combination of logic, persistence, and sheer will, Sherman solved his supply problem.

He might have been ready to advance against Joe Johnston in late April, the time he and Grant had originally agreed on to launch their simultaneous offensives in Georgia and Virginia. But Grant needed a few more days; Sherman not only acquiesced but asked for a launch date of May 5, because every day allowed him to build up his supplies. Grant agreed. Even as he prepared for his big move, Sherman looked to his rear and planned, as every good war leader must, for the worst. He knew that supply lines for his big army were vulnerable to enemy raids, and that the Rebel cavalry, especially under General Bedford Forrest, was bolder and better than his and would launch diversionary strikes in his rear. "The only danger I apprehend," he wrote Thomas on April 25, "is from resident guerrillas, and from Forrest," then in northern Mississippi. Against this menace Sherman early on developed a six-point plan:

1. Supported by navy gunboats, the Mississippi would be held by strong garrisons at Paducah, Cairo, Columbus, Memphis, Vicksburg, and Natchez. Sherman frankly hoped Forrest would operate against these garrisons and therefore stay in west Tennessee and away from the Nashville-Chattanooga railways. Sherman further expected his troops at Memphis and Vicksburg to launch diversionary activities of their own, thus keeping Forrest busy.

2. If they did not, and the enemy cavalry attempted "heavy swoops at our lines of communication," Sherman had ready a plan of elastic defense for his railroads. Main infantry reserves would be held at Nashville, Murfreesboro, and Columbia, Tennessee, as well as at Decatur and Stevenson, Alabama, "from which places they can be rapidly transported [by rail] to the point of danger." Lesser bodies of troops would be placed elsewhere along the line.

3. Vulnerable points on the route, such as bridges, would be protected by small detachments in blockhouses and redoubts. Throughout the spring Union engineers worked at constructing these blockhouses; fifty were built along the rail lines of the Nashville & Chattanooga Railroad, and fifty-four more on the Nashville, Decatur, and Stevenson road. Strengthened by double-log walls and dirt, these little forts were built to withstand artillery. They were to be manned by twenty to twenty-five men, who would be supplied with food, water, and fuel to hold out for up to seven days.

4. And hold out they were expected to do, until help could arrive. Sherman's orders stressed that "a small force in a block-house . . . can . . . protect their point against any cavalry force until relief comes. They should be instructed to fight with desperation to the last."

5. For their part, officers of garrisons along the rail lines were to keep cool, too, and not report mere rumors of enemy raids. "Actual facts should be reported to the headquarters at Nashville," Sherman advised; from there troops could be dispatched to meet any real threat.

6. Repair of damage to rail lines, bridges, and other strategic struc-
   tures if inflicted by the enemy, likewise would be directed from
   Nashville.[19]

With these preparations made and contingencies provided for, Sherman was ready to begin his offensive in the first week of May. True,
he had had to modify his plan slightly. Originally he wanted
McPherson to lead the Army of the Tennessee from Decatur toward
Rome, Georgia, crossing the Coosa River and flanking Johnston from
his position at Dalton. Thomas and Schofield would threaten the
enemy's front, engage his attention, and invite battle; Sherman even
pondered a cavalry raid around Johnston's right flank. The Federal
commander considered, too, the possibility of attacking Johnston
outright. "But," as he wrote to General Schofield on April 24, "I do
not propose rushing on him rashly." Sherman preferred instead to
see what McPherson could do in a flanking maneuver. His failure to
get A. J. Smith's hoped-for reinforcements and delays in bringing forward other troops returning from furlough meant that McPherson's
army would not be as strong as Sherman had anticipated. Thus, he
modified his plan slightly to bring McPherson in closer to the main
force. "I will not attempt to move on Johnston's rear at the start,"
Sherman told Major General Henry W. Halleck, the army chief of
staff, in a wire on April 28, "but collect the entire army in front of
Chattanooga, and make no detachments till the first issue at Dalton
is determined."[20]

The Union commander was robustly confident of his ability to
press Johnston back. A month before his campaign opened, Sherman was predicting that Johnston would retreat behind the Chattahoochee to Atlanta; he even outlined to Grant how he would then
"act on Atlanta" by cutting its railroads, feinting in one direction
while moving in another. Clearly, Sherman had the situation well
in hand and was confident for all the right reasons. He had a good
plan and had made the most thorough preparations. He knew he
had a firm numerical superiority; against his 100,000 or so, Sherman
correctly calculated from spies and other sources that Johnston's
army in late April numbered 45,000–60,000. He even knew when the
Rebels began moving reinforcements to Johnston (chiefly Polk's
corps from Mississippi and Alabama). Finally, the Federals knew
their opponent and suspected that they knew his plan as well.
"Johnston does not seem inclined to attack," Thomas understatedly

told Sherman in early April. This observation was of course no surprise to anyone, least of all to Sherman, who had faced Johnston the year before in Mississippi. "Johnston will hardly attack Thomas' fortified line," Sherman wrote on April 8. Moreover, the Federal commander reckoned that Johnston "will be compelled to hang to his railroad, the only possible avenue of supply to his army," just as Sherman would be compelled to hang onto his own railway lines.[21]

With all of these advantages, it is no wonder Sherman felt confident in early May. The very fact that he evinced so much concern for his rear suggests the extent to which he felt he had the situation in his front firmly in control. Numbers alone gave the Northerners an advantage in morale; Sherman knew his strength and believed he knew the enemy's, too. Their commander's self-confidence must have infected the troops in Sherman's three armies, who had the additional advantage of knowing how they had beaten the western Rebels in previous campaigns. Besides numerical strength and the self-assurance that comes from assiduous planning, the Federal commander had a third reason for confidence: he knew his opponent to be cautious, inclined toward the defensive, and likely to be cowed by a show of aggressiveness and determination. This combination of Union strength and Confederate weakness led Henry Watterson to predict, months before it happened, the inevitable fall of Atlanta. In other words, the three-way combination of Sherman's confidence and savviness, the heavy Northern battalions and, finally, Joe Johnston himself would lead to Atlanta's fall.

CHAPTER FOUR

JOHNSTON PREPARES TO FALL BACK

JUST AS GENERAL SHERMAN'S optimistic aggressiveness could be seen in his preparation and planning for the spring campaign, so too could the measure of General Johnston be discerned from *his* preparation and planning. But the measure of Johnston was nothing like that of Sherman. In fact, he was downright passive and pessimistic, as President Davis and others in both the government and the army could see, almost from the time Johnston took charge of the army in December 1863.

Johnston formally took command two days after Christmas of an army whose effective strength numbered some 33,600 infantry, 2,400 artillerymen with 112 guns, and between 3,000 and 4,000 cavalry. This count did not include several thousand more men present for duty but officially listed as sick. Nor did it include slightly over 3,000 Georgia militia and "State Line" stationed in the rear, at Rome and Etowah, which Governor Joseph E. Brown had placed at Johnston's disposal. The new commanding general took this fighting force and applied himself to preparing it for the spring campaign. The first task was to strengthen morale, which had plummeted after the rout from Missionary Ridge. Bragg's removal from command helped, and General Hardee, in his several weeks as interim army commander, accomplished some good. Johnston built on these beginnings and did more. He increased the supply of rations and forage by working with the governments of the state of Georgia and the Confederacy to improve the supply efficiency of the single-line railroad serving the army. The chief problem seemed to be a shortage of cars available to haul goods on the Western & Atlantic, the state-owned railway from Atlanta to Dalton. After appeals to Richmond failed to get cars reassigned to the Georgia line, Johnston acted on the matter himself. He sent a supply officer into Mississippi, who succeeded in bringing out a large number of freight cars for the Western & Atlantic, including twenty-five that originally had belonged to the railroad itself.

Johnston even involved himself in the quartermaster department's procedures for slaughtering and transporting beeves to the front. (Live cattle brought to Dalton took up more car space; Johnston suggested that the butchering and brining be done in Atlanta.) All of the commanding general's efforts and entreaties brought about a gradual improvement in the Western & Atlantic's operations, as freight trains ran more regularly from Atlanta to Dalton. Johnston was able to report to the president, January 23, that the railroad was serving the army more efficiently, bringing enough rations and forage even for a few days' accumulation. Johnston saw to the welfare of his men in other ways, such as scouring for shoes and granting more furloughs, and he began instituting reforms that improved discipline and morale. In early January he issued a long general order, specifying times for the troops' roll call, drill, mess, and other routines, and insisting on regularity of inspections, guard detail, and a host of other matters. He also looked after other administrative issues. The army's infantry, about 33,000 effectives, was organized into two corps, then commanded by General Hardee and, temporarily, General Thomas C. Hindman. In January, Johnston began asking the administration for another lieutenant general. Initially he sought the promotion and transfer of W. H. Chase Whiting or of Mansfield Lovell, then on inactive duty, but on February 18 he wired Adjutant General Cooper, asking for Lieutenant General J. B. Hood, whom he knew had recovered from his wounding at Chickamauga and was ready for active duty. That same day Johnston telegraphed Hood, then in Columbia, South Carolina: "We want you much."[22] The Senate had just approved Hood's promotion to lieutenant general and the War Department issued orders for his assignment to Johnston's army. When Hood arrived in Dalton on February 25, he replaced Hindman, who reverted to division command.

In his first four months of command, General Johnston also worked to strengthen his army. He took satisfaction in reporting that by the end of April some 5,000 absentees had returned to the ranks, so that the Army of Tennessee had present for duty 54,500 men—a 14 percent growth, no small achievement. Yet in those four months the army's "effective" strength rose only slightly. For this reason, in March, Johnston began suggesting to General Bragg that his army be reinforced not only from Leonidas Polk's department but also from Lieutenant General James Longstreet's command (then in east Tennessee), P. G. T. Beauregard's department along the South Carolina–Georgia coast, or the garrison of Mobile. In his correspondence Johnston applied himself particularly to asking General Bragg that Polk's infantry be transferred from Mississippi to his army. Initially rebuffed, Johnston's petitions for reinforcements from Polk's department gained more substance when Confederate intelligence reported Sherman's concentrations in April, especially his moving bodies of Union infantry from Vicksburg toward Chattanooga. Johnston further was aware of Schofield's Twenty-third Corps moving toward him from Knoxville and so informed Bragg on the 28th. In the face of this enemy concentration, Bragg directed Polk on April 23 to begin moving his forces toward a junction with Johnston's army.

Yet, much more than his infantry, Johnston worried about his cavalry, half of which, he reported to the president as he assumed command, had gone off with Longstreet into East Tennessee before the battles at Chattanooga. Eventually these mounted troops returned to the army's cavalry corps (commanded by Major General Joseph Wheeler) and thus helped contribute to the army's increased numbers by the end of spring. But Johnston repeatedly complained about their condition. In early April, though his returns showed some 6,300 cavalrymen present for duty, Johnston claimed that only about 2,000 were properly mounted for active service.

The army's artillery was another matter. In his first week of command Johnston wrote Davis that he had enough cannon—returns at the time showed 117 guns and about 2,500 artillery officers and men present—but that their horses were too weak to maneuver the guns. Johnston worked at finding replacement animals. Aided by an inspection report authorized by the War Department, Johnston's army received about 500. And after the inspector noted that the army had too many six-pounders and howitzers, steps were taken to replace them with superior guns, twelve-pounder Napoleons, and rifled cannon.

Thus, one could say that in winter and early spring 1864, Joe Johnston had snapped his army back into shape, improved its morale and discipline, ironed out some logistical weaknesses, and even increased its numbers (at least slightly in "effective" strength, and more impressively in the category of "present for duty"). For these accomplishments he had earned a reputation as a sound army administrator, one who was immensely popular with his officers and men. But in another key area, Johnston proved a disappointment—certainly to his government, maybe to his army, and perhaps even to the country as a whole.

Just before Johnston took actual command at Dalton, Davis wrote to him on December 23, expressing hope that after refitting the army Johnston could develop a plan for advancing back into middle Tennessee. With this letter, the president initiated a long string of correspondence back and forth between himself and Johnston and Bragg, and occasionally drawing in Longstreet, Beauregard, and a few others. The fifty or so letters exchanged between early January and early April 1864 reduce to a disagreement between the commanding general at Dalton and his superiors in Richmond on

the feasibility of a spring offensive. Johnston most thoroughly outlined his three reasons against such an operation in his reply to
Davis, January 2. First, leading an army of 43,000 effectives but faced
with at least 80,000 Federals in his front, he was outnumbered
roughly 2 to 1. Second, the Federals were well fortified at Chattanooga. Any offensive would require Johnston to go around them
by a long, hard, and risky flanking march—by either crossing the
Tennessee River to the left or crossing and entering the Cumberland
Mountains (a "rugged desert") on the right. And third, Johnston
noted, he had "neither subsistence nor field transportation enough
for either march." For these reasons, he suggested that if an offensive were to be made, Confederate forces might consider instead
"advancing from Northern Mississippi, avoiding the mountains."[23]

This suggestion was the closest General Johnston came to offering a plan for an offensive in spring 1864. He embellished it in a letter to Davis, February 1: he would move his army into northern
Mississippi, unite with Polk, and march into Tennessee from there.
This strategy would entail a far longer march than the shorter ones
to which he objected (which involved flanking the Federals at Chattanooga), but presumably the logistical problems would be easier.
In the meantime, once the Confederates abandoned north Georgia,
what would prevent the big Army of the Cumberland from marching on Atlanta? To this question Johnston put forth the astonishing
answer, expressed to Davis on January 15, that "two thousand or
3,000 cavalry could prevent a hostile army from reaching Atlanta in
less than a month." But he did not press hard for this plan; indeed,
it may be construed as a sop thrown to his superiors to assure them
that he possessed at least a little initiative. But throughout his correspondence Johnston made clear his belief that by far the best
course would be to *delay any advance until the enemy moved first.*
"I can see no other mode of taking the offensive here," Johnston
wrote on January 2, "than to beat the enemy when he advances, and
then move forward."[24]

General Johnston was right; Davis and Bragg were asking too
much of him, and in their enthusiasm for reclaiming middle Tennessee they were frankly unrealistic, given the very onerous difficulties and risks such an operation would pose for the Army of
Tennessee. At the same time, Johnston's plan of taking no action
and awaiting the enemy's advance reminded President Davis of the

cautious, defensive strategies he always heard from Johnston wherever he commanded—in northern Virginia, on the Peninsula, or in Mississippi. Moreover, Johnston sounded them again and again. One came on January 15: "Should the enemy attempt to penetrate Atlanta, and we be able to beat him and have then ready the means of marching across the Cumberland Mountains, as well as crossing the Tennessee, the offensive would be easy." And another on March 13: "The only practicable mode of assuming the offensive here [seems] to me to be to wait for the enemy's advance, and if we beat him, follow into Middle Tennessee."[25]

In short, Johnston's idea of taking the "offensive" was to stay on the defensive, prepare for the enemy advance, hope to beat him, and then seize the (counter-)offensive. Along the way, Johnston emphasized his difficulties. His cavalry was inadequate; he had too few artillery horses; he needed more wagons and bridge equipment. When Johnston claimed he would need heavy reinforcing before any offensive not just from Polk but also from Beauregard's forces in coastal South Carolina, Bragg actually considered the possibility, if only to keep the idea for an offensive alive. Specifically, the president and his adviser considered in early March reinforcing Johnston's army with troops from Polk and Beauregard as part of a plan for a spring offensive. With Johnston evidently bereft of any strong plan of his own, Davis and Bragg conceived the idea that Lieutenant General Longstreet, still in east Tennessee, march his forces to a junction with Johnston between Knoxville and Chattanooga, cross the Tennessee River and mountains, and enter the rich food-and-forage area of middle Tennessee before the Yankees could respond. The president ordered Longstreet to communicate this idea to Johnston by letter, which he wrote March 5; Bragg did so in a confidential letter, dated March 12, personally delivered to Johnston by an aide.

Johnston eventually replied to both letters. Of course he objected, pointing out (accurately) that a junction of his and Longstreet's forces would be close to impossible, given the enemy's two armies lying in between (at Chattanooga and Knoxville) and given the shortage of supplies and transport needed for such a long march. At the same time, Johnston rather liked two corollaries of the administration's plan. First, Bragg hinted that Johnston's army could be reinforced by 15,000 troops from Beauregard and Polk. Furthermore, to keep the enemy off balance, Confederate cavalry from Mississippi could ride into west or middle Tennessee—even then the intrepid Bedford Forrest was planning a raid that would carry his troopers all the way to Paducah, Kentucky, on the Ohio River within two weeks. There was a catch, however: Bragg made it clear that the reinforcements would be sent forward only when Johnston was prepared to set out in an offensive movement. But Johnston wanted those troops now, in order to defeat the enemy when he inevitably advanced. "To be ready we must have the troops you name immediately; otherwise we might be beaten, which would decide events. Give us those troops, and if we beat him we follow. Should he not advance we will thus be ready for the offensive."[26]

Bragg and Johnston wired and wrote back and forth. On March 19 Johnston reiterated his objections to the administration's plan for a spring offensive: the enemy had interior lines and could fall on either Johnston or Longstreet before they united; the route proposed, through East Tennessee, would entail a long and vulnerable line of communications; he did not have adequate field transportation to haul supplies needed for a long march; and furthermore, all signs indicated that the Federals were preparing to launch a massive campaign of their own against him. At the same time, Johnston urged the administration to order a cavalry raid from north Mississippi. Johnston reminded Bragg that a few weeks before, Polk had said he could send 15,000 horsemen into Tennessee. "Even two-thirds of that force," Johnston pointed out, "might injure the railroads enough to compel the evacuation of Chattanooga." And he asked again for those 15,000 reinforcements. Assuming Grant (whose arrival in Nashville had been reported), not Sherman, would be his opponent, Johnston urged, "I would have the troops assembled here without delay, to repulse Grant's attack and then make our own, or should the enemy not take the initiative, do it ourselves." When the letter arrived in Richmond, General Bragg passed it on to the president, who added his rather restrained endorsement, "read with disappointment. J.D."[27]

Back and forth it went. Bragg wrote on March 21: "Your dispatch of 19th does not indicate an acceptance of the plan proposed." Johnston replied on March 22: "In my dispatch of 19th I expressly accept taking offensive, only differ with you as to details." Bragg would have none of this, and in his communications with Johnston over the next several weeks he more or less let the matter drop.

It was clear both to him and to Davis that the Confederate army in Georgia would remain on the defensive that spring. In one last effort, however, to push his general to more aggressive action, Davis, on April 7, ordered Brigadier General William N. Pendleton (who had inspected the Army of Tennessee's artillery the month before) again to Dalton on "inspection duty." Privately, Pendleton was instructed to confer with Johnston and reiterate the president's desire for aggressive operations by the Army of Tennessee. Davis seems not to have imparted a specific strategic plan but only to have asked Pendleton to urge Johnston to take some action against the enemy so as "to break up his plans, . . . press him, . . . beat him," and finally, "to obviate the necessity of falling back likely to occur if the enemy be allowed to consummate his own plans." This last consideration was probably President Davis's main motivation, since he had seen before what Joe Johnston would end up doing whenever the enemy was allowed to "consummate his own plans": Old Joe would bow to "the necessity of falling back."[28]

General Pendleton met with Johnston at Dalton on April 15 and, predictably, did not get very far. The commanding general listened attentively and politely, then enumerated all the by-now familiar objections regarding logistics and transportation, as well as the enemy's build-up of numbers in his front. Based on intelligence brought in by Major General Wheeler, Johnston estimated 103,000 Yankee troops opposed to him, strung out from Decatur and Bridge-port in north Alabama (McPherson) to Knoxville in east Tennessee (Schofield). Against this host, Johnston stated that he had an effective strength of only 39,396: 34,500 infantry, 2,811 artillery, and 2,085 cavalry (though it was assumed that Polk would soon be sending some reinforcements). In the face of these facts and contentions, Pendleton could only dutifully record that Johnston's plan was chiefly "to stand on the defensive till strengthened; to watch, prepare, and then strike as soon as possible."[29]

When Pendleton finally returned to Richmond and reported to Davis and Bragg, they were not surprised by his findings. They already had received, unexpectedly, another personal report from the Army of Tennessee. Unknown to them as they dispatched Pendleton to make their case to Johnston, Johnston was dispatching one of his staff officers to make his own case to Davis and Bragg. This simulta-neous sending of envoys suggests the almost ludicrous breakdown in communication that characterized (and hobbled) the Confederate war effort in Georgia in late winter and early spring 1864.

On April 8 Johnston ordered his assistant adjutant general, Colonel Benjamin S. Ewell, to go to Richmond and explain his position. Ewell arrived in the capital and on the 13th met with Bragg and laid out Johnston's points. The general in Georgia, Ewell explained, was not opposed to an advance; he only objected to the administration's plan and wanted to wait until he was reinforced and had completed his logistical preparations before making final a more preferable plan. For example, the army needed a thousand or so wagons and numerous artillery horses if any offensive were contemplated. Besides, the best idea for a forward movement was first to beat the enemy south of the Tennessee River. If Johnston won, then he would want to advance. Furthermore, to increase his chances of success, Polk's infantry and artillery should be sent from Mississippi to the Army of Tennessee.

Bragg agreed that because Longstreet had been recalled to join Lee in Virginia, the administration's initial plan of the month before was no longer feasible. Ewell then asked to meet with Davis the next day and did so. "The President received me courteously and listened with apparent interest to the different statements I made," Ewell later related to Johnston. Davis still hoped for an advance by the Army of Tennessee according to any plan agreed upon by General Johnston and himself. To Johnston's hope for reinforcements, Davis could give no immediate answer because of the demands being made by other departments. The meeting ended cordially. By this time, the third week of April, it was clear that Johnston had won the argument: he had effectively justified his policy of cautious, defensive inactivity with a patently insincere commitment to offensive action. Johnston's telegram to Ewell, sent April 14 as a last-minute point-rehearsal, demonstrates this double-talk.

> Assuming offensive must depend on relative forces. I shall be ready to do it whenever they warrant it. It will be a month or six weeks before we can expect the necessary transportation. I cannot foresee what force the enemy may then have. I do not think our present strength sufficient for defensive since Longstreet's withdrawal. No one is more anxious than I for offensive operations by this army.[30]

At least part of this message, if it had reached Davis and Bragg, would surely have alarmed them: "I do not think our present

strength sufficient for defensive." In other words, not only had Johnston piled up reasons for staying on the defensive but he was hinting to his superiors his fears of being unable even to hold his lines
in north Georgia.

Actually Johnston had been sending similar messages all along.
On January 12 he had warned the president that "unless the management of the railroad from Atlanta is improved we shall be compelled to fall back." (Davis reminded him that such a move "would
be . . . seriously detrimental, both from military and political considerations" and argued that he at least put his men on short rations
as an "alternative . . . to the one you present.") Johnston assured the
president that he would not readily resort to retreat, and that it
would "not be thought of when it can be avoided." Then, in a letter to the president of February 1, as Federals in north Alabama
seemed to be preparing for a march on Rome, Johnston warned that
he would not be able to counter such a move without giving up his
position at Dalton. A week later, he wrote to Colonel William M.
Browne, the president's aide-de-camp, announcing that he would
have to retreat if Rome were uncovered; in fact, because "this position [Dalton] is too much advanced," he would prefer, he said, to
fall back immediately and would do so, "but for fear of effect upon
the country." A week after that, February 15, Johnston endorsed
onto an officer's letter being forwarded to Richmond, "I have only
to repeat what I have written more than once—that this army is
much too weak for the object for which it is here." On March 12,
Johnston told Bragg that if Sherman's forces in Mississippi joined
those of Major General Thomas in his front, "this army would
require re-enforcement to enable it to hold its ground." Indeed, as
Sherman's forces grew in his front—when the Army of the Cumberland was joined by its sister armies of the Tennessee and the
Ohio—Johnston kept Richmond well informed, to justify his continued need for reinforcements (and perhaps his possibly impending retrograde). On April 6 he passed on to Bragg the news from
Major General Wheeler that seventy-four cars of Union troops had
arrived in Chattanooga from Knoxville in the previous three days.
A week later Johnston warned that more Yankees were en route;
some 6,500 enemy troops, preparing to march, had just arrived
below Chattanooga. On the 17th, he advised Bragg that McPherson's corps was beginning to arrive from Mississippi. In the face of
this mounting evidence, the Confederate War Department could

send Johnston only 4,000 men (half from Mobile, half from the Atlantic coast). Federal troop transfers from the Mississippi also justified shifting at least some of Polk's forces eastward. On the 23d Bragg ordered Polk to send Johnston half of his infantry, the division of Major General William W. Loring. To be sure, all of Polk's infantry and artillery would eventually be ordered to the Army of Tennessee, but before they finished arriving, Sherman had already kicked off the campaign, with his armies' advances on May 5.[31]

By that time it was too late for Johnston to do anything other than react. But the idea of staying on the defensive and awaiting the enemy's first move had all along been the linchpin of Johnston's notion of "assuming offensive." Worse: throughout winter and early spring 1864, there were signals, some communicated directly to Richmond, that Johnston anticipated having to retreat through north Georgia. An alarming indication of his intent was that more than six weeks before Sherman got his troops moving, Johnston was already looking well to his rear. On March 12, 1864, Captain Lemuel P. Grant, the Confederate engineer who had supervised the construction of fortifications around Atlanta, received a message that he was to report to Confederate headquarters in the city the next morning. General Johnston was arriving in Atlanta to "make an inspection of the works in this vicinity." Had President Davis known about this visit (and there is no indication that he did), his worst fears about Joe Johnston's timidity would have been confirmed. The 1864 campaign was almost two months away, and already the Confederate commander in north Georgia was inspecting Atlanta's fortified defenses. Having signaled that he had no real offensive plan for the spring, Joe Johnston, it now seemed, was already taking preliminary steps for a retreat back to Atlanta.[32]

CHAPTER FIVE

JOHNSTON IS TURNED, I

NO WONDER JOHNSTON wanted Sherman to attack him. He had his army deployed in a commanding defensive position along Rocky Face Ridge, a thickly wooded series of heights rising up to some seven hundred feet and extending from seven miles northwest of

Dalton, almost to the Oostanaula River twenty-five miles to the south. The ridge got its name from its steep western face, almost perpendicular rock cliffs that presented an insuperable barrier to the Yankees to the north and west. There were, to be sure, gaps in the ridge, such as Mill Creek Gap, also called Buzzard Roost Gap because of the steep cliffs on both its sides; through it ran the Western & Atlantic Railroad and the main road to Chattanooga.

The army under General Bragg had stopped its retreat at Rocky Face the previous November, General Hardee had rested here and begun to refit that army, and here too Johnston prepared to meet Sherman. He had his infantry divisions aligned north-south along Rocky Face, then arcing eastward into Crow Valley. All were well supported by artillery, with cavalry pickets and patrols extending out front and on the flanks. General Johnston, of course, had no assurance that Sherman's troops would do as he hoped and butt up against the Confederate positions on Rocky Face; but at least once during the winter they did. Ordered in late February to create a diversion that would keep the Rebels from sending troops against Sherman on his march to Meridian, Thomas pushed forward a sizable reconnaissance-in-force. Predictably, in several days' skirmishing, February 24–26, the Federals realized the impregnability of Johnston's position. But they also learned its vulnerability to flanking. In addition to the main cut through the ridge, Mill Creek Gap, which the Confederates guarded very well, there were other gaps in the southern reaches of Rocky Face that were not so well guarded. About three and a half miles south of Mill Creek was Dug Gap; the reconnoitering Federals nearly broke through here before frantically called Southern reinforcements pushed them back. General Thomas deduced from this encounter the likely existence of other gaps. Sure enough, the Northerners soon learned of Snake Creek Gap, five miles south of Dug Gap, and far enough from the Rebel positions that it appeared undefended. So promising did this flanking avenue appear that Thomas drew up a plan for the spring campaign around it, which he proposed to Sherman in late March. The plan called for a demonstration along the Rebel line while Northern forces struck through Snake Creek Gap, flanking Johnston, threatening to cut the railroad in his rear, and ultimately forcing either his speedy retreat or a bloody repulse.

Sherman knew he would have to flank Joe Johnston. "To strike Dalton in front was impracticable," he later wrote, because of the inaccessible ridge, the Rebels' fortifications, and the by-now widely understood axiom, shared by commanders on both sides, that prepared defenses are impervious to frontal assaults.[33] Moreover, as one of Thomas's scouts reported in early April, the Southerners had dammed up Mill Creek and flooded the gap basin to impede an infantry advance. In the early stages of his planning (around April 10), however, Sherman thought not of using Snake Creek Gap (Thomas's idea) but of making a wider arc around Johnston, sending McPherson's Army of the Tennessee, then at Huntsville, across the Tennessee River by pontoon at Decatur and Whitesburg, Alabama, and marching toward Rome (about forty miles south of Dalton) to cross the Coosa River and so outflank the Rebel army. By late April, when it appeared he would not get all the divisions he wanted for McPherson's army—he had hoped for nine divisions, 30,000 strong—Sherman considered such a wide detachment too risky and determined to keep McPherson closer in, flanking the Rebels by way of Snake Creek Gap, after all. But as a big modification of Major General Thomas's plan, Sherman designated McPherson's army, not Thomas's Army of the Cumberland, as the flanking force. While McPherson maneuvered, Sherman's plan called for Thomas and Schofield to keep Johnston pinned and focused on his front.

General Johnston could hardly have been unaware of the enemy's intentions. As hard as he hoped for a blundering frontal attack against Rocky Face Ridge, the Confederate commander must have doubted that his Northern opponent would be so obliging and stupid. As early as late February, Longstreet had warned Johnston, "If you don't try some flank movement, the enemy will, and throw you out of position." Johnston's chief of staff, Brigadier General William W. Mackall, similarly recorded in early March his prediction that the Yankees "would try and go past Dalton." To prepare for such movements, Johnston had his topographical engineers mapping the whole area around Dalton. Captain F. R. R. Smith, for instance, was ordered to survey and map an area well to Johnston's right flank, fully ten miles east of his position along Rocky Face. Smith was at work on this exercise when he was captured, April 13; his orders and maps all fell into Union hands.[34]

On his other flank, Johnston had good maps as well. We know today that maps carried by Confederate Brigadier General Henry D. Clayton (whose brigade was in A. P. Stewart's division, Hood's corps) showed the area from Red Clay, on the Tennessee border, to Tilton, well south of Dalton. Ridges, gaps, roads, and streams were well marked on those charts; one in particular shows the course of Snake Creek (though unnamed) through Rocky Face, ten miles southwest of Dalton. Johnston therefore knew of the ridge gaps beyond his left flank. Wheeler had his cavalry picketing a wide front, from Ship's Gap in Taylor's Ridge on the left to the Conasauga River far to the right. The Confederate commander, in other words, had at least an adequate if not fully ample intelligence network in place when Southern scouts detected enemy troops on the march in the first days of May. On the 3d, dispatches sent in by Wheeler's scouts led Confederate staff officer Lieutenant Thomas B. Mackall to record, "preparations for movement on part of enemy [are] universally confirmed."[35]

The next day, May 4, Sherman ordered his three armies on the march early. Thomas moved on Ringgold while Schofield advanced on his left. McPherson's Fifteenth and Sixteenth Corps were well to the rear, leaving north Alabama and heading past Chattanooga toward Rossville. Sherman was pleased and confident. He had reason to be: after a winter of planning, his forces were on the move, well supplied and very strong (they would get stronger still, once the Seventeenth Corps, en route from the Mississippi Valley, joined McPherson's army). What was more, Johnston was doing nothing, save for the usual light skirmishing by Confederate cavalry in Schofield's and Thomas's fronts. "Everything very quiet with the enemy," Sherman recorded on the night of the 4th. "Johnston evidently awaits my initiative."[36] Thus, on the opening day of the campaign for Atlanta, the three decisive elements shaping the campaign's outcome—Sherman's aggressiveness, superior Northern numbers, and Johnston's passivity—were already evident.

The Federal plan unfolded in the next three days. Thomas and Schofield were to press down upon the Rebel positions along Rocky Face, diverting Johnston's attention from McPherson's turning maneuver to the south. Late on May 5 Sherman gave his good friend Mac orders for what he hoped to bring about: "I want you to move . . . to Villanow; then to Snake [Creek] Gap, secure it and from it make a bold attack on the enemy's flank or his railroad at any point between Tilton and Resaca." If Johnston retired, he continued, "you will hit him in flank. Do not fail in that event to make the most of the opportunity by the most vigorous attack possible."[37] If Johnston stayed at Rocky Face, slugging it out with Thomas, McPherson could descend on the Western & Atlantic in the Rebels' rear, wreck it, then retire westward to await the issue of battle to the north.

On the 5th Thomas pushed closer to Tunnel Hill; McPherson, with by far the longer route, moved his troops south of Chattanooga. Over in Confederate lines, General Johnston tracked these developments, but he did not know which flank to fear for most, his left or his right. Lieutenant Mackall, the staff officer, noted, "Scouts think attack will be made on our right."[38] At the same time, however, Johnston suspected the possibility of a wide enemy flanking march by McPherson toward Rome. On the night of the 5th Generals Johnston, Hood, Hardee, and Wheeler conferred at length at army headquarters, trying to divine Sherman's plans.

They were about to unfold. Though behind schedule, the head of McPherson's army camped at Lee and Gordon's Mill on the night of the 6th, and on the 7th moved to the southeast of Rock Springs Church en route to Ship's Gap. By then, Thomas had taken Tunnel Hill with little opposition—General Sherman seemed surprised that the Rebels had not tried to injure the critical railway tunnel—and begun skirmishing with the Rebels at Buzzard Roost. As he advanced on Rocky Face, so did Schofield's Twenty-third Corps, having advanced from Red Clay to cover Thomas's left flank. For the 8th, Sherman directed his army leaders to do more of the same: Schofield to feel down on the enemy, moving southwest from Varnell's to the northern reaches of Rocky Face; Thomas to threaten Mill Creek Gap but "not to lead to battle unless the enemy comes out of his works"; and McPherson to march by way of Villanow to occupy Snake Creek Gap.[39] All three objectives were accomplished on the 8th. In the process there occurred the "Battle of Dug Gap" (the first "battle" of the campaign deserving of the name), in which Brigadier General John W. Geary's division pressed hard against the Gap, defended at first by only a thousand Confederates, who were soon reinforced. In the end, Geary withdrew, leaving Johnston still in possession of the Mill and Dug passes.

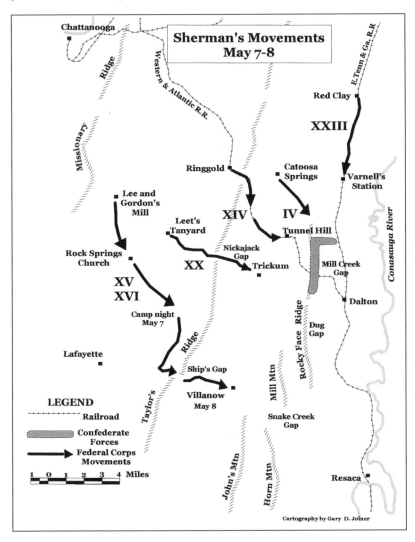

The seven infantry divisions of the Army of Tennessee were, as Lieutenant Mackall wrote, "all in hand for off[ense] or def[ense]," in an entrenched seven-mile line running from east of Dalton (Patrick R. Cleburne's division) to south of Mill Creek Gap (B. Frank Cheatham and W. H. T. Walker). Johnston knew Sherman's army stretched from Varnell's to below Trickum, and, from the repulse of

Geary's assault at Dug Gap, he knew that there was likely still more danger farther to the left. After reporting some of McPherson's troops way to the west near LaFayette (headed for Rome?), Wheeler's cavalry was ordered to be on the lookout well to the south. A Confederate infantry brigade at Resaca under Brigadier General James Cantey (the first reinforcements to Johnston's army from Alabama) was also instructed to "keep close observation on all routes leading from LaFayette to Resaca or to Oostenaula." Johnston warned Polk, who was moving toward Dalton from Alabama, that McPherson could be headed for Rome. Then the Southern vedettes seem to have lost contact with McPherson; on the 8th Johnston's headquarters received no word of his whereabouts. When Lieutenant Mackall recorded news of "Hooker's Corps crossing Taylor's Ridge this morning [May 8] at Ships Gap & Gordon Spgs Gap," the Southerners were confusing the Twentieth Corps with McPherson's column. General Cantey on the 8th wired from Resaca that cavalry scouts reported "Yankees in vicinity of Villanow to-day," but he could not identify their units. Nevertheless this movement toward Villanow—which McPherson reached that afternoon at two o'clock—was enough to concern Johnston's staff. Confederate cavalry under Colonel J. Warren Grigsby, having helped repel Geary at Dug Gap, was ordered to Snake Creek Gap that night. But there is nothing in the Confederates' correspondence to indicate their awareness that Grigsby's small brigade, fewer than 500 strong, was being sent against two corps of Yankee infantry, already entering the Gap.[40]

Had Sherman known this, he would have been less concerned for the safety of McPherson's column. As it was, though, he worried that Johnston was taking troops from his main line and shifting them southward to jump McPherson. "The reconnaissance to-day has not drawn a single gun of the enemy," he complained to Thomas on the night of the 8th. "I fear Johnston is annoying us with small detachments, whilst he will be about Resaca in force." The same message went to Schofield at midnight: "We must not let Johnston amuse us here by a small force whilst he turns on McPherson." Sherman therefore ordered Schofield the next day to "keep up the idea of an advance," with skirmishers to "act with boldness, but not rashness" to discern the enemy's strength in position. Thomas also planned demonstrations along Rocky Face beginning at six in the morning, which, with Schofield's, succeeded in arresting the Rebels' attention.[41]

If Sherman was concerned about locating the enemy army's main position, so was Johnston. Early on the 9th he instructed Wheeler to find out whether most of the Yankees were north of Rocky Face, or west of it; Wheeler's reconnaissance led to a run-in with Edward M. McCook's cavalry on Schofield's left, in which the Northerners received the worst of it. But by 10:00 A.M. Confederate headquarters turned eyes to the south, as word came in that Grigsby's troopers had encountered enemy forces at Snake Creek Gap. They were infantry of Brigadier General Grenville M. Dodge's Sixteenth Corps, leading McPherson's column, emerging from the southern opening of the Gap, fanning out. All Grigsby could do was retire fighting and call for help. Advancing eastward toward the railroad, Dodge not only pushed back the Rebel horsemen but routed a little group of maybe a thousand infantry, hastily assembled on a hill a mile west of Resaca. That place, with the vital railroad, was now in McPherson's reach. Mac wrote back to his commander at 12:30 that he proposed to cut the railroad, then according to his orders on the 5th fall back to a defensive position and await developments from Thomas and Schofield's front. McPherson was clearly worried that there were sizable enemy infantry before him. He had insufficient cavalry for scouting, and, besides, he had not established communication with General Hooker to the north (Thomas's right), who might warn him of a sudden enemy shift southward against him. For these reasons McPherson's advance probed tentatively toward Resaca, drawing fire from Rebels holed up in a fort overlooking the Oostanaula railroad bridge, and others well dug in (Cantey's brigade, Grigsby's tired troopers, as well as a Georgia regiment and battalion stationed at Resaca). The Southerners' stout resistance, coupled with McPherson's mounting uncertainty, led him after several hours of skirmishing to order Dodge's men to retire back toward the Gap, which they did by dark. Later, somewhat lamely, Mac told his friend Cump, "If I could have had a division of good cavalry I could have broken the railroad at some point." As it was, McPherson's forces disturbed not a single track of the Western & Atlantic that day, and the only damage done, by some mounted infantry near Tilton, was to snip the Rebels' telegraph wire.[42]

Both sides blundered on May 9. McPherson, having made a dramatic, surprise flanking march on Johnston, succumbed to his fears in not striking harder against the small enemy force holding Resaca. Similarly, Johnston at his headquarters in Dalton reacted just as tentatively and passively to the dangerous threat on his south flank. He, too, suffered from a lack of sure information. While Wheeler was earning accolades in the northern sector driving back Yankee troopers, his cavalry could have been engaged with Dodge, developing the enemy's strength and intent. At the same time, Johnston was remarkably lethargic in calling for more vigorous scouting of the Villanow–Snake Creek Gap sector. Throughout the several days Johnston seemed oddly oblivious to the crisis brought on by McPherson's march. "I do not think Resaca is in danger," Mackall, Johnston's chief of staff, wrote at 4:00 P.M. on the 9th; "we have 4,000 men there."[43] Informed as early as May 5 of enemy infantry marching southward by way of Lee and Gordon's Mill, Johnston thought Rome might be their objective. On the 6th this column was identified as Logan's corps. But after the 7th, when the Confederate high command fixed part of McPherson's army near LaFayette, Johnston seemed willfully to ignore McPherson, or hopefully to assume that Polk's troops arriving from Alabama could concentrate at Rome and so meet the threat. As a result, Johnston's only response was to send a weak cavalry brigade to Snake Creek Gap which, no surprise, found massed Yankee infantry marching through when it arrived on the morning of the 9th.

Thus, notwithstanding Johnston's understandable preoccupation with his Rocky Face front (as Sherman hoped), given the threat to the safety of his army posed by a strong enemy column marching beyond his flank and threatening his railroad and rear, Johnston must be blamed unequivocally for a huge tactical blunder. What response he made during May 7–8, the critical days of the enemy turning movement, was completely inadequate. As the threat to Snake Creek Gap developed, Johnston moved no infantry from his line. His hope that Polk, expected to arrive at Rome on May 9, might help meet the threat was unrealistic, as was the idea that 4,000 men assumed to be at Resaca could prevent McPherson from cutting his vital supply line to the rear.

General Johnston's apologists have steadfastly refused to impute negligence or blunder to the Confederate commander. In most of their writings Major General Wheeler has taken the blame. Chief of Staff Mackall led the way by spreading talk that someone (presumably Wheeler) was guilty of "a flagrant disobedience of orders." To be sure, beginning May 5, General Mackall had conveyed to Wheeler the commanding general's wish that cavalry bring in "the most accurate information" on enemy positions east of Taylor's Ridge. The next day, Lieutenant Mackall privately recorded, "Not a thing has been ascertained by Wheeler's cav—inactive.... But few scout reports rcd. from Gen. Wheeler—generally unsatisfactory." Yet for a long while afterward the Confederate leadership puzzled over whom to blame for the failure to guard Snake Creek Gap. "How this gap, which opened upon our rear and line of communications, from which it was distant at Resaca only five miles, was neglected I cannot imagine," Major General Patrick R. Cleburne wrote several months later. "Certainly the commanding general never could have failed to appreciate its importance."[44]

Johnston's biographers have accepted Cleburne's supposition and accused Wheeler and his troopers of faulty scouting of McPherson's movements. Gilbert E. Govan and James W. Livingood say, "The evidence points to the cavalry as the source of failure." Craig L. Symonds echoes their analysis: "Johnston's uncertainty about Federal intentions was largely a product of the weakness of his cavalry—the eyes of the army." Students of the Atlanta Campaign strongly supportive of Johnston accept Mackall's charge that Wheeler acted irresponsibly. An early writer, Wilbur G. Kurtz, concludes: "Johnston was a victim of ... overweening reliance upon subordinates who were derelict in duty." As if to exonerate both Wheeler and Johnston, however, others have suggested that Snake Creek Gap never appeared on the Confederate maps that the army used—a claim that, as the topographical maps in Brigadier General Clayton's possession show, cannot be supported.[45]

Still, other commentators have wondered whether it was Johnston, not Wheeler, who was derelict. Former National Park Service historian Edwin C. Bearss, for instance, asked himself why Johnston, trained in topographical engineering in the old army, could have been so blind to the importance of mountain passes on his southern flank. The characteristically outspoken Thomas Lawrence Connelly, even acknowledging the drawbacks in performance of

Wheeler's cavalry, resolved that "Johnston completely ignored Snake Creek Gap, and made no inquiries as to its status."[46] Nevertheless, Johnston's champions and critics agree that in Round One of the Atlanta Campaign, Sherman outgeneraled Johnston.

Sherman knew immediately. "I've got Joe Johnston dead!" he exulted on the afternoon of the 9th, when word came in that McPherson was closing in on Resaca. Early the next morning he wired Washington: "I believe McPherson has destroyed Resaca," breaking Johnston's line of communcations. The Union commander began thinking through various plans by which he could capitalize on McPherson's success, well aware, as he related to General Halleck, "Johnston acts purely on the defensive." As a good army leader has always been enjoined to do, Sherman early on May 10 planned to reinforce success: build on McPherson's flanking maneuver by throwing the bulk of Thomas's strength around Johnston by the same route so that he might "swing round through Snake Creek Gap, and interpose between him and Georgia." Johnston would try to retreat; then McPherson could attack the Rebels in flank. No wonder he believed he had Joe Johnston dead![47]

Mid-morning on the 10th, however, by 10:30, General Sherman received McPherson's dispatch of the night before and learned that the Army of the Tennessee had failed in its mission. "I regret beyond measure you did not break the railroad, however little," he wrote McPherson back, "but I suppose it was impossible." (Three days later, when the two officers met, Sherman is said to have told his friend, "Well, Mac, you have missed the opportunity of a lifetime."[48]) There was no time, however, for lamenting the lost opportunity. Sherman instructed McPherson to dig in where he was, await reinforcements (Hooker's corps), and resist any Rebel attack until Thomas and Schofield could march to meet him. In the meantime, Howard's Fourth Corps, helped by McCook's and Major General George Stoneman's recently arrived cavalry, would stay behind, keeping up enough of a demonstration against Rocky Face as to distract Johnston from the main movement. At his headquarters in Dalton, General Johnston was finally alive to the enemy's turning movement. Having impressed upon Cantey the "absolute necessity" of holding his position at Resaca and the railroad bridge across the Oostanaula, having dispatched a brigade of reinforcements to

Cantey, and having received positive reports that the enemy moving on Resaca were Dodge's and John A. Logan's corps (though Cantey and cavalryman Will Martin still said Hooker), Johnston on the night of the 9th ordered General Hood to take Cleburne's, Walker's, and Hindman's divisions to Resaca. Thus would begin the army's withdrawal from Rocky Face back to Resaca, where presumably it would again take up defensive positions. (Johnston also sent his chief engineer, Major Stephen W. Presstman, to stake out works around the place.) Arriving there, Hood found that McPherson's forces had withdrawn to the west, and he wired Johnston, "R[esaca]. all right Hold on to Dalton." Indeed, later that day Hood returned to Dalton with one of the divisions because the threat to Resaca, for the moment at least, appeared to have abated. Besides, the first of Loring's divisions arrived at Rome on the 10th, assuring Johnston that reinforcements would be coming by rail through Resaca itself. Johnston told Polk to concentrate there and assume command.[49]

With McPherson digging in, Sherman, skirmishing with Rebel cavalry but showing neither boldness nor haste, pushed his plan forward. He had stolen a march on Joe Johnston, as he told Halleck, and therefore he would be in no hurry to swing the rest of his forces southward. Accordingly, Thomas and Schofield slowly shifted by the right flank during May 11–12, so that by night of the 12th, five of Sherman's six corps were at Snake Creek Gap (Howard's Fourth would bring up the rear). Johnston became aware of their movements. To Polk at Resaca, Mackall on the morning of the 12th wired, "The enemy in our front is moving rapidly down the valley toward Snake Gap or Villanow." Wheeler's reconnoitering around the north end of Rocky Face confirmed most of the Yankees gone. Hence, in late morning Polk received a stronger message from headquarters: "The enemy seem to be abandoning this place." Although unsure of his opponent's precise objective (Resaca, Rome, or, now, Calhoun?), Johnston knew for certain it was time to leave Dalton. After telegraphing Richmond that the enemy was heading for the Oostanaula and that he intended to follow, the commanding general left Dalton by train on the evening of the 12th. The rest of the army, at least that part not already at Resaca or on its way thereto, evacuated in the night.[50]

CHAPTER SIX

THE BATTLE OF RESACA
(JOHNSTON IS TURNED, II)

ON MAY 13 THE OPPOSING FORCES lumbered into their new positions about Resaca. Building on Polk's position west of town, with its left flank secured on the Oostanaula, Johnston had the rest of his army dig a line of works three miles northward, bending around to the east to anchor on the Conasauga. Much of Walker's division was sent south to Calhoun, as a precaution against any raid in that direction; Martin's cavalry also guarded the area south of the river. Wheeler's horsemen, who had been opposing Howard's advance through Dalton, joined the army on its right flank. All in all, with 50,000 men dug in, Johnston again had reason to hope for the big defensive battle he had wished for at Dalton.

Sherman was mildly inclined to give it to him—not because he believed in the efficacy of force-of-arms but because he halfway expected Johnston to retreat on to Calhoun after making a show at Resaca. If so, perhaps a quick blow could send the Rebels running. But there was no quick blow. On the 13th, McPherson began advancing toward Resaca, combating Rebel skirmish lines along the way. The closer the Federals got to the railroad, the stiffer the opposition became, so that by the end of the day the Union forces had drawn up in fortified lines opposite the Confederates' positions. Sherman's hopes that the Rebels might continue retreating were dashed. But Cump was not daunted. The next day, May 14, he ordered McPherson to "renew the direct attack on Resaca, pushing it with vigor at all points till you draw the fire of artillery, if any, from the forts"—which really meant not so much an attack as a demonstration. McPherson would be supported by Schofield and Thomas on his left. Then, under this pressure, "should Johnston retreat south," Sherman planned to bring pontoons up and make a crossing of the Oostanaula so that his forces could at least follow Johnston, if not jump him in flank."[51]

Thus developed Sherman's plan at Resaca for May 14: (1) McPherson to press the enemy left; (2) Schofield and Thomas to attack the enemy right-center, keeping the Rebel line pinned; while (3) McPherson secured a crossing and bridgehead on the south bank of the Oostanaula. In the course of the day, the Federals achieved modest success in the first, suffered costly repulse in the second, and ended up first achieving, then failing in the third. Along the way, General Johnston was given the chance to launch a little attack of his own, which for a while promised to roll up the Yankee lines before it, too, was repulsed.

Skirmishing erupted at dawn, punctuated by artillery fire from both sides all along the line. Around eleven o'clock Schofield sent forward his two divisions in attack formation, supported by another from the Fourteenth Corps. The Northerners advanced over gullied and thick-brushed terrain, crossed a creek in their front, and then were stopped cold by fierce fire from the entrenched Rebels. The Federals' casualties, after they retreated around three o'clock: almost 1,400 killed and wounded.

With this part of Sherman's plan ended in miserable failure, brighter prospects loomed on the right flank. Brigadier General Thomas W. Sweeny, division commander in the Sixteenth Corps, moved men across the Oostanaula downstream from Lay's Ferry by pontoon raft (with only three sniper casualties). After scattering some dismounted Rebel cavalrymen, though, Sweeny received a message that Confederates were sending troops to cut him off (they were not), so he withdrew his bridgehead back across the north bank.

The day ended with two attacks, one by each side at opposite ends of the battlefield. When cavalry vedettes reported to General Johnston that the Federal left flank was in the air (without support or strong defensive position), he saw a chance to deliver a blow. To his credit, Johnston (long characterized by Sherman as acting purely on the defensive) seized the opportunity, ordering two divisions of Hood's corps, plus some units brought from the Confederate left, into an attack that began about 5:00 P.M. Hood's troops overran the Union trench line, sending its occupants running, but then were halted hard by resolute fire from a Union six-gun battery. Three separate charges against those guns had failed when a division of Union reinforcements, dispatched from Sherman's right-center, arrived to stabilize the situation. Hood's men withdrew.

On the other side of the line, McPherson heard the sound of Hood's battle and sensed the Rebels had weakened their lines in his front, and so he ordered an assault of his own. The Federals overran an advanced hilltop position held by one of Polk's brigades.

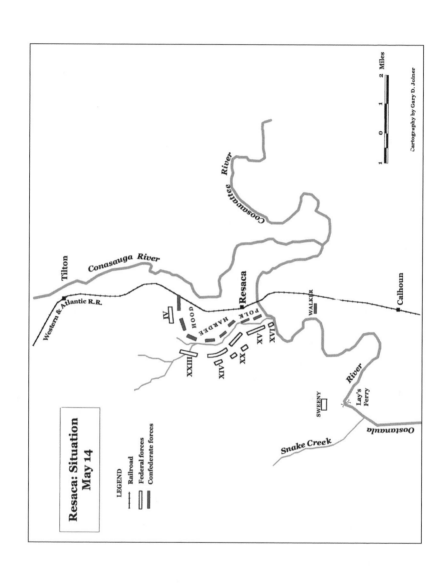

Resaca: Situation
May 14

LEGEND

Railroad
Federal forces
Confederate forces

Tilton

Conasauga River

Western & Atlantic R.R.

Coosawattee River

Resaca

HOOD

HARDEE

POLK

XXIII

XIV

XX

XVI

XV

WALKER

Calhoun

SWEENY

Snake Creek

Lay's Ferry

Oostanaula River

1   0   1   2 Miles

Cartography by Gary D. Joiner

The bishop-general ordered counterattacks; by darkness three of them had failed to retake the hill, which was east of Camp Creek and which allowed Union artillery even closer-range shots at the Western & Atlantic railroad bridge less than a mile to the northeast. This small topographical capture was the sole measure of Sherman's success for the day.

With Johnston apprehensive about his left flank and awaiting the Federals' next move, Sherman determined to maintain the initiative on the 15th. He planned another attack by Thomas down on the Confederate right (Howard's corps and Hooker's now swung around to the left flank). Schofield, then in the Union left-center, would stand ready to support Thomas's advance. McPherson was to hold his lines, "prepared at all times to assume the offensive," but concentrate on repeating Sweeny's achievement (subsequently undone) of throwing a pontoon bridge across the river near Lay's Ferry and securing "a good lodgment on the other bank."[52]

Hooker and Howard delivered their attack that afternoon. Its outcome, against veteran infantry in an entrenched position, was the predictable repulse, although the Federals overran an advanced battery position of four twelve-pounder Napoleons (which they subsequently retrieved). Hooker's men, the main attacking force, suffered the brunt of the casualties, around 1,200, though among Howard's three assault brigades, one lost 120 men in the first minutes of the attack, before they hit the dirt or drew back. Like the repulse the day before, this one led the Southerners to launch a counterattack. Intending to hit the Yankees in flank, Johnston ordered Major General A. P. Stewart's division forward. Stewart, however, ran frontally into the enemy position, suffering as sure a repulse as had Hooker, with almost as many (1,000) killed, wounded, and captured.

Amid this indecisive swapping of blows north of Resaca, only Union General Sweeny made headway. Assured that the previous afternoon's report of Rebels on the way was false, Sweeny got one pontoon bridge across the river at Lay's Ferry by noon. Another followed a few hours later, and soon Sweeny's division was over. A brigade from Walker's division attempted to drive the Yankees back across but was repulsed with help of U.S. artillery on the north bank. Nonetheless, by end of day Sweeny had advanced little beyond his bridgehead, still fearful of being attacked by greater force or (worse) cut off from the rest of the army.

But the damage was done. That evening Johnston met with his corps and a few division commanders, discussed the situation, and determined to retreat. According to Lieutenant Mackall, writing well after the event (and probably after the war), the logic of a retrograde was underscored by the Confederates' awareness of the enemy's numbers. With the entire Union army in their front, from the Oostanaula to the Conasauga, what, Mackall pondered, would keep Sherman from "detaching 40,000 and striking our communications, holding on at the same time to their works with a force equal to ours?" The Army of Tennessee was simply outmanned, "for we could not send a force sufficient to beat the force in our rear and at the same time hold present position."[53]

In this light the battle of Resaca, May 14–15, ranks strategically as a Confederate defeat, in that it led to a retreat by the Southern army. Purely tactically, though, the two days' fighting produced a draw, because both sides had had their main attacks repulsed. Staff of neither army prepared a conclusive tally of casualties, but partial reports and inferences lead to the conclusion that by this measure, too, Resaca was a draw. Sherman later counted his dead "up to that time" (which may have included the skirmishing at Rocky Face) as about 600; on May 16 at Resaca he reported 3,375 wounded.[54] Confederate killed and wounded at Resaca may be estimated as approaching 400 killed and 2,500 wounded, if only from the casualty report, May 7–20, of the Army of Tennessee's medical director, which gives the numbers for that two-week period as 444 and 2,828, respectively. To those figures could be added maybe 500–600 missing, which was the number of Rebel prisoners reported by Federal officers after the battle.

General Johnston's headquarters sent out orders for the nighttime retreat. The Confederate army stealthily withdrew and crossed the Oostanaula with a minimum of confusion in the darkness. Wagons, ambulances, and artillery used the pontoon bridge; troops marched on the railroad and wagon trestle bridges. By 3:30 in the morning, May 16, Johnston's army was across; engineers took up their pontoons and set fire to the two bridges. Sight of the flames and skirmishers' discovery of empty trenches alerted the Federals before dawn of the Rebels' retreat. Later, Confederate Brigadier General Arthur Manigault wondered why the Yankees were so inert. "I never could understand why it was that the batteries on the ridge

[McPherson's] did not open fire on the bridges, during the night, and whilst they were choked up with troops," he wrote. "They had the range of the bridges and had been practicing on it all the afternoon. . . . The demoralization and confusion they would have caused might have been serious in their consequences." Thus Johnston pulled off a masterful withdrawal in the face of the enemy. In this achievement, however, one must acknowledge General Sherman's own contribution, since the Federal commander apparently disregarded the possibility of Joe Johnston's slipping away. To Halleck that night he had wired, "I hope he will not attempt to escape." Sherman even planned the next day to push his infantry closer to the Rebel works with sorties and skirmishes. But despite his hope that Johnston should not "escape," General Sherman allowed his opponent to do just that. It would not be the last time during the Atlanta Campaign when the Union leader would permit the Rebel army to slip out of his grasp.[55]

CHAPTER SEVEN

TO CASSVILLE

SOUTH OF THE OOSTANAULA, the Georgia countryside changes. Gone are the mountains and ridges of the Dalton area that gave the Army of Tennessee its defensive positions and that both obstructed and directed the routes of march for the three Union armies. Taking their place are the rolling hills of the Piedmont, offering no such dramatically obvious defensive terrain features—as Johnston found out when his army began marching south at sunrise on May 16.

In crossing the Oostanaula, General Johnston had at least two possible courses. He could march along the railroad toward Atlanta, the Confederates' base and their railroad center and presumably Sherman's geographic target.[56] Or he could move southwest to cover Rome, the only industrial town of any importance north of the Chattahoochee River. (Rome was site of the Noble Brothers ironworks, one of only fifteen private enterprises manufacturing cannon in the entire Confederacy.) Yet given the far greater importance of Atlanta over Rome, and the Confederate army's reliance on the Western & Atlantic for its supplies, this latter course was a remote possibility. Thus, Johnston determined to drop back along the railroad, "find a favorable position near Calhoun" as he later wrote, and "await the enemy's attack there." As he looked for a position from which to do so, however, he did not find it at Calhoun, the little railway town five miles south of Resaca. Johnston therefore gave the order to continue retreating, on to Adairsville, another ten miles southward by railroad. Significantly, from Calhoun on the 16th he wired President Davis that he had been "compelled to fall back on this place" by the Yankees' crossing of the river on his flank. Typically, Johnston gave no hint to Davis of whether his intentions were to stand and fight the enemy or to continue retreating.[57]

General Sherman was prepared for his opponent to fall back all the way to the Etowah River. "We will pursue smartly to the Etowah," he telegraphed Washington on the morning of May 16.[58] Thomas with the Fourth and Fourteenth Corps took the direct route, aided by a relative smooth bridging of the Oostanaula on the morning of the 16th. McPherson's army followed its vanguard, Sweeny's division, across Lay's Ferry. The Twentieth and Twenty-third Corps made a wide arc on the other (left) flank, crossing first the Conasauga, then starting to bridge the Coosawattee well east of Resaca. On the Union right, McPherson (whose force was closest to the Rebel rear) ran into the heaviest skirmishing of the day when elements of Hardee's corps launched a brisk sortie west of Calhoun. The Confederates broke off the firefight at dusk, having bought the time needed for the rest of the army and trains to get through Calhoun. Johnston's army spent that night marching to Adairsville, which its advance units reached at dawn of May 17.

Sherman was at this point interested in wrecking the industrial facilities at Rome, fifteen miles southwest of Adairsville, and so dispatched an infantry division there. Thus, on the 17th units of his three armies were spread out on a wide ten-mile front, with five columns of foot soldiers marching generally southward. Sherman counted on his opponent's not making an effort to save Rome, believing that the Rebels would retreat by way of Cassville, across the Etowah, and on to Allatoona, where hillier country afforded defensive possibilities. But there was also the chance that Johnston might try to make a stand at Kingston, the railroad town nine miles south of Adairsville. If he did, Sherman would use flanking columns to "break his railroads right and left, and fight him square in front." "A real battle to-morrow," Sherman wrote Thomas on the 17th, "might save us much work at a later period."[59]

In truth, Johnston was about to offer battle, as he began to see how Sherman's widely scattered columns gave him a favorable tactical situation. By the evening of the 17th, the Union Fourth Corps was just north of Adairsville. The Fourteenth Corps was well behind. The Twentieth and the Twenty-third Corps, having had trouble getting their artillery across, were south of the Coosawattee. McPherson's column had covered more than a dozen miles south of Lay's Ferry. On the far Union right, Jeff Davis's division approached Rome. To Johnston this setup presented the opportunity for an attacking battle (although he did not of course know the precise positions of the enemy's various corps), one in which he could throw his strength against an isolated enemy column. Closest of the five was that of the Fourth and the Twentieth Corps, which on the 18th would be marching south from Adairsville. Calling his three corps commanders to his headquarters around 6:00 P.M. on the 17th, Johnston went over the situation on his maps. As the Yankees moved south, they could go in two directions, to Kingston or to Cassville; they would probably use both roads, for faster marching. But taking two roads would further divide them, leaving the column advancing on Cassville particularly vulnerable. This corps (Hooker's) was the one Johnston proposed to strike. Hardee and most of Wheeler's cavalry would proceed to Kingston, luring some of the Yankees down that road. The rest of the army, Hood's and Polk's corps, would march toward Cassville and, when the timing was right, turn and assault the Federals following them. Such an attack would surely succeed in at least stopping, if not routing, part of Sherman's forces. It was a good plan.

What made it better was that Sherman played into it, believing that Johnston was indeed moving his army back on Kingston. To be sure, Hardee's men were leaving a "plain, well-marked trail" behind them, which Sherman directed Thomas to follow; he was to attack with Hooker's corps if he made contact with the enemy. Schofield would be in supporting distance of Hooker; McPherson, too, was moving on Kingston. Sherman himself was near Kingston when, at 10:30 P.M., he wrote McPherson to expect a battle. It did not matter that Johnston might "fall on one or other of our columns" (the Confederates' precise plan). Sherman wanted a fight on the north side of the Etowah, and he was prepared to bring it on, "even at the hazard of beginning battle with but a part of our forces."[60]

On May 19, both sides wanted battle, but no battle occurred. Johnston certainly wanted a fight; on the afternoon of the 18th he

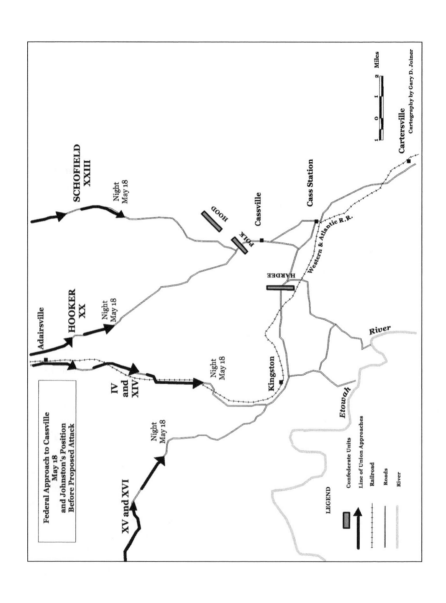

Federal Approach to Cassville
May 18
and Johnston's Position
Before Proposed Attack

Adairsville

SCHOFIELD
XXIII

Night
May 18

HOOKER
XX

Night
May 18

HOOD

POLK

Cassville

IV
and
XIV

Night
May 18

Night
May 18

HARDEE

Kingston

Cass Station

Western & Atlantic R.R.

XV and XVI

Night
May 18

River

Etowah

LEGEND

Confederate Units

Line of Union Approaches

Railroad

Roads

River

Cartersville

Miles

0   1   2

Cartography by Gary D. Joiner

aligned Hood's and Polk's corps, north of town in formation for the next day's work. Hardee, coming in from Kingston, deployed on Polk's left but would stay on the defensive, looking out for a Yankee advance from that direction. General Johnston even took the extraordinary step of issuing on the morning of the 19th a bellicose, blood-stirring general order to his troops: "Soldiers of the Army of Tennessee . . . you will now turn and march to meet his advancing columns. Fully confiding in the conduct of the officers, the courage of the soldiers, I lead you to battle."[61]

Johnston did not write out his battle plan with the meticulousness that so characterized Sherman; in fact, he seems not to have written it out at all, for no such document has come to light for publication. Meeting with his three corps commanders, Johnston conveyed instructions, as he later phrased them, for "the two corps at Cassville . . . to advance against the troops that had followed them at Adairsville, Hood's leading on the right."[62] Hood had in mind a flanking attack, and about eight o'clock on the morning of the 19th his infantry started marching to the area east of the Cassville-Adairsville road to be in position to assault the enemy flank when it began skirmishing with Polk. About 10:30 A.M., however, the Confederates' plan began to unravel when one of Hood's staff officers saw Yankee cavalry on the right flank, coming in from a road to the northeast and delivering some rifle and cannon fire against Hindman's division. Hood halted and even drew back, notifying headquarters of his need to do so. Johnston responded at first with disbelief but then accepted the situation. The Confederate commander felt he had no choice but to cancel the attack and order Hood to withdraw. Thus did the purely coincidental appearance of Union horsemen (McCook's and Stoneman's, ordered by Sherman to bear down on the Western & Atlantic east of Kingston) blow apart Joe Johnston's first real stratagem for a Lee-like pounce on part of Sherman's forces. By midafternoon Johnston had his army southeast of Cassville entrenching along a ridge in a new three-mile line, this time a purely defensive one.

General Johnston was naturally disappointed at the lost opportunity. The next day he wired President Davis that his plan for a general attack had been undone by credence given to a "false report" of enemy strength. "When the mistake was discovered" he explained, "it was too late to resume the movement." For a long time, years after the war, he argued that there could have been no Yankees on Hood's flank or rear. "The report upon which General Hood acted was manifestly untrue," he wrote in his memoirs (1874). Four years later he wrote, "[Hood's] erratic movement [was based] upon a wild report"; and later still, he claimed, regarding Hood's alleged sighting of the enemy, "Our whole army knew that to be impossible." Consequently, in not pushing forth his planned attack, Hood was guilty of "extraordinary disobedience." Hood responded with understandable vehemence, beginning in his official report, which was written in early 1865, after Johnston's report began to appear in the press. "It was not a mistake," Hood argued about the reported sighting of enemy cavalry; Hindman's division had casualties to prove it. Years later, General Hood went so far as to assemble letters from other officers to corroborate his position.[63]

However shaken out—and modern scholarship tends to favor Hood—Johnston's disappointment with Hood and the missed opportunity for attack on the morning of May 19 caused mistrust and eventually dislike between the two Confederate generals who opposed Sherman in the Atlanta Campaign. One might infer that a key reason for the force of Johnston's feeling against Hood was his resentment over being labeled a retreater and not a fighter, when Hood, the army's legendary fighter at Cassville proved not only to be a retreater but to be so in a way that reflected unfairly back on Johnston. Both of these officers would develop and build on their respective reputations in the weeks ahead.

CHAPTER EIGHT

TO NEW HOPE CHURCH AND BACK TO THE RAILROAD (JOHNSTON IS TURNED, AGAIN)

ON THE AFTERNOON OF MAY 19, 1864, as the Southerners fortified their new line southeast of Cassville, Howard's Fourth Corps came up, joined soon by Hooker's and Schofield's corps. Placing artillery on some hills, the Federals opened a severe barrage against Johnston's entrenched position. The Union cannonade caused such casualties among the men and damage to some batteries that Polk and Hood began to consider their positions untenable. In a conference that night with General Johnston, the two corps commanders contended that if the enemy opened up again with cannon fire, their lines could hold only two hours at the most; Polk's engineer confirmed that at several points in the line the troops were subject to lethal enfilade. They implied the need for a retreat to a better, safer position, an idea that Johnston at first resisted. After all, had he not just, that morning, proclaimed to his troops that he would lead them to glorious battle? Within an hour, however, Johnston gave the order for the army to withdraw, justifying his decision in three ways: the Yankees' artillery power in his front, their lengthening line, which threatened to overlap both his flanks, and, finally, the news that (as at Dalton and Resaca) troops had crossed the Etowah downriver (Kenner Garrard's cavalry had found a bridge southeast of Kingston). Again, Sherman had used his superior numbers and tactical agility to outflank Joe Johnston. And again, Johnston had been forced to retreat. The Southern army withdrew from its trench works between midnight and 2:00 A.M., while axmen cut trees as if for fortifying and skirmishers kept up their sporadic rifle fire. By dawn of May 20, the Confederates reached Cartersville, despite the usual confusion of a night march. They kept going, crossing the Etowah on train, wagon, and two pontoon bridges. By evening the army was across, and the bridges either taken up or burned. Yankees drawing up on the other side watched the flames.

Johnston understandably was bitter. In ordering the retreat from Cassville, "a step which I have regretted ever since," he later wrote, Johnston made it clear he was bowing reluctantly to pressure from both Polk and Hood to retreat. But there was not much he could say at the time to his men, who were of course disappointed at another retreat after having heard just that morning a hortatory battle address. To be sure, not all of this sentiment would have filtered up to the commanding general, but his staff was manifestly aware of it. "Troops dispirited and fagged," Mackall wrote, as well they should have been, after a night of marching and a day of standing on battle alert, digging in, skirmishing, more marching and enduring enemy shellfire. "Night retreat after issuing general order impaired confidence. . . . Troops think no stand to be made north of

Chattahoochee." Adding to these unhappy expressions emanating up from the ranks was a similar expression filtering down from President Davis. That afternoon, having established headquarters two miles north of Allatoona, Johnston received the telegram from Richmond that Davis had actually sent two days before and that in turn responded to news of two days before that—May 16, the day of Johnston's retreat from Resaca. "Your dispatch of 16th received; read with disappointment," Davis said with icy understatement. "I hope the re-enforcement sent will enable you to achieve important results."[64]

Indeed, the Confederate States War Department had strained mightily to reinforce Johnston's army. Added to his command since the first of May were troops from the Savannah-Charleston garrison (2,800) and Mobile (1,550) and 10,200 of Polk's "Army of the Department of Alabama, Mississippi and East Louisiana," now turned into Polk's corps, the Army of Tennessee. All of these additions, some 14,500 men, brought Johnston's strength up from his 54,500 present on April 30 to 69,000. Moreover, not all of Polk's troops had arrived. En route, Major General Samuel French's division (4,200) happened to be at Rome on the 17th, just in time to join the home defense troops and keep Jeff Davis's Yankees at bay. This infantry would join the army on May 19, bringing Johnston's command up to 73,250. Brigadier General William H. ("Red") Jackson's cavalry (4,500) had also ridden in by then. To be subtracted, of course, were the 3,000 or so casualties already sustained by the army. Thus, with a strength of 70,000–74,000 men, the Army of Tennessee in late May 1864 was the largest Confederate army ever assembled in the western theater, as well as in the Confederacy as a whole at the time, bigger than Lee's in Virginia.

Yet while Lee was holding his own against Grant in Virginia, Johnston was giving up territory and key points, such as northwest Georgia's principal city, Rome. After holding off the Yankees for a while, the last of French's division marched out of the city on the morning of May 18, whereupon Northern troops entered and began sacking the place. (The citizens had fled the day before.) Left behind, in fine order was the Noble Brothers foundry, which the withdrawing Southerners tried in their haste to wreck but failed. The Federals burned the shops, blew up the smokestacks, and eventually hauled away the machinery. The Confederates did a better job at salvaging the essentials of the Etowah Iron Works, whose machinery the Georgia militia managed to get on board trains before the town was abandoned. Nevertheless, the fall of Rome, coupled with the Army of Tennessee's seemingly chronic retrograde, contributed toward a public panic among many north Georgians. "Great alarm in country around," observed Lieutenant Mackall in his published journal.[65]

And well might there be alarm among the Southerners, for the Yankee armies at the Etowah were now less than fifty miles from Atlanta. Knowing this, and that their leader was demonstrating a pattern of outsmarting his Rebel opponent, Sherman's officers and men were "in splendid condition and spirits," observed one commentator on May 22.[66] They had marched and fought hard; so the commanding general offered them two days' rest and refitting before preparing to move out again on May 23. In the meantime, he summoned reinforcements, chiefly Major General Frank P. Blair's Seventeenth Corps from Decatur, Alabama, which was expected to add 10,000 infantry and artillerymen when it arrived in early June. He also expected newly organized militia from the several midwestern states to come down and free up those units of McPherson's and Thomas's armies detailed in the rear as railroad guards. Davis's division, having plundered Rome of enough provisions to subsist for twenty days, would rejoin the main body, too.

General Sherman's field orders intimated there was rough duty ahead. "The whole army must be ready to march by May 23, stripped for battle, but equipped and provided for twenty days." Sherman planned to leave the railroad for a week or two—not because he thought his men and animals could subsist entirely off the country (though they could be expected to draw much meat, forage, and vegetables). Rather, he knew the topography ahead, specifically at Allatoona, the rail village around which Johnston could be expected to draw up his next position. The Western & Atlantic cut through a pass in a ridge line that was just as imposing and militarily formidable as Rocky Face had been. "I knew the strength of Allatoona Pass, having ridden through it twenty years ago," Sherman later recorded. "Satisfied that the enemy could and would hold us in check at the Allatoona Pass, I resolved, without even attempting it in front, to turn it by a circuit to the right." As he outlined to Halleck on May 20, "On the 23d I will cross the Etowah and move on Dallas. This will turn the Allatoona Pass." Sherman was full of self-assurance. With new regiments and other soldiers returning from furlough adding to his ranks (and making good his casualties to date, estimated at around 4,000), he expected to cross the Etowah with 80,000 infantry. All were true effectives, because he had ordered the "sick, wounded, worthless men, and idlers" sent to the rear. Thus strengthened, he was already planning how he would feint and fool Johnston into crossing the Chattahoochee, another twenty-five miles southeastward. Privately, to his wife, Ellen, Cump avowed his intent to "take Atlanta and disturb the peace of central Georgia."[67]

The Confederates' situation was far less rosy. All that President Davis and others in Richmond could see was a lot of retreating. General Johnston sought to put the best face on it in a message sent from Etowah on the 20th: "In the last eight days the enemy have pressed us back to this place, thirty-two miles," he wrote, though his retrograde from Dalton, May 12, was actually closer to 45 miles. He did point out, though, that his forces "have repulsed every attack" of the enemy, albeit outflanked at Resaca and denied a chance to strike a blow at Cassville. The next day he corrected his mistake: "My dispatch . . . should have read thus: In the last six days the enemy has pressed us back to this point, thirty-two miles," which was indeed the distance covered retrogressively by the Army of Tennessee May 15–20 (that is, from Resaca to Etowah). Then, referring to Davis's message of the 16th (acknowledging "disappointment"), the general wrote candidly: "I know that my dispatch must of necessity create the feeling you express. I have earnestly sought an opportunity to strike the enemy. The direction of the railroad to this point has enabled him to press me back by steadily moving to the left and by fortifying the moment he halted. He has made an assault upon his superior forces too hazardous."[68]

Thrown thus on the defensive, and having deployed his army on the high ground around Allatoona Pass, Joe Johnston awaited Sherman's next move (though notice again the Confederate commander's decision not to contest the enemy's crossing of the Etowah, and his willingness to give the enemy those three days, May 20–22, to rest and refit). With the initiative thus firmly in hand, and in accord with Sherman's schedule, at dawn of the 23d all three Union armies broke camp and began to march. Sherman had selected the country town of Dallas, fifteen miles southwest of Allatoona Pass, as his objective, but for Thomas and Schofield most of the day was spent in just getting across the Etowah by bridge or ford.

Johnston knew from his cavalry that the Yankees were crossing the river in force downstream. Dust clouds alone showed that infantry and wagons were moving westward on the north bank. The Confederate commander, while holding Hood's corps near the railroad, therefore ordered Hardee and Polk to march toward Dallas early on the 24th. Hardee, in the lead, was later that morning just three and a half miles east of Dallas, about to beat the Yankees to that point. Polk eventually fell into line on his right; Hood, last of the three corps, marched toward New Hope Church, a Methodist crossroads four miles northeast of Dallas.

In war, knowing what the enemy is doing gives one an advantage; General Sherman had this advantage during his concentration on Dallas. On the afternoon of the 24th some of McCook's cavalry, skirmishing with Jackson's horsemen in the advance of Hooker's corps toward Burnt Hickory, captured a courier from Johnston to Jackson affirming that the Confederate army was moving toward Dallas. Thus, Sherman could infer that Joe Johnston knew his plan and was massing his troops to block it. Yet this intelligence seemed not to have registered with Sherman. On the morning of May 25 Hooker's corps, in the lead of Thomas's army, was marching not so much directly on Dallas as toward a point northeast of it, that is, toward contact with Hood at New Hope Church. As his men built logworks and brought up artillery, Hood sent two regiments and a battalion ahead as skirmishers. These not only peppered Geary's division (Hooker's van) as it approached after noon but charged it so smartly that Geary ordered a halt. From prisoners he learned that he had Hood's entire corps in his front. This information was enough to impel him, and Thomas, to order forward the other two divisions of the corps. Thomas also sent a staff officer to report Geary's precarious situation to Sherman, who was found to be "showing great impatience," presumably at his columns' lack of progress. Informed that Alpheus Williams's division was en route to support Geary, Sherman snapped, "Let Williams go in anywhere as soon as he gets up. I don't see what they are waiting for in front now. There haven't been twenty rebels there to-day."[69]

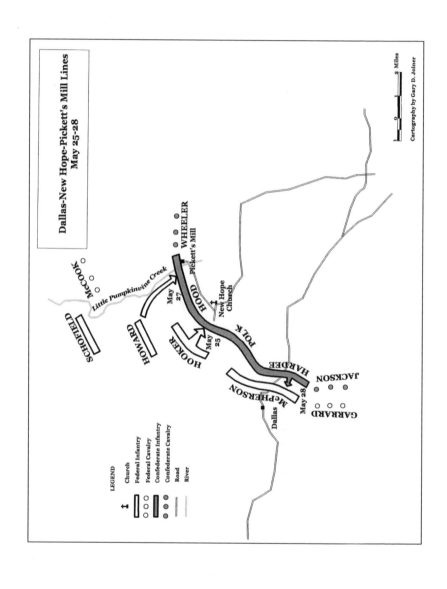

Dallas-New Hope-Pickett's Mill Lines
May 25-28

LEGEND

Church
Federal Infantry
Federal Cavalry
Confederate Infantry
Confederate Cavalry
Road
River

McCOOK
SCHOFIELD
Little Pumpkinvine Creek
HOWARD
WHEELER
HOOD
Pickett's Mill
May 27
HOOKER
May 25
New Hope Church
POLK
HARDEE
McPHERSON
May 28
Dallas
JACKSON
GARRARD

1   0   1   2 Miles

Cartography by Gary D. Joiner

These words were as close to an attack order as Thomas and Hooker received that day, and from it they inferred that it did not matter to the major-general in command whether they were faced by twenty rebels or by Hood's entire corps. So they ordered an attack, by all three divisions of the Twentieth Corps. The Confederates, meanwhile, had fortified their lines and prepared for an attack, based on information from a Yankee captured in the skirmishing earlier in the afternoon. Armed and ready, Hood's soldiers (more specifically, Peter Stewart's division) had little trouble repulsing the Yankee charge, begun around four or five that afternoon. It did not seem to matter that Hooker's corps numbered 16,000 and Stewart's division only about 4,000. By this time of the war, soldiers on the fortified defensive almost always enjoyed an easy victory. As one Confederate later observed, "It is fun for our troops to stand in their trenches and mow down their lines as they advance." Moreover, Stewart's soldiers were considerably buttressed by artillery that, according to Hood, "did great execution in the enemy's ranks." Casualties for the afternoon of May 25 at New Hope Church reflected these lopsided, customary odds: in Hooker's three divisions, 1,665 officers and men were reported killed, wounded, or missing; in Stewart's division the casualties were 300 to 400.[70]

Even General Sherman, having blundered in misjudging the enemy strength in Hooker's front and calling on him to attack it, acknowledged that the Twentieth Corps had "had a pretty hard fight" that afternoon. With the two armies hulking toward a possibly even greater showdown, Sherman brought his several corps closer together on the 26th: Howard's up on Hooker's left, Schofield's farther on that flank. McPherson, with the Fifteenth and Sixteenth Corps, occupied Dallas, forming the right of the Union line. Light skirmishing rattled throughout the day as the Union forces worked into position and both sides fortified further. Although Sherman could not verify whether more than Hood's corps was in his front, for the 27th he issued instructions for morning bombardment followed by movement around or against the enemy right flank.[71]

This movement would be done by Howard, supported by Schofield. If unimpeded, Sherman wrote, Howard could have as his ultimate goal Marietta or Acworth. At the very least he could maneuver into an advantageous position to deliver a flanking attack.

General Howard got his men marching in late morning, considerably hampered by the thick growth. This sight-blocking wilderness prevented the Fourth Corps commander from detecting the position of the enemy, who was, as it turned out, directly in his front and aptly placed to rebuff Sherman's hoped-for turning movement. Indeed, in the afternoon of the 26th, Johnston had extended his lines to the east by shifting Hindman's division (Hood's corps) but more notably by marching Pat Cleburne's division from Hardee's sector on the left all the way to Pickett's Mill, a mile and a half beyond New Hope. Worse for the Federals, Cleburne knew they were coming; a morning reconnaissance had disclosed the enemy moving toward his right. Thus Cleburne had time to prepare for an attack, placing his men along the top of a slope, where some of them erected slight works.

General Howard felt himself stumbling rather blindly through the woods. "No person can appreciate the difficulty in moving over this ground unless he can see it," Howard sent word back to Thomas at 4:35. Though he knew from prisoners that Hindman's and Cleburne's divisions were somewhere in his front, he nonetheless reported, "I ... am now turning the enemy's right flank, I think." Notice the *I think*, for General Howard was dead wrong, a gruesomely literal realization when he finally ordered an assault around five o'clock, propelled by a note back from Thomas: "General Sherman wishes us to get on the enemy's flank and rear as soon as possible." The Federals attacked resolutely and courageously but could not overcome the tactical advantages of veteran troops on the defensive. General Cleburne recorded that his men "were awaiting them, and ... as they appeared upon the slope slaughtered them with deliberate aim." Actually, Cleburne had to shift a brigade hurriedly because the Yankees for a while threatened to overlap his flank. These troops, H. B. Granbury's Texans, stood and fought without dirt- or logworks, shooting down the Yankees in murderous fire. The slaughter ended after two hours when Howard broke off the attack. Decisively repulsed, with no ground taken, Federal troops suffered casualties in the battle of Pickett's Mill, May 27, that numbered about 1,700, sustained chiefly by Thomas J. Wood's division of Howard's corps (212 killed, 927 wounded, 318 missing). Confederate losses did not even approach a third of the Federals'— Cleburne's division, 448 killed and wounded (mostly in Granbury's brigade), plus an undisclosed but small number of dismounted cavalrymen who helped out Cleburne's infantry. The resulting figure, Lieutenant Mackall observed, was "a fraction over 500."[72]

General Sherman was loath to disclose to Halleck in Washington the details of his repulses on the 25th and 27th, referring to the several days' activities as "many sharp, severe encounters, but nothing decisive." And while Sherman willingly acknowledged that he had been tactically stymied—"Johnston has chosen a strong line, and made hasty but strong parapets of timber and earth, and has thus far stopped us"—he could also assume strategic success in having turned Johnston's army out of its secure position at Allatoona Pass. Having done that, he contemplated sidling back to the railroad. Thus, early on the 28th he announced to Thomas his intention to "outflank the enemy by an enlarged movement by our left," building, in other words, on Howard's bloodied, attempted turning movement at Pickett's Mill the previous day.[73]

From their high ground, Confederate observers picked up some of this motion on the enemy right. General Johnston wondered whether it meant that Sherman was shifting back eastward. As a result, on the 28th Johnston ordered his leftmost division, that of Major General William B. Bate, supported by Brigadier Frank Armstrong's cavalry brigade, to develop the enemy position and attack if it were in any way weakened. It was decidedly not, as Confederates advancing around 3:00 P.M. quickly discovered: Logan's Fifteenth Corps was dug in behind log-and-earth fortifications. But by the time Bate knew the enemy was there and tried to cancel the attack, two brigades were already in motion. They were sharply repulsed, losing about 400 men. Added to Armstrong's 167 killed and wounded, Confederate casualties were probably 600. Logan reported a surprisingly high loss of 379.

Thus, both commanders in the several days of the Hell Hole (Union soldiers' nickname for the New Hope area) were reminded of the cruel lesson of Civil War tactics: how readily a flank or turning movement (such as Howard's, May 27) or a reconnaissance or demonstration (such as Bate's, May 28) could turn into a wasteful frontal attack. The pathetic result of both of these minor disasters was most trenchantly expressed by the soldiers themselves, including Union lieutenant Ambrose Bierce, who called the Union assault of the 27th a "criminal blunder." On the Confederate side, Bate's men also knew someone had blundered with their charge; one survivor, John Jackman, recorded how Bate (called "Old Grits" by his men) took the blame: "'Grits' 'catches it' from all sides and quarters."[74]

As the commander with the fewer troops, General Johnston was more mindful of the wastefulness of these frontal assaults. He certainly did not mind when Sherman ordered one on his lines. But among his own tactical alternatives, save maintaining the purely passive defense, there were just a few options, such as an infantry flanking movement or cavalry strike into the enemy's rear. On a very small scale, Johnston tried the latter when he sent Wheeler and some 800 men across the Etowah on May 23, ordered to reconnoiter the enemy's movements and, as Lieutenant Mackall recorded in his journal, to "cut communications."[75] Had he truly meant to disrupt Sherman's supply flow, General Wheeler would deliberately have struck the Western & Atlantic Railroad and torn it up. No; Wheeler contented himself with attacking a Yankee wagon train at Cass Station on the 24th, burning much of it, while carrying away seventy wagons and teams with 180 prisoners and more horses and mules, before returning to the army on the 26th. Wheeler's expedition, not so much a raid as a reconnaissance with a wagon-train burning thrown in, was as close to a cavalry strike on Sherman's communications as Joseph E. Johnston ever attempted while commander of the Army of Tennessee. The attack created only passing notice among the Federals, before their own cavalry drove Wheeler back across the river. For an army commander who had for months been calling upon the administration to send Polk's, S. D. Lee's, or Forrest's cavalry out of Mississippi into middle Tennessee, General Johnston was noticeably reluctant to dispatch his own mounted forces for the same purpose. To be sure, President Davis and General Bragg had included the idea of such a raid, if only as a diversion, in their plans for a spring offensive. General Forrest himself favored the idea as he made clear on April 6 when he proposed that Johnston send cavalry, with his own, in a combined raid on Nashville. There is no record of Johnston's reply.

Once Sherman had launched his campaign in early May, Johnston renewed his calls upon Polk for a cavalry expedition into middle Tennessee. S. D. Lee, his successor, actually directed Forrest to start for middle Tennessee on May 20 but had to countermand the order in a few days when Union forces out of Memphis looked as though they were launching an expedition of their own. This setback may have influenced Johnston in his decision to send Wheeler across the Etowah in his raid, May 23–26, but beyond that he made no bolder effort to block the Western & Atlantic's supply service to Sherman's armies. Had he really been determined to do so, we could speculate that two weeks earlier Johnston would have destroyed the railway cut through Tunnel Hill before evacuating his position at Dalton. In their retreat, though, the Confederates merely removed track at the underpass.

Back with the army, Wheeler reported on the evening of the 27th that the Yankees' left flank was vulnerable to attack. General Hood requested and received from Johnston permission to draw his corps out of line and deliver the blow. Marching well before dawn of the 28th, Hood's troops found the enemy had redeployed and even dug in. Word was sent back to headquarters; Johnston canceled the attack and ordered Hood to return to the main line. Both generals regretted the lost opportunity; but at least Hood was searching for a chance to deliver a coup de flank.

With both sides rapped and bleeding through the misplaced audacity of running up against prepared positions, neither attempted a move on the 29th or 30th. Instead, the two days and even nights were spent sniping and shelling through the woods all down the lines from Pickett's Mill to Dallas. As the more passive of the two army leaders, Johnston was reasonably content to maintain this watchkrieg (a term created to reflect General Mackall's statement that his boss's plan was "to keep close up to the enemy" and "watch carefully"). Watching, waiting, General Johnston could console himself that he was at least delaying Sherman's advance deeper into Georgia. "We are still confronting the enemy here," he wrote Bragg on the 28th. Perhaps this passive delaying was the only strategy Johnston had at this point, three weeks into the Georgia campaign. After the war, the general's admirers would begin to see Johnston's strategy as a masterfully deliberate program of delaying the enemy's advance, likening it to that of the old Roman general Quintus Fabius, dubbed Cunctator (the Delayer). (It is said that Johnston did not particularly like this Fabian allusion, probably realizing that mere cunctation is not the usual attribute of history's great military leaders. Gilbert E. Govan and James W. Livingood, the general's biographers, suggest his dislike of the Fabius moniker stemmed from his argument that throughout his campaign in north Georgia, Sherman's superior numbers gave him no choice but to retreat.)[76]

Thus, what some at the time saw as delaying, others saw as retreating. Johnston had retreated from Dalton, Resaca, and Cassville and been turned out of Allatoona. Would it ever end? Some Atlantans thought not, and that number seemed to grow daily as Sherman moved closer. "I find that very many people think it probable that this place may be occupied by the Yankees very soon," Louisa Pittman wrote on May 18. Events of the days following rattled more people in the city. On the 21st military officials ordered the army's hospitals and stores in Marietta to be evacuated to Atlanta. On the 23d Mayor James M. Calhoun ordered all able-bodied civilian men to report for military service or else leave town. As if in compliance, a whole slew of the citizenry began loading their possessions, making May 24 "a wild day of excitement," according to Cyrena Stone, whose house stood in the city's northeast suburbs. "Such packing up & leaving of those, who but a short time ago said with such great boasting & assurance, that Johnston would never fall back here, & allow the Yankees to step a foot on Georgia soil—is perfectly marvellous to behold." The very next day, for the first time ever, Atlantans heard the muffled thud of artillery (from New Hope Church, less than thirty miles away). The noise created more alarm among the townspeople, even though the *Intelligencer* downplayed the commotion by asserting that "our General, in whom we have the most implicit confidence, assures us that 'Atlanta is safe.'" Not everyone felt this way; for these "ravens" and "croakers" (as the *Intelligencer* called them), a reporter in town gave voice. He was Henry Watterson, writing as "Shadow" under date of May 24 and setting down his impressions of "the condition of Atlanta at this moment." He found the city "demoralized utterly; confused, bewildered." "The order of the Mayor calling everybody to the trenches," he reported, "is fast depopulating the principal thoroughfares. Wagons block up every way. . . .—All is tumult, consternation." So many people evacuating bespoke little public confidence in Joe Johnston's ability to defeat or repel Sherman's hordes. "Shadow" himself acknowledged doubt and pessimism when he added, "I observe my own feeling on the subject and I think Atlanta will fall."[77]

Watterson's gloomy opinion brought instant rebuttal from the *Intelligencer*, which accused the correspondent of "vivid imagination" and "hyperbolic assumptions." Probably many Atlantans agreed with Mary Mallard, wife of the minister of Central Presbyterian Church, who called "Shadow's" column "a most absurd piece," a gross exaggeration of a few people's exodus, and an utter "falsehood" in claiming that a panic had developed in the city.[78] Regardless of how many Atlantans were fleeing, however, both Watterson and Mallard would have agreed that at least part of the citizenry in late May doubted that Confederate general Joseph E. Johnston had the talent, manpower, or grit to keep the Yankees out of Atlanta. Their doubts and anxieties would have deepened if they knew that already Johnston had dispatched Major General Mansfield Lovell, now serving as a volunteer aide, to the Chattahoochee River to examine its ferries. With Brigadier General Marcus Wright, post commander at Atlanta, Lovell was already planning positions for artillery and infantry to contest enemy crossings. It was not a good sign for the populace of Atlanta. It was no sign at all of anything except Johnston's plan to retreat some more.

General Sherman, ever restless, desired to get to the Chattahoochee as soon as he could. And although, as he told Thomas on the 30th, there was no need for "undue haste" (because every day brought Blair's infantry corps closer to a junction with the army group), he had already formed his plan and wanted to push it.[79] Thus, he issued orders that started his troops moving northeast, back to the railroad. Garrard's and Stoneman's cavalry were sent ahead to Allatoona Pass; their securing of that place by June 2 meant not only that the Federals held a formidable position but also that they could advance their railhead south of the Etowah. On the 3d, Federal troops entered Acworth, five and a half miles southeast of Allatoona by the Western & Atlantic, advancing their control of the railroad that much farther.

With the exception of Wheeler's cavalry contesting the enemy movements with the usual skirmishing, Johnston offered no opposition to Sherman's sidling back to the railroad. "For several days he has been approaching railroad gradually, intrenching at every point," Lieutenant Mackall recorded on May 30. But with Sherman moving, Johnston also had to move and made plans to march his army to the area of Lost Mountain. In the meantime, both commanders characterized the previous week's activity in much the same way. "Thus far we have had no real battle, but one universal skirmish extending over a vast surface," Sherman wrote General Halleck, June 2. To Halleck's counterpart in Richmond, Braxton Bragg, Johnston reported on the 1st that his army was healthy and had enjoyed advantages in its recent "partial engagements," only the sum of which he judged would be equal to a full battle.[80]

Notwithstanding these advantageously fought "partial engagements," General Bragg—like some Atlantans, like some people throughout the Confederacy, like some soldiers in Johnston's own army—could not help concluding that Sherman's armies had advanced more than sixty-five miles into Georgia (the distance from Ringgold to New Hope Church) with no more than, figuratively speaking, a bloody nose. Thus, Bragg, in his reply to Johnston, pointed out: "General Lee, like yourself, has had no general battle lately, but in a series of partial engagements he has greatly damaged the enemy." Johnston's only response to this coy jab at his generalship, directed by his immediate superior in the nation's capital, was to ask what further assistance he could receive from S. D. Lee and Bedford Forrest in Mississippi. The latter especially, Johnston still hoped, could be thrown against the railroad between Chattanooga and the Etowah. "Cavalry on the rear of Sherman, this side of the Tennessee, would do him much harm at present," he advised, adding in a separate message to General Lee that even a division from Forrest's command, plus a horse brigade out of Alabama, sent against the railroad "may produce great results."[81]

General Johnston, however, had a hard time realizing that such assistance could not be sent. To be sure, he knew that Polk's arrival in mid-May had cleaned out Alabama and Mississippi of most Confederate soldiers; as Lieutenant Mackall acknowledged, "Southwest drained of troops to strengthen this army." The only forces available to defend what was left of Confederate authority in the region were, in effect, S. D. Lee and Forrest's cavalry, as well as the garrison at Mobile, though even it was being further tapped. (On May 21 the War Department ordered General Maury in Mobile to send another brigade, Brigadier General W. A. Quarles's, plus two regiments to Johnston. Quarles's brigade alone, arriving May 26, would add another 2,200, maybe as many as 2,800, effectives to the Army of Tennessee.) Sherman understood the situation: "I have no doubt Johnston has in my front every man he can scrape." Though his army was as strong as it could ever possibly be, Johnston could not relinquish the hope that some equestrian coup, launched from outside his department against Sherman's logistical lines, would bring about the strategic result that he himself felt incapable of producing. He was joined by others, such as the Confederate senator from Tennessee Gustavus Adolphus Henry, who asked War Secretary Seddon, "Now that the enemy are drawn far into Georgia would it not be a great move to order Forrest with his whole force to fall in behind the enemy and cut off his trains of supplies and make such a demonstration in his rear as will destroy his army?" On May 29 Forrest again offered to "attempt to cut enemy's communication in Middle Tennessee," but the Yankees kept getting in the way. On June 1 a strong Union column marched out of the Memphis area under General Samuel Sturgis with the express purpose of fighting Forrest and at least keeping him busy if not actually defeating him. This development caused General Lee to wire back to Johnston on the 3d that he could not dispatch Forrest till the enemy expedition had been dealt with. "So, the great results anticipated from a raid of the Mississippi cavalry in Sherman's rear," the faithful Mackall recorded, "are not to be fulfilled at an early day." Lee's message meant that General Johnston was once more informed that he would have to deal with Sherman on his own. With this news in mind, on the 4th Johnston ordered a night march of his army to the position he had already ordered his engineers to stake out along Lost and Pine Mountains. Because the former, from New Hope Church, was six miles more to the east than the southeast, the army's change of line June 4–5 might not have merited the name "retreat" or "retrograde." But as Johnston's soldiers slogged through the rain and mud that night, they could well have been excused for thinking of their march in those terms.[82]

When General Bragg in Richmond read Johnston's telegram of June 5, announcing very tersely the army's taking up of a new position about Lost Mountain, he well might have been undecided whether to interpret it as a sidewise maneuver or as another retreat. Indeed, playing a little loosely with words was a game in which both commanders indulged themselves just then. Johnston, for his part, fibbed in his message to Bragg of the 1st. When he said that his army in its "partial engagements . . . had had great advantage," he was ignoring entirely the bloody and blundering frontal assault that cost Bate's division around 700 men on May 28. Sherman was even more of a prevaricator. When he generalized to Halleck on the 5th that he had succeeded in turning Johnston's Dallas–New Hope–Pickett's Mill lines "with less loss to ourselves than we have inflicted on him," he was ignoring the 3,200 casualties of Hooker's and Howard's repulses, May 25 and 27. Sounding like his opponent, Sherman generalized to another officer that "in all encounters we had the advantage."[83]

Both generals thus toyed with notions of who had gained the most recent advantage. Behind all these exercises in semantics was the hard truth in war that numbers count beyond all else. And according to the numbers, the Union was superior by a ratio of almost 2 to 1: on June 1, Sherman's effective strength was 112,819; on June 10, Johnston's was 59,956. The Southerners' odds improved a little more in the category of "present for duty," adding in 6,500 officers and the men detailed away from the firing line: 120,229 Federals faced 69,291 Confederates "present." The ratio here was almost 10 to 6.

The Southerners would never have better odds in the Atlanta Campaign, for Confederate authorities, as Sherman himself knew, had "scraped" every available man into the Army of Tennessee. A few auxiliaries could be added eventually; on June 4 General Johnston learned that Governor Brown had organized a division of 3,000 state troops. But they were assigned to guard the Chattahoochee crossings.

In sum, having drawn his army to within twenty-five miles of Atlanta, Joe Johnston was still well outnumbered. Worse, he had given up two river barriers to the Yankees' advance (the Oostanaula and Etowah) and had only one more behind him (the Chattahoochee). Moreover, not only was Johnston running out of defensive strongpoints but Sherman had used his superior numbers repeatedly to get around them. At the same time, the Confederate leader had shown none of the boldness demonstrated by his opponent, and—if past performance was an indicator—would probably continue the same cautious, tepid defensive policy he had announced all along as his only recourse. For all of these reasons, "Shadow" predicted, "Atlanta will fall." General Bragg, though less ominously, warned President Davis on June 4, "the condition of affairs in Georgia is daily becoming more serious."[84]

It would get more serious still.

CHAPTER NINE

THE MOUNTAIN LINES, JUNE 5–JULY 2, 1864

ON JUNE 5, WITH HIS FORCES marching toward Gilgal Church and Pine Mountain, Sherman found that the Rebels were already in position in front of them. He was not surprised. The night before he had written: "Joe Johnston is shrewd enough to see that we have begun such a movement, and will prepare the way." Besides, Cump had a multiday plan in mind: wait for his engineers to finish rebuilding the railroad bridge across the Etowah (estimated completion time, five days), at which point he could begin transporting supplies down to Acworth and beyond; wait for the arrival of Blair's Seventeenth Corps, which had reached Kingston on the 6th and would join McPherson on the 8th; store up supplies for the next big push while letting the men rest; and then at daylight on June 9, get the whole army group marching. With Johnston's army blocking his path, Sherman expected a fight at Kennesaw Mountain, but he would be prudent. As he wrote to his wife on the 9th: "I will not run hot-headed against any works prepared for us." Cump's words would prove an uncertain predictor of his battle behavior.[85]

Sherman's preparations were not completed by June 9, the announced date for resumption of the Union offensive, but he sent his armies marching the next morning on a wide front generally heading southeastward to Marietta. McPherson, moving via the railroad, passed through and south of Big Shanty (the present-day town of Kennesaw); Thomas and Schofield came up on the Rebel lines at Gilgal Church and Pine Mountain. Sherman's orders were quite clear: "Intrenched positions will not be attacked without orders."[86] By entrenching at Pine Mountain, General Johnston hoped not only to take advantage of high ground (albeit with a somewhat vulnerable salient, held by Bate's division) but also to induce the enemy to do just what Sherman had given orders against—attack entrenched positions. After McPherson's army occupied Acworth on the 6th, the Confederates shifted their lines farther to the east, so that on June 8 their position ran from Gilgal across the Western & Atlantic to north of Kennesaw Mountain. Three days later, Johnston reported

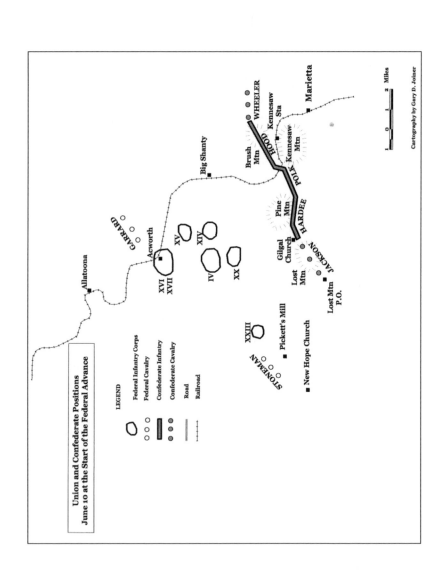

Union and Confederate Positions
June 10 at the Start of the Federal Advance

LEGEND

Federal Infantry Corps
Federal Cavalry
Confederate Infantry
Confederate Cavalry
Road
Railroad

Allatoona

GARRARD

Acworth

XVI
XVII

XV

XIV

IV

XX

XXIII

STONEMAN

Pickett's Mill

New Hope Church

Big Shanty

Brush
Mtn

HOOD

WHEELER

Kennesaw
Sta

Kennesaw
Mtn

POLK

Marietta

Pine
Mtn

HARDEE

Gilgal
Church

Lost
Mtn

JACKSON

Lost Mtn
P.O.

1   0   1   2 Miles

Cartography by Gary D. Joiner

to General Bragg no change, save a little more shifting to the right, corresponding to McPherson's advance south of Big Shanty.

No one, probably including Johnston himself, knew how long the commanding general intended to hold these lines. The question doubtlessly came up during Georgia governor Brown's visit June 8 to Johnston's headquarters west of Kennesaw Mountain. Five hundred miles away, President Davis also wondered what Johnston would do, especially because he had heard rumors that more reinforcements were heading for Sherman from as far away as Louisiana. And on the 9th he wrote to Robert E. Lee: "Unless General Johnston strikes before the enemy has brought up all the reinforcements reported to be moving, his chances will be greatly diminished for the success which seemed attainable before he retreated." The president added, however, that though Johnston's yielding of territory had reduced his tactical possibilities, "success . . . still seems to be practicable." General Johnston, who had announced no plan of achieving success against Sherman's advancing corps, at least knew their position: the Twentieth and Twenty-third on his left, the Fourteenth in the center, the Fifteenth on the right, backed by the Sixteenth and the Seventeenth, all from prisoners' information. (He even knew that the Seventeenth Corps, 9,000 strong, had arrived in Acworth on the 8th.) Johnston also knew their objective, Marietta. "Evidences have accumulated of designs to move to our right," Lieutenant Mackall recorded June 9. Southern scouts reported that Yankee engineers were mapping the terrain and roads all the way to the Roswell textiles factory on the Chattahoochee, eleven miles northeast of Marietta. This latter information portended a possible enemy cavalry raid around the Confederates' right flank.[87]

In truth, Sherman was considering just such a venture, motivated by the Rebels' success in slipping a regiment of Alabama horsemen behind his lines at Calhoun, where on the morning of June 10 they stormed in, set fire to the depot, and burned five train cars. This guerrilla-style attack and the Rebels' repeated sniping and ambushing of his rearward detachments led Sherman to characterize the fighting as "a big Indian war." It also led him to wonder why he could not get his own mounted troops to do the same thing. "Surely if this cavalry can make such marches ours should do something," Sherman stated to Kenner Garrard, in his written instructions, to ride out by the left and "threaten, if not attack" the railroad south of Marietta.[88]

Garrard never carried out such a raid, but the threat of one caused General Johnston to ask Major General G. W. Smith, commanding the Georgia state troops guarding the Chattahoochee, to watch for the enemy up to the Roswell factory bridge. At the same time, Johnston pondered the possibilities of launching a substantial cavalry strike of his own against Sherman's railroad. But all he did was ponder, apparently afraid that sending off too much of his mounted force would deprive him of reconnaissance. On or about the 7th Johnston also contemplated dispatching Jackson's division on an expedition, but by June 10 nothing had happened. Instead, the Confederate commander returned to his pet notion of having Forrest do the raiding. It did not matter—as the president and Bragg had tired of explaining—that with Polk's departure Forrest's cavalry were the only defenders of north Mississippi (they were busy that very day fighting, and decisively defeating, Sturgis's column at Brice's Cross Roads). But like a bee in a bonnet, the notion of Forrest raiding Sherman's rail lines buzzed incessantly in Johnston's mind. On the 11th he wired S. D. Lee: "I respectfully urge the importance to the cause of breaking the railroad between Dalton and the Etowah. Your cavalry can do it while ours employs that of the enemy." The next day he asked Bragg to order Lee to launch the rail-breaking raid. In response, Bragg reminded him that Forrest was occupied with the enemy out of Memphis; as soon as Forrest has disposed of that threat, he wrote, "your suggestion will have attention." Johnston responded by shifting his message a bit, and, on the 13th, he asked that Forrest be sent off on a raid but only with cavalry forces presumed to be in east Alabama. He even had Lieutenant General Polk, Jefferson Davis's good friend, write to the president, urging the same thing. Polk went so far as to say he was informed (by Johnston, no doubt) that there were 9,000 horsemen in Alabama who could make the raid. Then, to add more weight, the army's senior corps commander, Hardee, endorsed Polk's letter: "I concur in the above."[89]

Leave it to Joe Johnston to lecture the Confederate States War Department on what troops it had in Alabama. Compounding the situation was Johnston's failure to do anything more than annoy the enemy with his own horsemen. One example was the raid by 75 Confederate cavalry, sent out by Red Jackson on June 14 to cut the railroad between Kingston and Resaca. This laughably small effort was of course inconsequential, especially because Sherman, intercepting orders to Jackson, knew it was coming and warned his post commanders at Allatoona, Etowah, and Resaca. Chagrined by this and other equally inconsequential efforts, Johnston, on the 16th, again wired Bragg: "I repeat the suggestion that the cavalry in Alabama be put in the enemy's rear"; he said the same thing once more to Lee, with a reference to the cavalry posted at Blue Mountain, Alabama. In the face of this irritating fusillade of almost childlike insistence, General Bragg attempted to close the matter, June 18, by informing Johnston that the only significant cavalry in Alabama was General Philip Roddey's, defending the munitions works at Selma against the sizable enemy forces in the northern part of the state. The president himself sought to close the matter more firmly still with a note to Bragg, dated the 23d, affirming that Lee's cavalry had to stay in defense of his department. Johnston had already received all the available infantry (Polk's) from Alabama and Mississippi, which had been sent, Davis wrote, "on the supposition that the enemy would be met at Dalton or in front of it." Now, however, Johnston's retreat had so exposed the region that Lee was required to retain the forces he had left. Pointedly, the president responded: "General Johnston should be notified of the condition of things in that department so that he may not count on aid from General Lee, but rather perceive that the drafts upon the Department of Alabama, Mississippi, and East Louisiana have been already too great." Bragg could only add, to Adjutant General Cooper, that the president's message should be communicated directly to Johnston and S. D. Lee. Presumably it was. Nevertheless, General Johnston did not cease his clamor for a raid by Forrest and his cavalry.[90]

While Johnston was placing such great importance on a cavalry strike against the Federals' rail lines, Sherman was heedful of the prospect, yet scarcely fretful. "All well," he wired Washington on June 13. And well it was, since Sherman had a huge number of troops, over 88,000, in garrisons at Nashville, Memphis, Chattanooga, Bridgeport, and other points, all poised to parry an enemy raid. Thus, while Bedford Forrest could and did annoy Sherman (who termed him "the very devil"), the Federal commander did not allow the Rebel saddle-wizard to deter him from his mission of browbeating and bludgeoning the enemy in his front.[91] He was confident he had troops enough in Memphis and elsewhere to handle Forrest in his rear, and troops enough to handle Joe Johnston in his front.

At the same time, Johnston, with no help coming from without, and with the sure prospect of another necessary retreat, would have considered his position along the Gilgal–Pine Mountain line merely temporary. Looking rearward, he thus gave renewed attention to fortifications along the Chattahoochee. On June 7 he ordered at least another artillery redoubt built at the river bridge; already forts and rifle pits lined both banks for some distance. On the 10th he directed that all engineers and slave laborers improving the defenses around Atlanta be shifted to work at the Chattahoochee. The next day he took the ominous step of ordering all the army's wagons except those carrying ordnance to south of the river. Doubtless he expected to be there in a few weeks.

Several days of rain, June 10–13, impeded the Federal armies' movements and threw General Sherman behind schedule. To be sure, he was elated, June 14, by news that a chance artillery shot had killed Leonidas Polk, the high-ranking Rebel general, Episcopal bishop, and longtime corps commander of the Army of Tennessee. But the commanding general, U.S. Military Division of the Mississippi, was becoming impatient, to the point of violating the pledge he had earlier made to his wife, that he would not "run hot-headed against any works." Indeed, after Southern deserters reported a weakening will in Johnston's army, one of Schofield's division leaders suggested that now might be the time to storm the Rebel lines somewhere. Mindful of Polk's death and Johnston's constant retrograde, General Sherman gave heed to the idea and ordered for June 15 activity all along the front: artillery barrage in the morning, cavalry probes on the flanks, strong demonstrations by McPherson and Schofield on the left and right, and, by Thomas in the center, an attack to "break the enemy's center" near Gilgal Church.[92]

It did not matter that Johnston evacuated Bate's division from its Pine Mountain salient that night (Thomas's cannonade and gradual encroachment had made the position untenable). Sherman knew of the Rebels' withdrawal by at least 7:30 A.M., but his plans went forward. On the Union left, a division of Logan's Fifteenth Corps overran an outer line of Rebel works, capturing 350 officers and men while losing only 45 killed and wounded. At the other end of Sherman's line Schofield's demonstration felt up on the Rebel position, taking some rifle pits and prisoners too. In the center, after troops from Stanley's division, the Fourth Corps, occupied Pine Mountain and planted batteries on its crest, General Hooker pressed his afternoon attack. Against an enemy entrenched, supported by artillery and protected by abatis (felled trees) and chevaux-de-frise (pointed stakes), the Federals in this, the "battle" of Gilgal Church, were predictably repulsed, with over 600 casualties in the two divisions, John Geary's and Daniel Butterfield's, mounting the assault. In the Confederate lines, manned by Cleburne's division, losses were so slight as apparently to go unreported, though Lieutenant Mackall noted that the day's toll of wounded for the entire army was 230.

With Federal troops entrenched along an eight-mile front, Sherman directed that the "grand skirmish" (his term for the fighting June 15) be continued on the 16th. It was. While his artillery banged away at the Rebel lines, Schofield's troops advanced about a mile. Stoneman's cavalry on the flank also made headway against Jackson's. These gains posed such a turning threat to his left that Johnston ordered Hardee to pull back during the night of the 16th–17th to high ground southeast of Gilgal Church. "The enemy has, as usual, been approaching by fortifying," Johnston telegraphed Richmond. "I can find no mode of preventing this." Discovery of the Rebels' retraction of their left led Sherman to order more pressing down on that enemy flank. But even though his forces occupied Lost Mountain and the Rebels' abandoned trenches ("Six miles of as good field-works as I ever saw," Sherman observed), and even though they brought up artillery to pound Hardee's new line, all these efforts were not good enough. Either the Rebels were not retreating fast enough, or his own Northern soldiers were not pressing hard enough. "The troops seem timid in these dense forests of stumbling on a hidden breast-work," Sherman complained. To Grant on the 18th he vented vexation not only at his cavalry leaders ("Garrard is over-cautious and I think Stoneman is lazy"), but also at the entire Army of the Cumberland, from Major General Thomas down to the privates. "A fresh furrow in a plowed field will stop the whole column, and all begin to intrench," he lamented. "Still I have all the high and commanding ground, but the one peak near Marietta, which I can turn."[93]

That peak was Kennesaw Mountain, which was really a two-mile ridge with three peaks: Big Kennesaw, Little Kennesaw, and Pigeon Hill, rising above the surrounding terrain seven hundred,

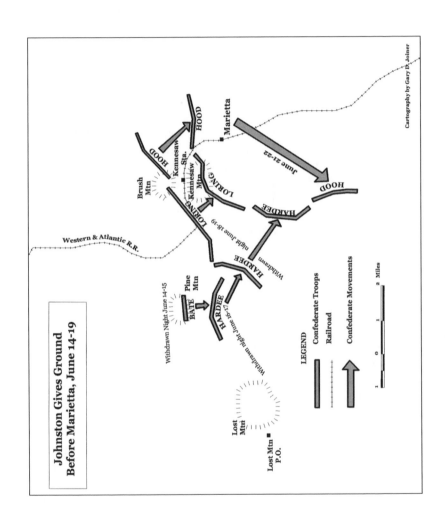

Johnston Gives Ground
Before Marietta, June 14-19

Brush Mtn

HOOD

HOOD

Kennesaw Sta.

Kennesaw Mtn

LORING

LORING

HOOD

Marietta

HARDEE

June 21-22

HOOD

Withdrawn night June 18-19

HARDEE

Western & Atlantic R.R.

HARDEE

Pine Mtn

BATE

Withdrawn Night June 14-15

HARDEE

Withdrawn night June 16-17

Lost Mtn

Lost Mtn P.O.

LEGEND

Confederate Troops

Railroad

Confederate Movements

1   0   1   2 Miles

Cartography by Gary D. Joiner

four hundred, and two hundred feet, respectively. To this commanding terrain Johnston withdrew his army on the rainy night of June 18–19 as soon as his engineers had laid out a new defensive line along the ridge and to its south. The next day Johnston reported to General Bragg in Richmond: "We have shifted our position to Kenesaw Mountain. The enemy has been moving his forces to his right."[94] Neither Bragg nor Davis sent back any reply. Johnston's seemingly perpetual retrograde had become so predictable that it apparently was no longer remarkable to the Confederate government, and perhaps also the people at large.

At least the Georgia rain was helping the Southerners. It certainly slowed the "pursuit" that Sherman so hopefully announced on the morning of the 19th, when he believed that Johnston was retreating more precipitately than in fact he was. By nightfall the Union commander acknowledged to General Halleck that the enemy had merely fallen back a mile or so to a new position. "We have pressed him pretty close to-day," Sherman added, "although the continued rain makes all movements almost an impossibility."

Nonetheless, with lines pressed up "pretty close," skirmishing and cannonading continued despite the rain. Spur-of-the-moment sorties would erupt over possession of a section of rifle pits or some hill; in one such fight on June 20, over a "bald knob" south of the Kennesaw Ridge, the Union brigade commander involved reported 273 killed, wounded, and missing.[95] Also on the 20th, as if to keep the Rebels on their toes, Sherman ordered his cavalry leader on the left, Garrard, to advance against Wheeler. In the resulting two-hour fight, considered the biggest all-cavalry engagement of the campaign, the Confederates drove back the Yankee horsemen, taking down 65 and losing probably about the same number of their own. On the other flank, however, Schofield's infantry pushed back some Rebel cavalry and presented such a threat that on the 21st Johnston had to extend his lines southward, by ordering Hood's corps from his right to his left.

Thus, on June 22 the Confederate infantry corps of Hood, Hardee, and Major General William W. Loring (temporary successor to General Polk), faced the Union armies of Schofield (on the right), Thomas (center), and McPherson (left). With the weather at last beginning to clear, Sherman ordered more pressing on his right by Schofield's and Hooker's corps. By 2:00 P.M. Williams's division (Twentieth Corps), with Milo Hascall's (Twenty-third) on its right,

had reached Widow Kolb's house, Sherman's desired objective for
the day, and begun to dig in. They dug deeper upon hearing from
captured Rebel skirmishers that Hood planned to attack. Across
no-man's-land, Lieutenant General Hood interpreted the Federals'
activity as their preparation to attack. Perhaps also—the documentary evidence is scant—he perceived an opportunity to strike the
Yankees in flank. Nonetheless, Hood ordered Major General Carter
Stevenson to charge the Yankees, which his division did at 5:00 P.M.,
supported by Hindman's division on its right. The Confederates
very definitely did not catch the enemy in flank; they delivered a
bloody, brutal frontal assault. Against prepared enemy infantry positions with artillery support, Stevenson's men met sharp repulse, losing 807 killed and wounded, with 63 missing. Hindman's troops,
which advanced only partway, suffered, mostly from cannon fire,
35 killed, 170 wounded, and 10 missing. In contrast to the Southern
casualties of more than 1,000, on the Federal side, Williams's and
Hascall's divisions sustained not even 200 casualties, a 5-to-1 ratio
in hors de combat that was almost customary when even veteran soldiers charged defensive positions of dug-in infantry and artillery.

Why did General Hood order the attack at Kolb's Farm? In a
brief report to General Johnston, Hood speaks only of first repelling
the enemy's advance, then counterattacking—a very skewed view
of the situation. The unequal ratio of casualties that day attests to the
Federals' quite defensive posture. Actually, in the morning and early
afternoon, Hooker's Federals had driven in Hood's skirmish line
and taken two hills. But without formal reconnaissance, Hood could
only guess whether this activity presaged a heavier attack, or
whether the enemy simply intended these positions to anchor his
flank. In short, Hood was left to weigh the tactical situation and
respond. Clearly, he saw an opportunity for attack and chose to act
on it, without seeking permission from army headquarters (which
were at the Atkinson house in Marietta's west suburbs, several miles
away). It is possible also that he envisioned Stevenson as actually
catching the Yankees in flank. Indeed, Union general Williams
believed the Rebels' purpose in charging his line had been to "take
advantage of the woods" in front of one of his brigades and "turn
that flank."[96]

Some commentators on the Atlanta Campaign, however, have
judged Hood more harshly. In Hood's order for a costly, fruitless

assault, one local writer, looking ahead to Hood's accession to army command, goes so far as to see in the attack a "rehearsal for Atlanta's doom." A more balanced perspective, though, would take in what Hood knew at the time. Having just marched his corps during the night of June 21–22 into new position on the Confederate left, and immediately having had his skirmishers pushed back from high ground in his front, he would have been well justified in ordering a "counter"-attack without seeking approval from General Johnston. Then there is the possibility that Hood envisioned the always-desired flanking attack. According to the former Kennesaw Mountain historian Dennis Kelly, "It is quite possible he gambled that his [night-time] march [to the Confederate left] had put him beyond the Union army's flank, and by wheeling toward his right, he would crash into their flank and win a great victory." Albert Castel agrees that Hood on the afternoon of June 22 probably understood the Union deployment as one against which he could attempt what he had "been trying to do since the campaign began—deliver a crushing flank attack." Even the Atlantan William R. Scaife, locally known as a harsh critic of Hood, acknowledges that Hood, in ordering his "impetuous and ill-advised attack," might have "thought he was striking the enemy's flank or rear."[97]

Yet to understand Hood's decision at Kolb's Farm, we must look beyond his previous failures to deliver flank attacks at Cassville, May 19, or at New Hope Church, May 28, and consider his entire experience as a Confederate general. Trained and promoted in "the Lee and Jackson school," as he phrased it—that is, the Virginia theater of 1862–63—John Bell Hood had learned that battlefield success required not just attack but flanking attack. After having directed the Confederates' assault against the enemy left at Resaca on May 14, Hood had become critical of General Johnston's subsequent lack of aggressiveness against the enemy. Borrowing on his friendship with Jefferson Davis, Hood had written the president on May 21, asking that his aide, Colonel Henry Brewster, be granted an interview to explain Hood's perspective on the campaign to date. Neither Davis nor Brewster kept notes on their conversation in Richmond in late May, but Brewster evidently revealed the gist of it in a chat, June 4, with his friend Mary Chesnut: Johnston, "overcautious," refused to fight; "so much retreating" was demoralizing the army and "breaking Hood's heart." In this context, then, given a chance to strike a blow (and do that which he had criticized his superior for not doing), Hood was justified in his decision to order the attack. Later in the campaign, General Hood would have many opportunities to prove himself a disciple of the Lee and Jackson school.[98]

For a while both sides believed that another pupil of that school, Lieutenant General Richard S. Ewell, would come from Virginia to take command of Polk's corps. The rumor floated in Johnston's army, and prisoners reported it to Sherman's, before it proved to be false. On June 23, Major General Peter Stewart, division commander in Hood's corps, was promoted to lieutenant general and named to succeed the dead bishop. While it would be another two weeks before Stewart formally took command, his first informal day on the job proved to be like all the rest: cannonading and skirmishing on his as well as on Hardee's front. On Hood's flank, Schofield continued probing and testing but found that the Rebel line extended so far to the south that he could see no immediate prospect of turning it. Ultimately turning a flank was Sherman's purpose, but for the present the Federal commander satisfied himself with the situation: "lines . . . in close contact and the fighting incessant, with a good deal of artillery."[99]

Such constant skirmishing brought daily casualties and exhausted the troops, but the relatively static nature of the fighting around Kennesaw in late June suited Joe Johnston's purposes of delay. Every day spent holding Sherman north of Marietta gave Southern engineers more time to work on their fortifications along the Chattahoochee; on the 24th a Union spy reported having seen 500 slaves working on artillery embrasures on the north bank. It was only a matter of time before the Confederate commander, who might well have been called Johnston the Delayer, Johnston Cunctator, would order his army back to this line.

As he well knew by this time, however, such passive strategy was not what his superiors (and probably many people in the South) wanted. This fact was borne down upon him by two events in late June. On the 21st, Atlanta's leading newspaper, the *Intelligencer*, ran a column in which General Lee's successes in Virginia were contrasted with General Johnston's lack of success against Sherman in Georgia. The article doubtless passed under Johnston's eyes or at least those of many in his army: "The *great* secret of *their success* (Lee's army) seems to be in the fact that General Lee always fights the enemy when he gets the opportunity, and never permits his men to become dispirited by the disorganizing influences of retreat—a movement, however, which that great General [Johnston] does not seem to understand." The next day an embarrassed editor, John H. Steele, apologized profusely to his readership, explaining that the article had slipped into press without his having seen it, that he had only "admiration for, and confidence in" Johnston's leadership. But the damage had been done.[100]

Then, on the 24th, Johnston's good friend from Texas, Senator Louis T. Wigfall, passing through Georgia on his way home, stopped at army headquarters in Marietta for a frank discussion. Wigfall confided to the general that concern in official Richmond over his retreats and over rumors that the army was becoming demoralized had reached such a crescendo that the president was considering relieving him of his command. Johnston was probably not surprised; there is evidence that he already knew it. (Just two weeks before, one of Johnston's aides, Lieutenant Richard Manning, had written, "I understand that in consequence of the General not having provoked a *General Engagement*. . . the *enemy* at Richmond . . . are busy criticising-blaming-abusing & undermining. What does our General think of all this? He thinks little of it."[101])

Thus, instead of being distressed by Wigfall's news, Johnston used the senator's visit as another occasion to insist that a cavalry strike against Sherman's supply lines was the only alternative to his continued retreating back to Atlanta's fortifications. But Wigfall, one of Davis's known enemies in the Confederate States Congress, did not relay this message to Davis directly; it would have been a wasted effort. Instead, he seems to have persuaded Governor Brown, to whom Davis had to listen, to write and make the case for the raid by Forrest. In addition, apparently also at Wigfall's urging, the governor of Alabama, Thomas H. Watts, and Major General Howell Cobb, in charge of Confederate reserve troops in Georgia, wrote to add their support to the proposal for the raid. When another member of Congress, Senator Richard W. Walker of Alabama, sent a letter to the War Department also calling for a cavalry strike, Joe Johnston could feel satisfied that he had done everything possible to exculpate himself from responsibility for his constant retreating through Georgia. As he had done at Harpers Ferry in summer 1861, he made sure that when he had to fall back on Atlanta, fault would lie with the government and not with him.

While General Johnston shirked a decisive battle, the big engagement that he knew his superiors desired, General Sherman contemplated just such an engagement. As early as the 16th he had envisioned an assault against Johnston's center as a faster means of achieving his strategic end. "It may cost us dear," he wrote, "but in results would surpass an attempt to pass around. . . . If, by assaulting, I can break his line, I see no reason why it would not produce a decisive effect." Moreover, in the past few days he had suspected that Schofield's probes to the right had caused Johnston to detach troops from his center, thereby making it even more vulnerable. Besides, the impatient Sherman was tiring of his flanking game, at least with its recent lack of results. When Schofield on June 24 reported that the Rebels had extended their lines farther than he could safely envelop, Cump snapped, "I suppose the enemy, with his smaller force, intends to surround us." Seeing the commanding general in such a mood, no one, not even Thomas and McPherson, whose troops would be making the assault, dared to raise objections.[102]

During the next few days Sherman issued instructions for the attack, which would be aimed at Johnston's left-center, to step off at 8:00 A.M. on the 27th. Generals Thomas and McPherson were directed to reconnoiter the enemy lines and select the most advantageous target sectors. Schofield would do his part, too; he was directed to "feel well to his extreme right and threaten that flank of the enemy with artillery and display." Altogether, something would have to give, for on the 26th Sherman wrote home, "We are now all ready and I *must* attack direct or turn the position. . . . I . . . to-morrow will pitch in at one or more points."[103]

The multipointed pitch-in had two objectives: Rebel salients at Pigeon Hill and an unnamed prominence to the south that soon took its identity from the Southern troops dug in on it—Cheatham's. Against the former, after a brief cannonade, 8:00 A.M. June 27, three brigades of Logan's Fifteenth Corps, 5,500 men, aligned in the warm morning sun and advanced. Overrunning and capturing Rebel pickets, the Federals then floundered amid craggy rocks, underbrush, and abatis, not to mention cannon fire and murderous riflery. They did not even make it to the enemy trenches before General Logan ordered them to retire. To the south, again after a cannonade, Thomas gave the word to advance. Most of John Newton's division

(5,000) and two brigades from Davis's (4,000) did only a little better than their comrades of the Fifteenth Corps. Facing the same obstacles, compounded in some places by the angled lines of stakes and rows of chevaux-de-frise, the Federals fell before withering musketry. A few actually managed to reach the parapet of the Rebel works before being shot or dragged down captive. Within an hour the attack had failed, although Thomas made one last try, sending in the last brigade of Newton's division. But it began to retreat ten minutes after it stepped off.

By 10:30 A.M., just two and a half hours after it had begun, Sherman's attack had collapsed. Only its brevity kept the Northern casualties down to slightly more than 2,000 killed, wounded, captured, or missing. Sherman that night noted "the loss particularly heavy in general and field officers." It would eventually total one brigadier general (Charles Harker), three colonels (including Dan McCook), and four lieutenant colonels killed or mortally wounded; many other officers, including company commanders of lesser rank, were also wounded. Along the rest of the U.S. line demonstrations by supporting units plus postattack sharpshooting and cannonading brought the day's Federal casualties to over 2,900.[104]

Confederate losses that day were only a fifth of that, estimated at 600. The three divisions (Cleburne's, Cheatham's, and French's) facing and repelling the main Union assaults suffered 392 killed, wounded, and missing. Against the more than 2,000 Federals lost in the eight attacking brigades, this ratio of about 1 to 5 represented a defensive/offensive imbalance similar to that at New Hope Church and Kolb's Farm. No wonder Major General Thomas, in a rare display of feeling, wrote Sherman that night, "One or two more such assaults would use up this army."[105]

General Newton, whose division had suffered severely, was more caustic in his message to the commander: "Well this is a damned appropriate culmination of one month's blundering." That night, to Halleck, Sherman acknowledged the failure of his assaults, though later he added that if Harker and McCook had not been killed, or if the men had attacked with "one-fourth more vigor," he could have broken Johnston's line. Later still, with more chivalry, he accepted full responsibility for the doomed attack. Yet he continued to justify having ordered it, "as it demonstrated to General Johnston that I would assault and that boldly."[106]

General Johnston was justifiably content when he wired Richmond the results of the day's activity: enemy assault repulsed, their loss supposed great, ours known to be small. That night he reinforced his telegraphic communication with a rare, long letter to General Bragg in which he sought to explain why he and his army "have been pressed back so gradually but continually." He reminded the administration that, through General Pendleton in April, he had warned of Sherman's numerical superiority. Then he explained that the enemy had used his superior numbers to outflank him at Dalton and Resaca; that he had found no position north of the Etowah so good for defense "as our inferior numbers required"; that Sherman's "engineering operations, . . . superior numbers and the character of the country" had all conspired to force his withdrawal from successive positions; and that since May 7 the "almost daily skirmishes and . . . attacks" had cost him 9,000 killed and wounded (and that did not count the many men made sick from the long, cold, rainy weather). In short, the enemy's "numerous army and the character of the country" had brought the campaign to this point, from whose unhappy continuation Johnston forecast no relief except through the use (once again) of "strong parties of cavalry to cut his railroad communications." He might have emphasized *strong*, because all such Confederate equestrian efforts so far had had little effect. Just recently S. D. Lee, because of "the urgent and repeated request of General Johnston," had authorized Brigadier General Gideon Pillow, with 1,500 men at Blue Mountain, Alabama, to attempt a raid on Sherman's rail line in north Georgia. Setting out June 20, Pillow got only as far as LaFayette, about eighteen miles west of Dalton and the Western & Atlantic, before he was turned back by the Yankees, his "raid" clearly ending in failure.[107]

Even though Johnston had all along maintained that his own cavalry was too weak to detach, at least one small raiding party, 100 men under Captain Addison Harvey, had set out from Red Jackson's division on June 11 to strike at the enemy rear. Already little bands of guerrillas were at work; it may have been they or Harvey's men who took up a rail and cut the telegraph north of Allatoona on or about June 18, and who attacked and burned part of a forage train near Resaca the next day. After the expedition hovered in the Union rear for more than a week, Johnston on the 26th reported the "very good news" that Harvey's men had broken the railroad briefly and burned a train or two. Such sorties, however, did little more than annoy Sherman's supply officers and apparently did not even irk Sherman himself. (Just a rumor, patently false, that Johnston had sent out 2,000 horsemen on a raid caused one Union officer to comment off-handedly, "Can't harm us; if so, it's too late.") What the Confederates therefore needed, Johnston insisted to Bragg, was a major cavalry raid out of Mississippi (Forrest?) or East Tennessee (Morgan?). Bragg patiently telegraphed Johnston again that there was no cavalry in east Tennessee and that the horse force in Mississippi was busy against Yankees there in great numbers. But Johnston kept to his message: because he himself was "unable so far to stop the enemy's progress," he had to hope for mounted raids from outside his department to bring about "Sherman's speedy discomfiture."[108]

It had indeed to be speedy, for Johnston knew from six weeks' experience that his antagonist would not give up the initiative (and certainly there was no chance of General Johnston's assuming it). The Confederate commander knew that Sherman, repulsed in his attacks, would soon resort to maneuver. Actually the maneuvers were taking place even as the attacking and repulsing were going on. Schofield, according to Sherman's plan for the 27th, continued to probe the enemy's flank. His right-most division, Cox's, was up early that morning, before four o'clock even, pushing back Rebel cavalry vedettes, assisted by Stoneman's troopers. By noon the Federals had advanced so far south of Johnston's main line they were actually closer to the Chattahoochee (within five miles) than the Confederates were. Sherman told Cox to dig in and hold his advantageous position. He did not intend for the Twenty-third Corps to extend farther, because he suspected his lines, already ten miles long, would be drawn too thin. Instead, Sherman planned for McPherson's army to swing around from left to right and be the main flanking force. The Army of the Tennessee, Sherman's old command, had played this role repeatedly (at Dalton and Resaca) and it would continue to do so. For the march here, at Kennesaw Mountain, General McPherson advised Sherman he would need several days to fill his wagons with supplies. Sherman, with no recourse but to attack again (which he could not do), granted McPherson the time.

Johnston expected the enemy to turn his left; Lieutenant Mackall, the staff officer, recorded headquarters' belief on this point as early as June 24. Thus, even before the battle of Kennesaw Mountain,

General Johnston had his engineers laying out a new line south of Marietta to which the army could fall back. Meanwhile, he did the best he could to guard his left, ordering Major General Smith to bring up his Georgia State Troops to bolster Jackson's cavalry on that flank. With a line stretching eight miles, the Confederate commander (like Sherman) worried that he was being drawn too thin. He eagerly accepted two regiments of Georgia cavalry, 1,500 men, which Bragg sent up from Savannah, and explained to Richmond why he could not send back three other regiments that had been given to him only temporarily. Governor Brown of Georgia did his part, too, keeping up his peppery correspondence with President Davis, urging more and more help to Johnston. Telegraphing from Atlanta June 28, Brown almost scolded Davis, reminding him, unnecessarily: "This place is to the Confederacy almost as important as the heart is to the human body. We must hold it." Brown, with his frequent proclamations to his citizenry, felt he had done all he could to raise troops (two regiments of the Georgia State Line and Smith's 3,000 militia, about 5,000 men in all). Thus he asked Davis to do more: send Forrest or Morgan against Sherman's rail lines or send more troops to Johnston. The president wired back, patiently explaining that Forrest and Morgan were already at work, that all available reinforcements had already been sent, and that, for these reasons, "the disparity of force between the opposing armies in Northern Georgia is less as reported than at any other point"—meaning, all Confederate armies were outnumbered, but Johnston's was less so. (End-of-June returns support this point. Johnston had 62,700 officers and men present for duty, whereas Sherman had 106,000 men, a ratio of 59 Confederates to 100 Federals. In Virginia, the South's other big army faced worse odds, 47 to 100; Lee's present for duty numbered 52,200 to Grant's 110,300.) On the day Davis wrote to Brown, he received a letter from General Bragg confirming Johnston's relative strength. Bragg pointed the president to the Army of Tennessee's returns of early June, which showed 62,000 effectives, a number that did not include the two horse regiments recently sent, or the auxiliary state troops. "No doubt he is outnumbered by the enemy," Bragg conceded, "as we are everywhere, but the disparity is much less than it has ever been between those two armies."[109]

Johnston was so overwhelmed by his sense of numerical inferiority, however, that he could only grudgingly concede Bragg's point.

When, on July 1, Georgia Senator Benjamin H. Hill visited him at his headquarters, Johnston stressed that Sherman's superior numbers enabled the Federals repeatedly to flank his position and compel him to fall back. Because Sherman would probably not launch another frontal attack, and because Johnston certainly would not do so, all the Confederates could do was to hold their Kennesaw lines until (inevitably) they were flanked. His only hope, Johnston maintained, was for Forrest or Morgan to lead 5,000 cavalry to descend on the Western & Atlantic Railroad between Dalton and Marietta and so damage it that Sherman's army would have to retreat or starve.

In truth, this explanation was what Senator Hill wanted to hear; he had come to Johnston at the request of Governor Brown and presumably also of Senator Wigfall to gather information for an appeal to President Davis for just such a cavalry raid. But along the way Hill asked several pointed questions. (1) Why did Johnston not send out Wheeler and the Army of Tennessee's cavalry to raid Sherman's rear? Johnston answered that they were needed with the army. (Wheeler disliked this rather stationary role for his cavalry, and he said so to General Bragg in a private letter that coincidentally was dated July 1: "I have begged General Johnston to allow me to go to the enemy's rear nearly every day for the last three months and he is anxious that it should be done but states that my presence is necessary upon the flanks.") (2) Did Johnston believe that Sherman would attempt to launch a cavalry raid of his own, especially on the important rail line from Alabama bringing food to Johnston's army? Johnston said no he did not. (Johnston would be proven wrong. Already Sherman was planning to send Major General Lovell H. Rousseau, then at Nashville, with a strong mounted force to cut through east-central Alabama to break up the railroad to Atlanta bearing supplies to Johnston's army.) (3) Even if the War Department authorized a cavalry expedition, it would take time to get it going. How long did Johnston think he could hold Sherman at bay north of the Chattahoochee? Johnston, Hill later recalled, "did not answer this question with directness." (4) One question was so crucial that Hill asked it three times: "And I understand you to say, General Johnston, that Sherman cannot be defeated except by the proposed attack in his rear, and that this work must be done by Forrest or Morgan or by some such force?" Johnston answered with an unequivocal yes and with that, he thanked the senator for carrying his message to Richmond. As the president's friend, Hill would surely be taken seriously. All would know in the government's high circles that Johnston was powerless to stop Sherman by himself. In the words of Albert Castel, "Rarely if ever has a military commander striven harder to persuade the head of his government that he [was] incapable of defeating by his own efforts the army he [opposed]."[110]

Having assured Senator Hill on July 1 that he could keep the enemy back for a while, General Johnston proceeded to retreat again. The Union Twenty-third Corps that day continued to press down hard on the Confederate left. George Stoneman's cavalry swung so far around as to reach the Chattahoochee River sixteen miles southwest of Atlanta. The next morning, the 2d, with Lieutenant Mackall recording intelligence of enemy wagons seen and heard rumbling to the left and Yankee cavalry concentrating on that flank, General Johnston determined that his Kennesaw lines were now untenable. At 1:30 P.M. his headquarters announced that the army that night would drop back to the new position already engineered, some five miles south of Marietta. The retreat went as planned, allowing Johnston to wire Bragg on the 3d, "The extension of the enemy's intrenched line several miles nearer the Chattahoochee than our left has compelled us to fall back about six miles." It also allowed Northern troops, ascending Kennesaw Mountain to the abandoned Rebel lines, to whoop and holler in exultation, celebrating not just their triumph but also, prematurely, the national holiday that would mark the morrow.[111]

CHAPTER TEN

JOHNSTON IS YET AGAIN TURNED, AT THE CHATTAHOOCHEE

JOHNSTON'S RETREAT FROM Kennesaw Mountain on the night of July 2–3 led Sherman to cancel his plans for McPherson to swing around by the right flank. Instead, Sherman announced to Halleck that he would "press the enemy close till he is across the Chattahoochee River." With the Rebels on the run, Sherman even confidently forecast his plans once Johnston had crossed to the south bank of the river—he would rest, accumulate supplies for the campaign's next phase, and "better guard my rear" against the threat of an enemy cavalry raid, rumors of which were always afloat from Rebel deserters coming into the lines.[112]

Thomas did as he was told and pressed the enemy close July 3. The closer he pressed, the more excited Sherman became at the prospect of mauling Johnston's army as it tried to cross the Chattahoochee. That evening he vented his excitement. "We will never have such a chance again," he wrote Thomas, " . . . of a large army fighting at a disadvantage with a river to his rear." He was absolutely determined therefore that the next day the Army of the Cumberland would "press with vehemence at any cost of life and material." His other two armies would do the same. "I have ordered McPherson and Schofield to cross Nickajack at any cost and work night and day to get the enemy started toward his bridges. . . . You know what loss would ensue to Johnston if he crosses his bridges at night in confusion with artillery thundering at random in his rear."[113] Johnston was not crossing the Chattahoochee, though, at least not yet. This much Thomas's men learned when on the 4th they pressed up close against the Confederates' entrenched positions. At two separate points strong Union skirmish lines advanced, took cannon and rifle fire, and fell back and dug in. Sure enough, the Rebels were securely entrenched, as the Federals' 270 casualties attested. Farther to the Union right, Dodge's Sixteenth Corps was the front of McPherson's army as it marched toward Nickajack Creek. That afternoon, too, elements of two of Dodge's divisions tested the Rebel lines in a brief charge that brought the same results as Thomas's efforts: 140 killed and wounded; and, again, the Rebels were entrenched. On the other side of the ledger, the Federals captured about 150 Rebels that day as they overran the outlying rifle pits, before being knocked back.

These little repulses, however, could not cloak the really important tactical development of the day, the threat of the Confederate left being flanked. McPherson and Schofield were pressing down; by 2:30 P.M. Confederate headquarters knew that at least one enemy corps had crossed Nickajack Creek in front of Hood. Johnston's chief of staff, Brigadier General Mackall, rode out to Hood's sector to see for himself the danger posed by the enemy's encroachments. Then, after four, Lawrence S. ("Sul") Ross, one of Jackson's brigadiers, sent

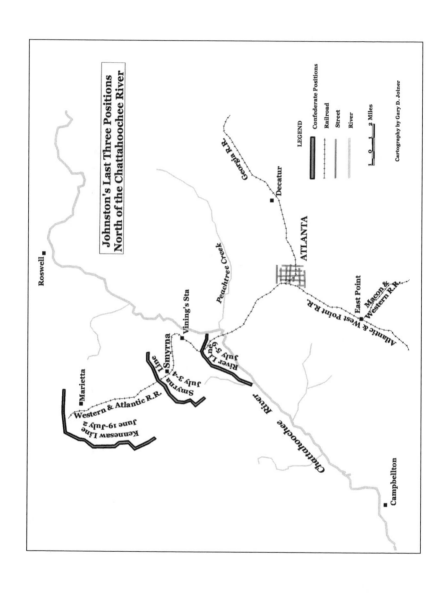

Johnston's Last Three Positions
North of the Chattahoochee River

word that "the enemy is moving around my flank. . . . My position here is now no longer tenable. . . . I am moving back."[114] Finally, that evening G. W. Smith, whose state troops were also on the left, wrote in to headquarters that he would have to withdraw no later than daybreak. All this news swayed the commanding general, roughly thirty-six hours after his troops had occupied the Smyrna line, to order them to abandon it.

The Confederates marched back to a line that once again had already been prepared. Two weeks before, in fact, when the army was at Kennesaw, work had begun under the direction of the army's chief of artillery, Brigadier General Francis A. Shoup. According to Shoup, Johnston told him "it was but a question of time, and that a short time" before the army would retreat across the Chatta-hoochee.[115] Chagrined, Shoup asked whether he might supervise construction of fortifications on the north bank of the river at the rail-road bridge. Johnston, eager for anything that would aid his cunc-tation of Sherman's advance, agreed. Thereupon Shoup directed the army's engineers and hundreds of slaves in tree cutting, digging, and building log-and-earth infantry forts. There were some three dozen of these "Shoupades" (G. W. Smith's term), connected by log pali-sades for more infantry and studded with artillery forts, all arced in an almost six-mile line around where the Western & Atlantic bridge crossed the river near Peachtree Creek. During the night of July 4–5 Johnston's army marched into these defenses.

Sherman was frankly surprised when his morning picket reports informed him that Johnston was entrenched near the river. "No general, such as he," the Federal commander had written on the 3d, referring to his opponent's trademark cautiousness, "would invite battle with the Chattahoochee behind him."[116] He had to see for himself on the morning of the 5th that the Rebels had indeed not fled across the river. He was content that day with Thomas's drawing closer to the enemy's new line. McPherson and Schofield were probing to the right along Nickajack Creek, while the cavalry on both flanks fanned out toward the Chattahoochee's various crossings.

These crossings were numerous: six ferries in the fourteen downstream miles from the Western & Atlantic bridge, another seven fords or ferries upstream, plus a wagon bridge at Roswell,

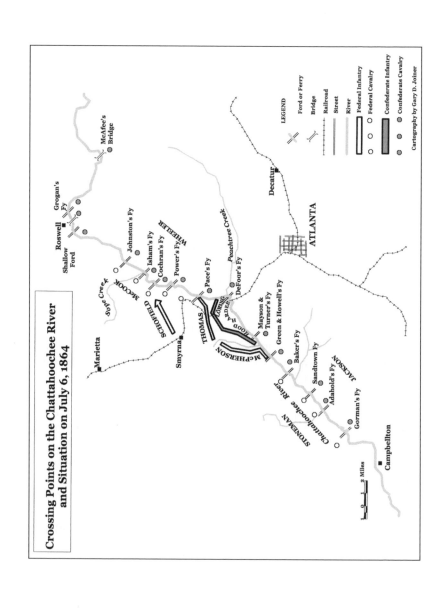

Crossing Points on the Chattahoochee River and Situation on July 6, 1864

Cartography by Gary D. Joiner

LEGEND

Ford or Ferry
Bridge
Railroad
Street
River
Federal Infantry
Federal Cavalry
Confederate Infantry
Confederate Cavalry

McAfee's Bridge
Grogan's Fy
Roswell
Shallow Ford
Johnston's Fy
Isham's Fy
Cochran's Fy
Power's Fy
Sope Creek
McCOOK
SCHOFIELD
Marietta
Smyrna
WHEELER
Pace's Fy
DeFoor's Fy
Peachtree Creek
THOMAS
LORING
HARDEE
HOOD
McPHERSON
Mayson & Turner's Fy
Green & Howell's Fy
Baker's Fy
Sandtown Fy
Adahold's Fy
Gorman's Fy
JACKSON
STONEMAN
Chattahoochee River
Campbellton
Decatur
ATLANTA

0   1   2 Miles

and another one six miles farther up at McAfee's. All these possibilities for an enemy cavalry crossing had long drawn General Johnston's attention. As of the 4th, at least a few of the crossings, especially downstream (because Sherman seemed to show a disposition to flank by his right), had little guard posts, some fortified. For example, at Adaholt's Ferry, ten miles down from Johnston's river line, the one hundred or so dug-in state troops repelled a Union cavalry reconnaissance (Stoneman's) on the afternoon of the 3d; two brigades of Confederate cavalry were sent downriver to reinforce the local troops defending the various crossings. On the other flank Garrard's cavalry was doing the same thing, feeling toward Roswell.

General Sherman viewed Atlanta for the first time from a hill at Vining's Station on July 5. Although some Federals had caught their first glimpse through a telescope atop Kennesaw Mountain the day before, on the 5th Sherman espied the church steeples and house chimneys of Atlanta, about nine miles off to the southeast. Brigadier General Geary could see them that day, too, from high ground near Turner's Ferry; soldiers of the Twentieth Corps climbed trees for their view. As word passed through the ranks, cheers went up so loud, one Northern officer reflected, that they might have been heard far off in Atlanta, "the doomed city itself."[117]

Atlantans may not have agreed that their city was doomed, but many of them had so little confidence in Joe Johnston's ability to stem Sherman's smart combination of numbers and flanking that they fled the city. The press tried hard to calm the citizenry, especially when word spread of the army's retreat from Kennesaw. "Speculation was rife yesterday to establish the reason for our retreat," the *Intelligencer* acknowledged on the 5th. "To-day it is more eagerly agitated—what will we do next? Our street Generals have it that we will be flanked to the Gulf."[118]

General Johnston himself did nothing to gird public confidence that day when he ordered Atlanta's military hospitals and munitions works to be evacuated. At once ordnance, medical, and quartermaster officers began vying for space on train cars, and the infectious confusion spread. Even Governor Brown, then in the city, got caught up in the panicky presumption of Atlanta's doom and sent a telegram to President Davis. "If your mistake," he said, referring to Davis' failure to unleash cavalry on Sherman's supply line, "should result in loss of Atlanta . . . , the blow may be fatal to our cause and remote posterity may have reason to mourn over the error." He threw in jabs about how "the whole country" expected a cavalry raid, and that, as he saw it, the Richmond authorities were deceived about Johnston's strength relative to Sherman's. An angry Davis lectured back: "Most men in your position would not assume to decide on the value of the service to be rendered by troops in distant positions. When you give me your reliable statement of the comparative strength of the armies, I will be glad also to know the source of your information as to what the whole country expects, and posterity will judge."[119]

While Davis and Brown, as well as many Atlantans, and probably many soldiers in Johnston's army itself all worried that Atlanta might fall, General Sherman thought ahead of how he would make it happen. He had already announced his plan in April and on July 6 merely reiterated it to Halleck: once across the Chattahoochee, "instead of attacking Atlanta direct, or any of its forts, I propose to make a circuit, destroying all its railroads."[120] The first task was to cross the river, which was running high at the moment because of the rains. Until the water fell to a safer level for pontoon bridging, Sherman would spend a few days studying information brought in by his cavalry on the various crossing points.

He received some intelligence on the night of the 6th, when Garrard reported from Roswell: though the bridge was destroyed, there remained a good ford. Downstream General McCook found both Power's and Isham's Ferries guarded with artillery. Schofield's Twenty-third Corps marched from Smyrna toward a proposed crossing somewhere downstream from Roswell. Farther below, O. O. Howard's Fourth Corps had reached Pace's Ferry, where they saw retreating Rebels cut a pontoon bridge. McPherson's army held the right, with some of his troops down as far as Howell's Ferry; Stoneman's cavalrymen stretched farther downriver toward Campbellton. All told, from Campbellton to Roswell, Sherman had his forces spanning over thirty miles. Such a broad front was well calculated to confuse Joe Johnston about where the Federals planned to make their main crossing. Sherman kept up the impression that he might try to push his right wing; for that reason on the 7th he told McPherson to "display as much anxiety to cross as possible and as low down, but keep your masses ready to move to the real quarter when required." The real quarter would be on the other flank, where he directed Schofield to make a foothold on the south bank near Sope Creek or anywhere else in the vicinity. In the meantime, there were indications that Johnston was being fooled. Judging by the light force against him, Garrard reported: "Johnston will make no attempt on this flank; . . . his cavalry has gone to his left." Sherman accepted this news, and it allowed Schofield to anticipate a virtually unopposed crossing. It was therefore a confident commander of the Military Division of the Mississippi who wired General Halleck July 7: "Johnston is maneuvering against my right, and I will try and pass the Chattahoochee by my left."[121]

What was Johnston doing? He knew Sherman was planning to cross, but aside from strengthening Shoup's line and enjoining Wheeler to observe the river closely, he was doing nothing. Unfortunately every signal out of army command portended a retreat across the Chattahoochee. On the 6th Johnston moved his headquarters to a house on the south bank. He also instructed his corps commanders to keep their ordnance trains and most wagons on the south bank, too. The apparent imminence of another retrograde moved President Davis to telegraph a warning against retreating across the river. Johnston's reply, July 8, had the three well-worn elements of his earlier correspondence: (1) "Our falling back was slow. Every change of position has been reported to General Bragg." (2) "We have been forced back by the operations of a siege, which the enemy's extreme caution and greatly superior numbers have made me unable to prevent. I have found no opportunity for battle except by attacking intrenchments." And (3) "It is believed here that there are 16,000 cavalry for defense of Mississippi and Alabama. . . . Might not 4,000 of this cavalry prevent the danger by breaking up the railroad between the enemy and Dalton, thus compelling Sherman to withdraw?"[122]

Johnston's telegram of July 8 summarized as well as any other contemporary communication why the Union armies had so far succeeded in north Georgia. Sherman, if not acting quite with "extreme caution," was at least prudent in not squandering his strength with the kind of massed, head-on attacks that Grant was attempting in Virginia. As a consequence, the enemy's "greatly superior numbers" had forced the Confederates back, albeit slowly.

Professing himself helpless in the face of this combination of smart generalship and heavy battalions, Johnston looked for others (Forrest, Morgan, Davis, Bragg, anybody) to save him and Atlanta. His repeated insistence upon an outside cavalry raid in Sherman's rear had become so well known that Southern political leaders and newspapers were now echoing it even more shrilly. Governor Brown spoke out once more on the 7th, warning the president of the calamity to ensue "if Atlanta is sacrificed and Georgia overrun while our cavalry are engaged in distant raids." And Atlantans themselves continued to fear that their city would fall. Johnston's order for evacuation of the city's munitions works and military supplies created among the citizenry a palpable "alarm," as Lieutenant Mackall observed after he and Major General Lovell returned from a trip into town on the 7th.[123]

The next day, July 8, the *Intelligencer* recognized the likelihood that the Army of Tennessee would fall back across the Chattahoochee. To be sure, the paper reported, the soldiers were as "defiant and confident as ever," only hoping that General Johnston would "issue the order of battle," whereupon they would "attack Sherman's flank, centre or rear" regardless of "whether his insolent Yankee troopers were twice the number they are." But because there was so little chance of Johnston's issuing that attack order, the *Intelligencer* advised Atlantans to prepare for the Confederate army's occupation of the defenses surrounding the city. Fainthearted residents were encouraged to leave for the safer environs of the countryside because "almost all the houses will be required for army quarters and it will be difficult for those who remain, who have no connection with the army to get subsistence."[124]

If General Johnston had read this column, he probably would have reacted with the same indifference that he gave the president's dire expressions of anxiety, and that he gave the increasingly worried warnings of his Congressional friends that his job was at stake. It was the same indifference he seemed to give to the very imminent prospect of Sherman's troops fording the river. And they did so midafternoon of the 8th. With Thomas ordered to "stir up the enemy" with demonstrations and Garrard to attempt a crossing at Roswell, Schofield was Sherman's main hope for a foothold on the south bank.[125] Cox's division of the Twenty-third Corps not only found a convenient fish dam near Isham's Ferry that allowed them to wade across the river but found on the other side just a handful of Rebel pickets, who fled. A pontoon bridge was thrown across so that by 7:00 P.M. Schofield was able to report that Cox's whole division was on the south bank and entrenching. That night a Southern scout informed Confederate headquarters that the Yankees had crossed at least two brigades of infantry plus artillery at Isham's, and that they had pushed more than a mile from the riverbank. Johnston responded predictably: early on the 9th he directed Wheeler to contain the Yankee bridgehead while he issued orders for the army to retreat across the river that night. By the time that it did so, more of Schofield's corps had crossed, and so had at least two brigades of Garrard's cavalry division. The Federals' crossing of the Chattahoochee, which had been the focus of Sherman's anxious thoughts for days on end had, thanks to Joe Johnston's indolence, proven surprisingly easy.

Having laid grass and straw on their bridges to soften the sounds of their wagons, the Southerners were able to get across on the night of July 9–10 without arousing the Yankees. At 4:45 the next morning Thomas reported, "The enemy has left my front and burned the railroad and wagon bridge over the river." After getting across, the Rebels had also taken up their several pontoon bridges. Sherman was content to watch the wooden trestles burn, because he knew that eventually his engineers would rebuild them easily. Moreover, he had instructed Schofield to have a bridge built and was sending Dodge's Sixteenth Corps to reinforce Garrard at Roswell; he would have the wagon bridge there rebuilt. With these preparations made, for which he allowed up to three days, General Sherman could afford to pause in his campaign and see to the buildup of supplies and the strengthening of his railway garrisons, even as he planned his next move. General Johnston, for his part, could only wire Bragg on the 10th that the enemy crossing at Isham's had forced his retreat to the south bank of the Chattahoochee. Brigadier General Shoup, who had placed such faith in his line of fortifications, later lamented that Johnston's "abandonment of the works at the Chattahoochee River ... was, in my opinion, the final turning point in the fate of the Confederacy." In Richmond, President Davis knew also that a turning point had been reached, and he was coming to the conclusion that he would have to act boldly if defeat and disaster at Atlanta were to be averted.[126]

CHAPTER ELEVEN

THE GOVERNMENT CONCLUDES JOHNSTON HAS FAILED: DELIBERATIONS AND THE DECISION TO REPLACE HIM, JULY 10–17

"WE ALL FEEL much dejected and low spirited at our prospects," Captain W. L. Trask, of Hardee's staff, wrote on July 10. "Everything indicating the giving up of Atlanta." General Johnston, of course, did not even think of indicating this possibility to his superiors in Richmond, although he must have been thinking of it as his eventual necessity. All President Davis had to go on—the only military intelligence he had from Atlanta—was Johnston's wire announcing his withdrawal to the south bank, supported by another one, also of the 10th, from Brigadier General Wright telling Bragg that "Hooker's [sic] corps crossed to this side of the river at Isham's Ferry" and was entrenching. Virtually starved for information on his commanding general's intentions, Davis on the 9th (before he even knew of the army's crossing), dispatched Bragg to Atlanta to meet with Johnston. It would be several days before Bragg could send any report, but in the meantime Senator Hill of Georgia arrived.[127]

After conferring with Johnston on July 1, Hill traveled to Richmond to speak directly to the president, which he did on the 10th, and to Secretary of War Seddon the next day. Hill's message was clear: Johnston felt he could not stop Sherman with his present force, and that only a raid against the enemy's supply lines by cavalry outside his department would compel Sherman's retreat. Years later, Hill recalled that in the meeting Davis had emphasized the pressures faced by other commands in the western theater. Everyone was pleading for reinforcements. Davis read some of their telegrams to Hill, who understood then that the administration had done all it could to aid Johnston.

Having made these points to Senator Hill, who was acting as General Johnston's informal secretary, President Davis made them to the general himself in a telegram of July 11. "If it be practicable for distant cavalry," the president wrote with studied irony about Johnston's hoped-for raid, "it must be more so for that which is near, and former experiences have taught you the difference there would be in time, which is now of such pressing importance."[128] That same day, July 11, Davis and Seddon received yet another alarming wire from General Johnston, urging the War Department to dismantle the prison camp at Andersonville, 110 miles south of Atlanta, and send the prisoners elsewhere to places of greater safety. This disturbing message, suggesting the vulnerability of southwest Georgia to Yankee raids, may have been Johnston's first, oblique way of warning his superiors of an inevitable evacuation of Atlanta.

It was probably Johnston's telegram of July 11, coupled with Senator Hill's visit, that compelled the Confederate president to admit, after months of frustrations and fears, that he had blundered in appointing Joseph E. Johnston to army command. Another message from the general, July 12, replying back why he could not detach his own cavalry to operate in Sherman's rear and complaining again that he was greatly outnumbered, added only more weight to the unhappy impression already formed. Davis confessed his dismay and anxiety in a telegram to his trusted commander, Lee.

12th July 1864

Genl. R. E. Lee,
Petersburg, Va.

   Genl. Johnston has failed, and there are strong indications that he will abandon Atlanta. He urges that prisoners should be removed immediately from Andersonville. It seems necessary to relieve him at once. Who should succeed him? What think you of Hood for the position?

Jefferson Davis[129]

That the nation's chief executive should so boldly broach the name of Hood as Johnston's successor reflected not just Davis's fondness for the young lieutenant general (nurtured during his convalescence in Richmond the previous winter) but also the confidence Hood had inspired through his correspondence with the president since he had joined the army. Even before Hood sent his aide Colonel Brewster to call on the president in late May, he had written five letters to Davis, Bragg, or Seddon, emphasizing his desire to take the initiative while General Johnston was sitting by. Yet Davis on July 12 was far from resolved upon Hood as a possible successor to Johnston. And Lee's reply to the president's telegram, received in Richmond just before 9:00 P.M. on the 12th, offered little reassurance: "I regret the fact stated. It is a bad time to release the commander of an army situated as that of Tenne. We may lose Atlanta and the army too. Hood is a bold fighter. I am doubtful as to other qualities necessary."[130]

In this uncertain setting, General Bragg's visit to Georgia proved crucial. Officially, Davis had instructed his adviser on the 9th to "proceed to Georgia, confer with General Johnston in relation to military affairs there," and continue his inspection tour into Alabama.[131] Just what Davis and Bragg discussed before the latter's departure from Richmond has never been documented, but their telegraphic communication during Bragg's stay in Atlanta has led historians to assume that Bragg had a very definite mission. Most probably, he was to verify that the military situation at Atlanta required Johnston's removal, assess which of the Army of Tennessee's two senior corps commanders, Hardee and Hood, would be more suitable as successor, and maybe even discuss with one or more of the three generals the administration's inclination toward appointing a new army commander. Part of Bragg's charge would also have been to keep President Davis informed of changes at the front; with Sherman so close to Atlanta, every day counted, and if the administration were to act, it would have to act fast.

It is not likely, however, that Bragg would have been authorized to appoint Hardee or Hood on the spot, for at least three strong reasons: (1) On July 9, when Davis ordered Bragg to Georgia, Johnston's army still held Sherman's forces on the north bank of the Chattahoochee, a formidable barrier to the enemy's further progress. Moreover, the president had not yet met with Senator Hill, and Johnston had not yet sent his warning about Andersonville. The military situation in mid-July, in other words, was very fluid; changing army commanders, always a dire step mid-campaign, might not be necessary after all. (2) As the president indicated in his message to General Lee of July 12, he was genuinely undecided whether Hood would be better than Hardee, and he wanted opinions from all his closest advisers—Lee, Bragg, and the Cabinet—before making the choice. That process had only begun with the dispatch of Bragg to Georgia. (3) Davis knew that Johnston, ever the stickler on matters of rank and protocol (recall his famous preoccupation with seniority in 1861) would never have recognized any verbal order from Bragg, technically his junior in rank, especially one relieving him from command. Any such order would have to be in writing and would have to come from the War Department in Richmond. In the meantime, Bragg followed through on the mission Davis gave him to visit the scene and make recommendations.

We can assume, however, that Bragg arrived in Atlanta on the morning of July 13 with his mind made up that Joe Johnston would have to be relieved. He knew that Governor Brown was putting pressure on the president to do something. Georgians in general were calling for action; Senator Hill told Major General S. G. French that the president said that he was regularly beset by deputations of citizens pleading for the defense of the state. Bragg had also heard rumors that Johnston's retreat was demoralizing the army and that some had begun to predict that the general would have to be fired. He would also have been mindful of the opinions expressed by corps commanders in the Army of Tennessee, written privately to Richmond and behind Johnston's back. Among the letters was Stewart, newest corps commander, to Bragg, March 19: "Are we to hold still, remaining on the defensive in this position until ... [the enemy] comes down with his combined armies to drive us out?"; Hood to Bragg, April 13: "I have done all in my power to induce General Johnston ... to move forward. He will not consent"; and Hardee to Davis, June 22, well after Johnston had established the passive pattern of his campaign: "If the present system continues we may find ourselves at Atlanta before a serious battle is fought." Arriving in Atlanta, therefore, Bragg knew that many in Georgia, in Richmond, and in the Army of Tennessee itself had built a case for Johnston's removal.[132]

If the choice over Johnston's successor were between Hardee and Hood, Bragg also probably had his mind made up. Hardee was no friend of Bragg's, or at least Bragg was no friend of Hardee's. The latter had been among those discontented generals of the Army of Tennessee who after Murfreesboro wanted Bragg removed. Hardee had bluntly expressed his opinion in a letter to Bragg in January 1863. Obviously hurt, Bragg immediately characterized Hardee as "a good drill master, but no more, except that he is gallant. He has no ability to organize and supply an army, and no confidence in himself when approached by an enemy."[133] There is no reason to believe that Bragg's judgment of Hardee had changed since then. If anything, Hardee's decline of permanent command of the army in December 1863 had strengthened Bragg's perception that he was no man to succeed Johnston.

When Bragg stepped off the train in Atlanta on the morning of July 13, harboring these preconceptions, he immediately would have seen signs of turmoil over Johnston's most recent retreat. The local press had even begun to prepare the citizenry for the fall of the city. Albert Roberts, editor of the *Southern Confederacy*, in a column of July 8, suggested hopefully to readers: "If Atlanta should fall, the campaign . . . is by no means at an end." John R. McClanahan, chief editor of the *Appeal*, said the same thing on the 8th: "We are not among those who believe that the fall of Atlanta or Richmond, or both of them, would prove disastrous or fatal to our cause." Not so fatalistic in predicting Atlanta's fall, John H. Steele, editor of the city's other major daily, the *Intelligencer*, on the 9th spoke only of Sherman's "determined policy . . . not to fight a regular battle, but to take this city by strategy and merely outweighing us." Steele could only hope that General Johnston would soon find "the turning point" of the campaign and expel the invader.[134]

The public mood darkened further when rumors circulated on the morning of the 10th that Johnston's army had retreated and that the Chattahoochee was no longer a barrier to the Yankees' approach. The effect of the news was electric. "I can give you no idea of the excitement in Atlanta," a correspondent for the *Mobile News* wrote. "Everybody seems to be hurrying off, and especially the women. Wagons loaded with household furniture, and everything else that can be packed upon them, crowd every street, and women, old and young, and children innumerable, are hurrying to and fro. . . . Every train of cars is loaded to its utmost capacity. . . . The excitement beats anything I ever saw, and I hope I may never witness such again." "This has been a sad day in our city," Samuel P. Richards recorded in his diary on the 10th, "for . . . there is a great probability of Atlanta falling into the hands of the enemy and the city has been in a complete swarm all day and for several days. All the Govt stores and Hospitals are ordered away and of course the citizens are alarmed and many have left and others are leaving." Probably more than at any other time since the beginning of the campaign, General

Johnston became the subject of open criticism among the Atlantans who had not fled. Brigadier General Mackall in army headquarters observed on July 11, "There is much discontent arising among the people around Atlanta and they are beginning to abuse the General." The public's loss of trust in Johnston was most tellingly measured by the speed at which residents fled the city. An officer of Lieutenant General Hardee's staff visited Atlanta on the 12th and found it "nearly deserted. Government workshops all removed, Newspapers (except the Appeal) all gone." In truth, the *Intelligencer* and *Southern Confederacy*, the city's longstanding dailies, had succumbed to the public panic they had for so long tried to still and packed up their presses after publishing their issues of the 10th. Thus, there was very little press coverage of Governor Brown's proclamation of July 9, which called on men enrolled in the state's reserved militia forces to rush to the front. In the message Brown took another shot at Jefferson Davis: "If the Confederate Government will not send the large cavalry force ... to destroy the long line of railroad over which General Sherman brings his supplies from Nashville, and thus compel him to retreat with the loss of most of his army," Georgians must rely on themselves to beat back the invader.[135]

With the newspapers clearing out, the army hospitals and ordnance machinery gone, the citizenry by and large packing up—even the City Council on July 11 ordered removal of the government's papers and municipal mules—Bragg found plenty of evidence, upon his arrival in Atlanta on the 13th, to support his and the president's sense that Johnston had to be replaced before he gave up the city. Even before he met with the army's commander, Bragg telegraphed Richmond that "indications seem to favor an entire evacuation of this place." Then he set out to meet with Johnston. Publicly, of course, he simply announced that he was on a tour of inspection, passing through Atlanta on his way to Alabama. Veteran reporter Henry Watterson, writing as "Grape" for an Augusta paper, reported that as he encountered Bragg, riding in a carriage to Johnston's headquarters outside the city, the general looked "as grim and wired as ever" but that he was understood to be only on a routine tour. Nonetheless, there was widespread speculation about his purpose. Another newspaperman attested to the public curiosity but tried to be reassuring: "It is not to be supposed for a moment that either the

President or Gen. Bragg would attempt to interfere with the plans of Gen. Johnston."[136]

Did Johnston on the 13th suspect that Bragg's visit held a darker motive? Probably. "Joe looks uneasy this morning. I am sorry to see him so fretted," the chief of staff, Mackall, noted. To his wife, Mackall offered his own guess about what was happening: "I fancy it is the design of Mr. D. . . . to make a display of his distrust of Johnston & if he can infuse it into the army, to relieve him." When Johnston and Bragg met, however, neither confessed any of these concerns. Apparently Bragg received a briefing on the tactical situation from Generals Johnston and Wheeler and returned to the city planning more extensive interviews with the army's leaders on the morrow. At 1:00 P.M. he telegraphed the president with what he had learned. Fully two corps of enemy infantry were across the Chattahoochee; Johnston's army was significantly reduced in strength; "I find but little encouraging," he concluded.[137]

In Richmond, Davis received Bragg's two telegrams and compared his adviser's tactical appraisal with that described by General Johnston in his latest message, of the 12th. Johnston said merely that the Federals held several fords eight to twelve miles from the city, that they were entrenched on the south bank, and that "everything [was] quiet," save for a little skirmishing and artillery fire. While Bragg's view was depressing and bleak, Johnston's seemed almost complacent. Most important, Johnston gave no hint of any plans for offensive action to disrupt the crossing of more Federal troops across the Chattahoochee. (Even Sherman was mystified by Johnston's inactivity along the Chattahoochee. Years later Sherman wrote, "I have always thought Johnston neglected his opportunity there, for he had lain comparatively idle" while the Federals secured their crossing points.) Adding to the president's worries was the letter he received sometime on the 13th from Lee, written the night before, expanding on the shorter telegraphic message sent earlier. General Lee repeated his regret that the crisis in Georgia was so grave as to require a switch in army leadership: "I am distressed at the intelligence conveyed in your telegram of today. It is a grievous thing to change commander of an army situated as is that of the Tennessee. Still if necessary it ought to be done." To the president's question wired on the 12th, "What think you of Hood?" Lee responded by reinforcing his characterization of his former division commander: "Hood is a very good fighter very industrious on the battle field, careless off & I have had no opportunity of judging of his action, when the whole responsibility rested upon him. I have a high opinion of his gallantry, earnestness and zeal." Then he added the unexpected: "Genl Hardee has more experience in managing an army." It is no wonder that Lee, knowing Davis was leaning toward Hood as Johnston's replacement but that he also had to consider Hardee, closed his letter, "May God give you wisdom to decide in this momentous matter." But Davis did not immediately decide. Having hoped that Lee would make his decision in favor of Hood easier, Davis now could only telegraph back to Lee that Bragg was in Atlanta and that he would have to await the latter's advice. "It is a sad alternative," the president wrote, "but the case seems hopeless in present hands."[138]

With Lee complicating, not simplifying, his decision making and with more detailed assessments expected from Bragg in Atlanta, Davis turned to another body of advisers, his Cabinet. The Cabinet met at least once during this testy period of mid-July; because of the lack of any minutes for the high-level meeting we cannot date it. Craig Symonds, Johnston's biographer, has guessed that it occurred on the morning of July 17, but he offers no documentation. Instead, a strong case can be made that the president convened the Confederate Cabinet sometime on July 14, the day Senator Hill wrote out, at Secretary of War Seddon's request, his record of General Johnston's admission on July 1 that he had no plan for defeating Sherman. Hill recalled Seddon's saying that his damning memorandum would be submitted to the Cabinet and that he was comfortable with their seeing it. Indeed, the senator expressed his willingness "to give any further information in my possession and to do anything in my power in this critical juncture."[139] For this reason, and because Hill was the only man in Richmond who had recently talked with Johnston and could describe his state of mind—certainly the general himself was unwilling to reveal anything—Davis and Seddon invited him to the Cabinet meeting. Present were Seddon, Secretary of State Judah P. Benjamin, probably Postmaster General John H. Reagan, and possibly the other members, too (Treasury Secretary George Trenholm, Attorney General George Davis, and Naval Secretary Stephen R. Mallory). Only Vice President Alexander H. Stephens would certainly have been absent, having now reclused himself at his farm in middle Georgia out of disgust over Davis's handling of the government.

At the Cabinet meeting, Davis received the unequivocal support he had been unsuccessfully seeking from Lee: Johnston had to be relieved of his command. All our information on the meeting comes from postwar recollections of the attendees, which reveal that Seddon and Benjamin were most vehement. Secretary of War Seddon had several reasons for wanting to fire Johnston. First was his "disappointment and mortification" at the general's "ineradicable tendencies . . . to the strategy of defense and evasion" that had led to the abandonment of north Georgia. Just as annoying, Johnston "had been strangely reticent with the Government as to his plans and purposes" and "would not give satisfactory information or assurances" on how he proposed to handle Sherman. Finally, there was some sense of guilt, too, because Seddon realized that his and the president's decision the previous December to appoint Johnston to army command had been a mistake. Thus, as Senator Hill remembered, Seddon wanted to atone for it by relieving him "even at this late day."[140]

To Benjamin (who had been secretary of war from September 1861 to March 1862), Johnston's retreat through north Georgia was a reminder of his retreat up the Peninsula toward Richmond two springs before. Benjamin also was resentful that after "we had drained every resource of the Confederacy" to reinforce the Army of Tennessee, Johnston had retreated "practically without resistance on his part, through the whole mountainous country down to Atlanta." Benjamin had thus come to size up Johnston's weakness of character. "From a close observation of his career I became persuaded that his nervous dread of *losing a battle* would prevent at all times his ability to cope with an enemy of nearly equal strength." For these reasons, annoyed and chagrined that "day after day, and week after week his telegrams reached us announcing his abandonment of his positions one after the other," Benjamin actually had wanted Johnston removed earlier. Now, in mid-July, he "was most anxious and urgent that he shd. be replaced by some other commander."[141]

At some point Senator Hill added his voice to these discussions. Probably Seddon would have asked him to reaffirm the gist of his conversation with Johnston of July 1 and of his debriefing and memoranda with Davis and Seddon July 10–14. Indeed, with his state being overrun by the enemy, the Georgia senator's testimony would have been quite moving, recounting his change of opinion, from originally urging more cavalry help for Johnston to now advocating the general's removal, which he seems to have done forcefully.

Thus, Seddon, Benjamin, and Hill made the argument for Johnston's relief from command. The Cabinet apparently took a vote, and it was unanimous in favor of removal. Everyone remembered that the president sat back and allowed the consensus to develop: "Mr. Davis was the last man in the Cabinet to agree to the order of removal" (Hill); "The conclusion [to relieve Johnston] had ... been arrived at by him [Davis] slowly and not without much hesitation, misgiving, and, even to the last, reluctance" (Seddon); "When you [Davis] were appealed to ... to remove Gen. Johnston from the command ..., you hesitated to do so, and called attention to the danger of doing so in the midst of a campaign" (Postmaster Reagan). Reagan recalled that the president had resisted all the letters and personal solicitations from people who had been urging Johnston's removal. James Lyons, a friend of the president's, remembered his saying, a few days after the Cabinet meeting, that he had approved Johnston's removal only with the greatest reluctance: "I could not help it—Hill urged it on behalf of the people of Georgia and Benjamin and Seddon were so violent that they would listen to nothing." Probably the main reason Davis resisted change in commanders was the problem of whom he would name as successor: Hood or Hardee? Within days of the Cabinet meeting Hill told Congressman Lyons that, after the vote for removal had passed, Davis "said with great feeling 'Gentlemen it is very easy to remove the Genl. but when he is removed his place must be filled and where will you find a man to fill it?'"[142]

In the choice between Hardee and Hood, the Cabinet may have expressed a slight preference for Hood. Secretary Seddon recalled that the Cabinet would have preferred Hardee had he not manifested distrust of himself by declining permanent command of the Army of Tennessee after Missionary Ridge. Reagan also cited Hardee's refusal as a reason for recommending Hood for the appointment. The president, however, was not ready to promote Lieutenant General Hood. In fact, as of July 14, he was not even ready to fire Johnston and would not take this step until he heard

further from either Bragg or Johnston himself. The latter unfortunately persisted in conveying an almost blithe complacency as more
Union troops crossed the Chattahoochee. In a wire to Adjutant
General Cooper on the 14th, Johnston reported that now fully three
corps of enemy infantry plus cavalry were on the south bank of the
river. Bragg, busy in meetings with Johnston, Wheeler, Hood, and
other officers, sent no telegram that day. For his part, Davis wired
Bragg on another matter, evidently part of Bragg's mission in tour-
ing Georgia and Alabama: selecting another possible site for a prison
camp. Cahaba, Alabama, was under consideration; Davis directed
Bragg that "if C. is thus indicated," he was to follow through.[143]

With the Cabinet having voted to remove Johnston, Davis continued to agonize over whom to promote as successor. So on July 15
he sent Secretary Seddon on a 5:00 A.M. train to Petersburg to get
more of Lee's advice. After meeting with the general, Seddon
returned to Richmond by 11:00 A.M., went straight to the president's
offices, and conferred with him for at least an hour. Again, Lee only
added to the burden of Davis's decision. According to Major General
Wade Hampton, Lee's chief of cavalry, Lee urged that Johnston not
be fired, saying that if he could not command the army "we had no
one who could."[144] The president was thus placed in a quandary,
torn between his most respected general, Lee (who favored keeping
Johnston or replacing him with Hardee) and his most respected
adviser, Bragg (who favored relieving Johnston and replacing him
with Hood).

Bragg had spent the 14th in various meetings with the army's
key generals. At nine o'clock he was at Johnston's headquarters
conferring with corps commanders Hardee, Hood, Stewart, and
Wheeler. Captain Trask, on Hardee's staff, recorded that Bragg "has
. . . been in close consultation with Johnston and other generals to-
day. Bragg, Johnston, Hardee, Hood and Stewart were to-gether for
several hours." Then he seems to have gone off and met with them
individually; we know that he spent a long time with Hood, who
wrote out, probably at Bragg's request, a lengthy personal assessment of the campaign to date that emphasized General Johnston's
reluctance to combat Sherman and also emphasized his own desire
to attack the enemy. Given the circumstances, such a memorandum
was in effect Hood's request to be placed in command of the army,
an action that by this time Bragg was evidently hoping to bring

about. On the 15th the president's adviser apparently stayed in the city, because Lieutenant Mackall noted he did not visit headquarters during the day. Bragg would have been writing a report of his meetings with the army's senior officers. Also during that day he sent four telegraphic messages to Davis relating what he had learned so far: "Another corps of infantry has crossed above. Nearly all available stores and machinery are removed, and the people have mostly evacuated the town"; "I have made General Johnston two visits [July 13 and 14], and been received courteously and kindly. He has not sought my advice, and it was not volunteered. I cannot learn that he has any more plan for the future than he has had in the past." Nonetheless, General Bragg added the hopeful note, "It is expected that he will await the enemy on a line some three miles from here, and the impression prevails that he is more inclined to fight."[145]

Bragg also told Davis in a wire: "Lieut. Col. H. W. Walter leaves here this evening, bearer of a letter for you."[146] Walter, a staff officer and the general's friend, would carry to Richmond a long, very important letter to the president—too long for transmission by wire and too important to be trusted to the mail. It was Bragg's official report on what he learned and what he advised the president to do. Its message, in short: if Atlanta is to be held, or at least not given up without a fight, Johnston must go, Hardee should be passed over and Hood named to command. In Walter's packet Bragg probably also enclosed the memorandum Hood had written him the day before. This packet of correspondence was vital, and Walter had to get it to Richmond as fast as he could. Then, his work done, Bragg packed up. He left Atlanta by train on the night or early morning of July 15–16, headed for Alabama and a continuation of his tour of inspection.

In Richmond, the president was indeed anxious to learn all he could. Aware that Sherman was moving his armies across the Chattahoochee virtually at leisure, he was aware too, from Bragg's telegrams of the 15th, that Johnston and his army were dug in some three miles north of Atlanta, apparently waiting for the enemy to attack them. To be sure, Bragg had conveyed, "the impression prevails that he is now inclined to fight," but Davis did not know whether that meant offensively or defensively.[147] He did know, however, that while Johnston apparently sat by, the enemy was encroaching upon Atlanta. On the 15th Bragg wired his military secretary in

Richmond, Colonel John B. Sale, that the Federal infantry south of the Chattahoochee were extending their entrenched lines three or four miles eastward, not only expanding their bridgehead but also approaching the Augusta railroad, one of the three lines serving Atlanta and supplying its Confederate defenders. Clearly, Sherman was probing at the rail lines around Atlanta, foreshadowing an envelopment and possible siege of the city. How was Johnston going to stop him? The commanding general was appallingly silent, sending no wired message at all on the 15th, while Bragg sent five (including the one to Sale). The crisis seemed to be worsening, through both the enemy's activity and Johnston's silence. In these straits—with the Cabinet already on record with unanimous support for Davis's decision to relieve Johnston but with General Lee expressing misgivings at such a step, and with Bragg's written report somewhere on its way from Atlanta—the president had to act on his own. By this time, though we have no private memoranda as confirmation, Davis had made up his mind on Hood as Johnston's successor—the preference he had indicated to Lee as early as the 12th. Still, reflecting his anxiety, his lingering vacillations, and, above all, his logical quest for every last bit of supporting information, Davis simply asked Johnston what he intended to do.

Richmond, July 16, 1864

General J. E. Johnston:

A telegram from Atlanta of yesterday announces that the enemy is extending intrenchments from river toward railroad to Augusta. I wish to hear from you as to present situation, and your plan of operations so specifically as will enable me to anticipate events.

Jefferson Davis[148]

Johnston was too intelligent, too aware of the president's long-standing mistrust of him, and too suspicious of Bragg's motives not to have sensed the gravity of this telegram. For one thing, it confirmed that Bragg had been in direct communication with Richmond, because Johnston had never reported to the president on the enemy's movement toward the Augusta railroad; that information had to have come from Bragg. Thus, General Johnston's reply to the president, wired back the same day (probably in the evening), must be seen as a dramatic instance not so much of naïveté (though Symonds and a few others have so contended) as of studied indifference, even callousness to his superior's implicit wishes and expectations. Joseph E. Johnston in effect made his own case to be relieved from command.

> Near Atlanta, July 16, 1864
>
> His Excellency the President,
> Richmond:
>
> Your dispatch of to-day received. The slight change in the enemy's dispositions made since my dispatch of the 14th to General Cooper was reported to General Bragg yesterday. It was a report from General Wheeler that Schofield's corps had advanced eastwardly about three miles from Isham's Ford and intrenched. As the enemy has double our number, we must be on the defensive. My plan of operations must, therefore, depend upon that of the enemy. It is mainly to watch for an opportunity to fight to advantage. We are trying to put Atlanta in condition to be held for a day or two by the Georgia militia, that army movements may be freer and wider.
>
> J. E. Johnston[149]

President Davis and Secretary Seddon probably received this message, after transmission and deciphering, sometime on the morning of July 17. Overriding all else in what would have been a troubling message was that Johnston's strategic attitude had not changed since the opening of the campaign. At Dalton the previous winter he had said that his plan was mainly to watch for an opportunity to fight to advantage; now that this strategy had brought him to the very gates of Atlanta he was, with remarkable obliviousness to the crisis his retreats had brought on, still saying the same thing. Furthermore, Johnston's adding detail to Bragg's message of the day before on enemy movements did little more than remind the authorities in Richmond of just how reticent Johnston was about communicating daily developments at the front. More significant was the Confederate commander's belief that because Sherman outnumbered him 2 to 1, he was paralyzed on the defensive. To be sure, from his returns of July 10, Johnston knew his strength (59,000 officers and men present), of whom, even General Bragg conceded the number of effectives would not reach 52,000. But what about the enemy's numbers?

Even though Bragg downplayed them, estimating on the 15th, for example, that Sherman's strength totaled 75,000 (60,000 infantry, 10,000 cavalry, and 5,000 artillery), still Davis and Bragg were right in judging that Johnston faced less onerous odds than any other army in the Confederacy. At issue was what Johnston intended to do with his army. For instance, returns of July 10 showed that the Army of Tennessee now had over 10,000 effective cavalrymen, its largest mounted force of the campaign. Given Johnston's frequent calls for a raid into Sherman's rear, his failure to announce a more aggressive use of his mounted troops was telling.

Most telling of all—and here was the jarring surprise of his telegram—General Johnston closed by informing Richmond that he would entrust Atlanta's defense to the few thousand Georgia state troops while he maneuvered the army "freer and wider." President Davis's alarm in reading these lines may well be imagined, as he and Seddon huddled over the decoded message. Davis had told the Cabinet and others all along that he was determined that Atlanta would not be given up without a fight; now here was Joe Johnston intimating that this was the very thing he would do. The administration had to act at once, without even waiting for Bragg's report borne by Colonel Walter (who probably did not arrive until the 18th, since the trip from Atlanta to Richmond would have taken almost three days); thus, Bragg's long letter did not influence President Davis's eventual decision to relieve General Johnston.

No, if Atlanta were to be saved, or at least merely fought for, the time had come to implement the decision ratified by the Cabinet and concurred in if not advocated by Senator Hill and other Georgians. Hence the telegram from Adjutant General Cooper, probably written out just as Davis and Seddon had phrased it:

Richmond, July 17, 1864

General J. E. Johnston:

> Lieut. Gen. J. B. Hood has been commissioned to the temporary rank of general under the late law of Congress. I am directed by the Secretary of War to inform you that as you have failed to arrest the advance of the enemy to the vicinity of Atlanta, far in the interior of Georgia, and express no confidence that you can defeat or repel him, you are hereby relieved from the command of the Army and Department of Tennessee, which you will immediately turn over to General Hood.[150]

Sent from Richmond probably on the afternoon of the 17th—
assuming Davis, Seddon, and Cooper mulled and resolved for at
least several hours after receipt of Johnston's suicidally evasive
reply—Cooper's wired message was received that evening at the
army telegraph office in a downtown Atlanta hotel. Major Charles
W. Hubner, chief of the Telegraph Corps, would have waited while
the dots and dashes punched on paper tape by the machinery of the
time were transcribed and key words were deciphered. Then Hubner himself rode the message out to Johnston's headquarters at the
Dexter Niles house, three miles northwest of the city center. Lieutenant Mackall of the headquarters staff recorded the time of its
arrival at 9:00 P.M.; Johnston recalled it was closer to ten when Hubner walked in, interrupting Johnston and his chief engineer, Colonel
Stephen Presstman, as they looked over maps of Atlanta's fortifications. In his postwar writing Johnston does not reveal his feelings
at the time. We know only that he and his staff promptly drafted
and sent out that night the circulars formally announcing to the
army its change of commanders.

News of this sort travels fast. It is likely that even before Major
Hubner rode up to the Niles house, Atlanta's downtown residents
had heard it. Samuel Richards, who lived three blocks away from
Hubner's telegraph office, received the news in time to enter it into
his diary entry for that Sunday night, after his customary notice of
the day's worship service: "All of a sudden Gen Johnston has been
relieved of the command of the Army and Gen Hood or 'old Pegleg'
as the soldiers style him placed in command, so that there is thought
to be a prospect for a fight before Atlanta is given up, as Hood is said
to be a fighting man, if he *has* only one leg."[151]

Thus, even the man on the street realized immediately the
import of the news. The fall of Atlanta by that time may have been
inevitable, but the South did not want Atlanta to be given up without a fight. So the government put a general in charge to see to it.

NOTES TO PART ONE

1. "Shadow" [Henry Watterson], "Letter from Atlanta," May 24, 1864,
Mobile Advertiser and Register, May 29, 1864.

2. Johnston to "Fellow Soldiers," July 9, 1863; to Davis, July 12–15, U.S.
War Department, *The War of the Rebellion: A Compilation of the Official Records*

of the Union and Confederate Armies, 128 vols. (Washington: Government Printing Office, 1880–1901), 24, pt. 1, 201–2, 207; pt. 3, 994. All references to the *Official Records (O.R.)* are to series 1 unless stated.

3. Memorandum Orders, July 14, 1863; Sherman to Grant, July 14, *O.R.* 24, pt. 3, 510; pt. 2, 524.

4. Sherman to Grant, July 12–14, 1863, *O.R.* 24, pt. 2, 523–24.

5. Ibid., July 15, 17, 527–28.

6. Gen. Samuel Cooper to Johnston, June 13, 1861, *O.R.* 2:924.

7. Davis to Johnston, Mar. 15, 1862; S. Cooper, General Orders, No. 14, Mar. 13, *O.R.* 5:527–28, 1099.

8. Johnston to Lee, Apr. 29, 1862, *O.R.* 11, pt. 3, 473; to Davis, quoted in Craig L. Symonds, *Joseph E. Johnston: A Civil War Biography* (New York: W. W. Norton, 1992), 153.

9. McClellan to his wife, May 22, 1862, quoted in Stephen W. Sears, *To the Gates of Richmond: The Peninsula Campaign* (New York: Ticknor & Fields, 1992), 110; Lee to Johnston, May 21, Clifford Dowdey and Louis H. Manarin, eds., *The Wartime Papers of R. E. Lee* (Boston: Little, Brown, 1961), 176–77.

10. Johnston to Lee, May 28, 1862, *O.R.* 11, pt. 3, 555.

11. Ibid., Apr. 30, 1862, 477; Lee, quoted in Steven E. Woodworth, *Davis and Lee at War* (Lawrence: University Press of Kansas, 1995), 167.

12. John S. Tucker diary, quoted in Sears, *To the Gates of Richmond,* 69; 13.

13. Symonds, *Johnston,* 163.

14. Davis to Johnston, May 17, 1862, Dunbar Rowland, ed., *Jefferson Davis, Constitutionalist: His Letters, Papers, and Speeches,* 10 vols. (Jackson: Mississippi Department of Archives and History, 1923), 5:247.

15. Johnston to Louis T. Wigfall, Jan. 26, 1863; to Seddon, May 13, June 15; to William W. Mackall, June 7; and Brigadier General Josiah Gorgas diary, quoted in Symonds, *Johnston,* 199, 205, 214–15; Davis to Johnston, July 8; to Lee, July 21, quoted in Rowland, *Jefferson Davis, Constitutionalist,* 5:540, 574.

16. Cooper to Hardee, Dec. 2, 1863, *O.R.* 31, pt. 3, 775.

17. Grant to Sherman, Apr. 2, 1864; Sherman to Grant, Apr. 10, 1864, *O.R.* 32, pt. 3, 246, 313.

18. Quoted in Albert Castel, *Decision in the West: The Atlanta Campaign of 1864* (Lawrence: University Press of Kansas, 1992), 92.

19. Sherman to Thomas, Apr. 25, 1864; Special Orders No. 35, Apr. 25, *O.R.* 32, pt. 3, 490, 496–97.

20. Sherman to Schofield, Apr. 24, 1864; to Halleck, Apr. 28, ibid., 292, 294.

21. Sherman to Grant, Apr. 10 and 24, 1864; Thomas to Sherman, Apr. 8; Sherman to McPherson, Apr. 8, ibid., 314, 466, 474, 521.

22. Johnston to Hood, Feb. 18, 1864, *O.R.* 52, pt. 2, 624.

23. Johnston to Davis, Jan. 2, 1864, *O.R.* 32, pt. 2, 511.

24. Ibid., Jan. 2 and 15, 511, 559.

25. Ibid., Jan. 15, 559; Johnston to Longstreet, Mar. 13, *O.R.* 32, pt. 3, 618.

26. Johnston to Bragg, Mar. 18, 1864, *O.R.* 32, pt. 3, 649.

27. Ibid., Mar. 19, 1864; Bragg to Johnston, Mar. 12, ibid., 654; Davis's endorsement to Johnston, Mar. 19, quoted in Symonds, *Johnston,* 263.

28. Bragg to Johnston, Mar. 21, 1864; Johnston to Bragg, Mar. 22; Special Orders No. 82, Apr. 7, *O.R.* 52, pt. 2, 644; 32, pt. 3, 666, 755.

29. Brig. Gen. W. N. Pendleton, "Memorandum of conference held at request of President Davis . . . with General J. E. Johnston . . . ," Apr. 16, 1864, *O.R.* 38, pt. 3, 623.

30. Ewell to Johnston, Apr. 29, 1864; Johnston to Ewell, Apr. 14, *O.R.* 32, pt. 3, 781, 840.

31. Johnston to Davis, Jan. 12, 1864; to Browne, Feb. 8; Davis to Johnston, Jan. 13, 16; Johnston to Davis, Jan. 17; Johnston's endorsement, Feb. 15; Johnston to Bragg, Mar. 12, *O.R.* 32, pt. 2, 549, 698; 52, pt. 2, 596, 601, 603; 32, pt. 2, 618; pt. 3, 614.

32. Adj. A. W. Harris to Grant, Mar. 12, 1864, L. P. Grant Papers, Box 7, Folder 5 (Letters Received 1864), MSS 100, Atlanta History Center Library and Archives.

33. Sherman's report, Sept. 15, 1864, *O.R.* 38, pt. 1, 63.

34. Longstreet to Johnston, Feb. 27, 1864, *O.R.* 32, pt. 2, 810; Mackall to his wife, Mar. 4, quoted in Gilbert E. Govan and James W. Livingood, *A Different Valor: The Story of General Joseph E. Johnston, C.S.A.* (Indianapolis: Bobbs-Merrill, 1956), 266.

35. Richard M. McMurry, "The Mackall Journal and Its Antecedents," entries of May 3, 1864, typescript, courtesy of the author. Further references to this key manuscript source use McMurry's designations of Lieutenant Thomas B. Mackall's Journal A for the shorter version and Journal B for the longer.

36. Sherman to Grant, May 4, 1864, *O.R.* 38, pt. 4, 25.

37. Sherman to McPherson, May 5, 1864, ibid., 39–40.

38. Mackall Journal B, May 5, 1864.

39. Sherman to Thomas, May 7, 1864, *O.R.* 38, pt. 4, 56.

40. Mackall Journal A, May 7–8, 1864; W. W. Mackall to Brig. Gen. James Cantey, May 7; Cantey to Mackall, May 8, *O.R.* 38, pt. 4, 675, 678.

41. Sherman to Thomas, May 8, 1864; to Schofield, May 8, *O.R.* 38, pt. 4, 71, 84.

42. McPherson to Sherman, May 9, 1864, ibid., 106.

43. Mackall to Wheeler, May 9, 1864, ibid., 682.

44. Ibid., May 5, 661; report of Maj. Gen. Patrick R. Cleburne, Aug. 16, 1864, *O.R.* 38, pt. 3, 721; Mackall Journals A and B, May 6.

45. Govan and Livingood, *A Different Valor,* 266; Symonds, *Joseph E. Johnston,* 272–73; Wilbur G. Kurtz, "Why Was Snake Creek Gap Left Unguarded?" manuscript, ca. 1935, Wilbur G. Kurtz, Sr., Papers, Atlanta History Center Library and Archives.

46. Thomas Lawrence Connelly, *Autumn of Glory: The Army of Tennessee, 1862–1865* (Baton Rouge: Louisiana State University Press, 1971), 336.

47. Sherman, May 9, 1864, quoted in Castel, *Decision in the West,* 141; Sherman to Halleck, May 10, *O.R.* 38, pt. 4, 111.

48. Sherman to McPherson, May 10, 1864, *O.R.* 38, pt. 4, 125; Maj. Rowland Cox, "Snake Creek Gap and Atlanta," in Sydney C. Kerksis, comp., *The Atlanta Papers* (Dayton, Ohio: Press of Morningside Bookshop, 1980), 341.

49. Mackall to Cantey, May 9, 1864, *O.R.* 38, pt. 4, 684; Mackall Journal B, May 10.

50. Mackall to Polk, May 12, 1864, *O.R.* 38, pt. 4, 698, 700.

51. Sherman to McPherson, May 13, 1864, ibid., 170.

52. Special Field Orders No. 6, May 15, 1864, ibid., 199.

53. Lt. T. B. Mackall, "Journal of Operations of the Army of Tennessee May 14–June 4 [1864]," *O.R.* 38, pt. 3, 981.

54. William T. Sherman, *Memoirs of General William T. Sherman,* 2 vols. (New York: D. Appleton and Company, 1875), 2:36.

55. R. Lockwood Tower, ed., *A Carolinian Goes to War: The Civil War Narrative of Arthur Middleton Manigault, Brigadier General C.S.A.* (Columbia: University of South Carolina Press, 1983), 183; Sherman to Halleck, May 15, 1864, *O.R.* 38, pt. 4, 189.

56. I say presumably because "Atlanta" is virtually unmentioned in the United States–Confederate States correspondence early in the campaign. As pointed out in a previous discussion, Grant's instructions to Sherman were simply to get into the enemy's country as far as he could. And the Confederate administration's expectations of Johnston did not entail a retrogressive defense of Atlanta; they focused on an offensive into Tennessee.

57. Joseph E. Johnston, "Opposing Sherman's Advance to Atlanta," in Robert Underwood Johnson and Clarence Clough Buel, eds., *Battles and Leaders of the Civil War,* 4 vols. (New York: Century, 1888), 4:267; Johnston to Davis, May 16, 1864, *O.R.* 38, pt. 4, 201.

58. Sherman to Halleck, May 16–17, 1864, *O.R.* 38, pt. 4, 219–20.

59. Sherman to Thomas, May 17, 1864, ibid., 716.

60. Sherman to Thomas, Schofield, and McPherson, May 18, 1864, ibid., 233, 242, 244.

61. General Orders No. ———, May 19, 1864, ibid., 728.

62. Johnston's report, Oct. 20, 1864, *O.R.* 38, pt. 3, 615.

63. Johnston to Davis, May 20, 1864, *O.R.* 38, pt. 4, 728; Joseph E. Johnston, *Narrative of Military Operations* (New York: D. Appleton, 1874), 321n.; Joseph E. Johnston, "The Dalton-Atlanta Operations," in Edwin L. Drake, ed., *The Annals of the Army of Tennessee* (Nashville: A. D. Haynes, 1878), 5; Johnston, "Opposing Sherman's Advance," 268; Hood's report, Feb. 15, 1865, *O.R.* 38, pt. 3, 634–35.

64. Johnston's report; Mackall, "Journal of Operations," entry of May 20, 1864, *O.R.* 38, pt. 3, 616, 984–85; Mackall Journal A, May 20; Davis to Johnston, May 18 (received at Allatoona, May 20), *O.R.* 38, pt. 4, 725.

65. Mackall, "Journal of Operations," May 20, 1864, *O.R.* 38, pt. 3, 984.

66. Van Duzer to Eckert, May 22, 1864, *O.R.* 38, pt. 4, 260.

67. Special Field Orders No. 9, May 20, 1864; Sherman to Halleck, May 20, ibid., 272, 282; Sherman's report, June 8 and Sept. 15, *O.R.* 38, pt. 1, 60, 65; Sherman to his wife, May 20 and 22, M. A. DeWolfe Howe, ed., *Home Letters of General Sherman* (New York: Charles Scribner's Sons, 1909), 291, 293.

68. Johnston to Davis, May 20–21, 1864, *O.R.* 38, pt. 4, 728, 736.

69. Henry Stone, "From the Oostenaula to the Chattahoochee," in Kerksis, *Atlanta Papers,* 79.

70. Lt. Andrew J. Neal to his sister, quoted in Castel, *Decision in the West,* 225; Hood's report, *O.R.* 38, pt. 3, 761.

71. Sherman to McPherson, May 25, 1864, *O.R.* 38, pt. 4, 312.

72. Howard to Thomas, May 27, 1864, ibid., 324; Lt. Col. Joseph S. Fullerton's Journal; Cleburne's report, May 30; Mackall, "Journal of Operations," *O.R.* 38, pt. 1, 865; pt. 3, 706, 724–25.

73. Sherman to Halleck; to Thomas, May 28, 1864, *O.R.* 38, pt. 4, 331–32.

74. Bierce and Jackman quoted in Castel, *Decision in the West*, 236; William C. Davis, *The Orphan Brigade: The Kentucky Confederates Who Couldn't Go Home* (Garden City, N.Y.: Doubleday, 1980), 223.

75. Mackall, "Journal of Operations," May 23, 1864, *O.R.* 38 pt. 3, 986.

76. Mackall to his wife, quoted in Castel, *Decision in the West*, 247; Johnston to Bragg, May 28, 1864, *O.R.* 38, pt. 4, 745.

77. Louisa Pittman to John Neal, May 18, 1864, Andrew Jackson Neal Collection, Box 1, folder 7, Emory University Special Collections; "Miss Abby" Diary, in Thomas G. Dyer, *Secret Yankees: The Union Circle in Confederate Atlanta* (Baltimore: Johns Hopkins University Press, 1999), 309; "The Situation: Army of Tennessee," *Atlanta Intelligencer*, May 25; "Shadow," "Letter from Atlanta," *Mobile Register and Advertiser*, May 29.

78. "'Shadow,'" *Atlanta Intelligencer*, June 1, 1864; Mary S. Mallard to Mary Jones, May 27, June 3, Robert Manson Myers, ed., *The Children of Pride: A True Story of Georgia and the Civil War* (New Haven: Yale University Press, 1972), 1174, 1176.

79. Sherman to Thomas, June 2, 1864, *O.R.* 38, pt. 4, 352.

80. Sherman to Halleck, ibid., 362–63, 385; Mackall, "Journal of Operations," May 30, 1864; Johnston to Bragg, June 1, *O.R.* 38, pt. 3, 988; pt. 4, 753.

81. Bragg to Johnston, June 2, 1864; Johnston to Bragg and S. D. Lee, June 3, *O.R.* 38, pt. 4, 343, 747.

82. Sherman to Halleck; Forrest to Lee, May 29, 1864, ibid., 755–56; Mackall, "Journal of Operations," May 30, June 4; G. A. Henry to Seddon, May 25, *O.R.* 38, pt. 3, 988, 990; 52, pt. 2, 672.

83. Sherman to Halleck, June 5, 1864; to Brig. Gen. Joseph D. Webster, June 6, *O.R.* 38, pt. 4, 408, 418.

84. Bragg to Davis, June 4, 1864, ibid., 762.

85. Sherman to Thomas, June 4, 1864, *O.R.* 38, pt. 4, 401; Sherman to his wife, June 9, Howe, *Home Letters*, 294.

86. Special Field Orders No. 21, June 9, 1864, *O.R.* 38, pt. 4, 445.

87. Davis to R. E. Lee, June 9, 1864, Rowland, *Jefferson Davis, Constitutionalist*, 8:270; Mackall Journal A, June 9.

88. Sherman to his brother John, June 9, 1864, Rachel Sherman Thorndike, ed., *The Sherman Letters: Correspondence between General and Senator Sherman from 1837 to 1891* (New York: Charles Scribner's Sons, 1894), 236; Sherman to Garrard, June 10, *O.R.* 38, pt. 4, 450.

89. Johnston to S. D. Lee, June 11, 1864; Hardee's endorsement, Polk to Davis, June 13; Bragg to Johnston, June 13, *O.R.* 38, pt. 4, 769, 774; 52, pt. 2, 678.

90. Johnston to Bragg, and to S. D. Lee, June 16, 1864; Davis to Bragg, June 23, *O.R.* 38, pt. 4, 774; 39, pt. 2, 658.

91. Sherman to Halleck, June 13, 1864; to Stanton, June 15, *O.R.* 38, pt. 4, 466.

92. Special Field Orders No. 25, June 14, 1864, ibid., 480.

93. Sherman to Halleck, June 15, 17, 1864; to Grant, June 18; Johnston to Bragg, June 16, ibid., 481, 498, 507, 777.

94. Johnston to Bragg, June 19, 1864, ibid., 519.

95. Sherman to Halleck, June 19, 1864, ibid., 780.

96. Williams's report, *O.R.* 38, pt. 2, 32.

97. Eldon B. Richardson, *Kolb's Farm: Rehearsal for Atlanta's Doom* (n.p., 1979), 16; Dennis Kelly, "Mountains to Pass, a River to Cross: The Battle of Kennesaw Mountain, and Related Actions from June 10 to July 9, 1864," *Blue and Gray* 6, no. 5 (June 1989): 23; Castel, *Decision in the West,* 294; William R. Scaife, *The Campaign for Atlanta* (Saline, Mich.: McNaughton & Gunn, 1993), 66.

98. J. B. Hood, *Advance and Retreat: Personal Experiences in the United States and Confederate States Armies* (New Orleans: Published for the Hood Orphan Memorial Fund, 1880), 130; C. Vann Woodward, ed., *Mary Chesnut's Civil War* (New Haven, Conn.: Yale University Press, 1981), 616.

99. Sherman to Halleck, June 23, 1864, *O.R.* 38, pt. 4, 573.

100. "Explanation," *Atlanta Intelligencer,* June 22, 1864.

101. Manning to his mother, June 8, 1864, quoted in Richard M. McMurry, "'The *Enemy* at Richmond': Joseph E. Johnston and the Confederate Government," *Civil War History* 27, no. 1 (March 1981): 29.

102. Sherman to Halleck, June 16, 1864; to Thomas, June 24, *O.R.* 38, pt. 4, 492, 582.

103. Special Field Orders No. 28, June 24, 1864, ibid., 588; Sherman to his wife, June 26, Howe, *Home Letters of Sherman,* 298.

104. Sherman to Halleck, June 27, 1864, *O.R.* 38, pt. 4, 607.

105. Thomas to Sherman, June 27, 1864, ibid., 610.

106. Newton, quoted in Castel, *Decision in the West,* 321; Sherman to Halleck, July 9; Sherman's report, Sept. 15, *O.R.* 38, pt. 1, 69; pt. 5, 91.

107. Johnston to Bragg, June 27, 1864; Lee to Cooper, June 22, *O.R.* 38, pt. 4, 795–96; 39, pt. 2, 658.

108. Johnston to Wheeler, June 26, 1864; J. C. Van Duzer to Eckert, June 18; Johnson to Bragg, June 27, *O.R.* 38, pt. 4, 517, 792, 795–96.

109. Brown to Davis, June 28, 1864; Davis to Brown, June 29; Bragg to Davis, June 29, *O.R.* 52, pt. 2, 680–81; 38, pt. 4, 805.

110. Wheeler to Bragg, July 1, 1864, quoted in David Evans, *Sherman's Horsemen: Union Cavalry Operations in the Atlanta Campaign* (Bloomington: Indiana University Press, 1996), 243; Senator Benjamin H. Hill to Secretary of War Seddon, July 14, *O.R.* 52, pt. 2, 704–6; Castel, *Decision in the West,* 329.

111. Johnston to Bragg, July 3, 1864, *O.R.* 38, pt. 5, 9, 860.

112. Sherman to Halleck and to Thomas, July 3, 1864, ibid., 29.

113. Sherman to Thomas, ibid., 30–31.

114. Ross to Jackson, July 4, 1863, *O.R.* 38, pt. 5, 864.

115. F. A. Shoup, "Dalton Campaign—Works at Chattahoochee River— Interesting History," *Confederate Veteran* 3 (1895): 262–63.

116. Sherman to Thomas, July 3, 1863, *O.R.* 38, pt. 5, 30.

117. Maj. James A. Connolly to his wife, July 12, 1864, in Paul M. Angle, ed., *Three Years in the Army of the Cumberland: The Letters and Diary of Major James A. Connolly* (Bloomington: Indiana University Press, 1959), 234.

118. "The Position in Georgia," *Atlanta Intelligencer*, July 5, 1864.

119. Brown to Davis and Davis to Brown, July 5, *O.R.* 39, pt. 2, 688.

120. Sherman to Halleck, July 6, 1864, *O.R.* 38, pt. 5, 66.

121. Sherman to McPherson, and to Halleck, July 7, 1864; Garrard to Sherman, July 6, *O.R.* 38, pt. 5, 68, 73, 80.

122. Johnston to Davis, July 8, 1864, ibid., 868–69.

123. Brown to Davis, July 7, 1864, *O.R.* 52, pt. 2, 68; Mackall Journal A, July 7, 1864.

124. *Atlanta Intelligencer*, July 8, 1864.

125. Sherman to Thomas, July 8, 1864, *O.R.* 38, pt. 5, 86.

126. Thomas to Sherman, July 10, 1864, ibid., 102; Shoup, "Dalton Campaign," 264.

127. W. L. Trask journal typescript, entry of July 10, 1864, Kennesaw Mountain National Battlefield (KMNBP); Wright to Bragg, July 10, *O.R.* 52, pt. 2, 691–92.

128. Davis to Johnston, July 11, 1864, *O.R.* 38, pt. 5, 875.

129. Davis to Lee, July 12, 1864, ibid.

130. Lee to Davis, July 12, 1864, in Douglas Southall Freeman, ed., *Lee's Dispatches: Unpublished Letters of General Robert E. Lee, C.S.A. to Jefferson Davis and the War Department of the Confederate States of America 1862–1865* (New York: G. P. Putnam's Sons, 1915), 282.

131. Davis to Bragg, July 9, *O.R.* 39, pt. 2, 695–96.

132. Maj. Gen. Alexander P. Stewart to Bragg, Mar. 19, 1864, quoted in Richard M. McMurry, *John Bell Hood and the War for Southern Independence* (Lexington: University Press of Kentucky, 1982), 98; Hood to Bragg, Apr. 13, *O.R.* 32, pt. 3, 781; Hardee to Davis, June 22, Jefferson Davis Papers, Emory University Library Special Collections (Box 1, folder 38).

133. Bragg to Col. B. S. Ewell, Jan. 14, 1863, *O.R.* 52, pt. 2, 407.

134. "Invasion Is Not Subjugation," *Atlanta Southern Confederacy*, July 8, 1864; "Richmond and Atlanta," *Atlanta Appeal*, July 8, quoted in *Macon Telegraph*, July 11; *Atlanta Intelligencer*, July 9.

135. "Getting Out of Atlanta," *Mobile News* (undated), quoted in *New York Times*, Aug. 7, 1864; Samuel P. Richards Diary, July 10, Atlanta History Center Library and Archives, MSS 176, vol. 10 (July 1864–Apr. 1865); Mackall to his wife, July 11, 1864, quoted in William W. Mackall, *A Son's Recollections of His Father* (New York: E. P. Dutton & Company, 1930), 219; Trask journal, July 13, KMNBF; Brown's proclamation, July 9, *O.R.* 52, pt. 2, 688–91.

136. Bragg to Davis, July 13, 1864, *O.R.* 38, pt. 5, 878; "Grape," "Letter from the Georgia Front," *Augusta Constitutionalist*, July 16; "Ora" in *Montgomery (Alabama) Advertiser*, July 16.

137. Mackall to his wife, July 13, 1864, quoted in Symonds, *Johnston*, 323.

138. Johnston to Bragg, July 12, 1864, *O.R.* 38, pt. 5, 877; Sherman, *Memoirs*, 2:70; Lee to Davis, July 12, Freeman, *Lee's Dispatches*, 283–84; Davis to Lee, July 13, Rowland, *Jefferson Davis, Constitutionalist*, 6:292.

139. Hill to Seddon, July 14, 1864, *O.R.* 52, pt. 2, 707.

140. Seddon to Davis, June 17, 1872; to W. T. Walthall, Feb. 10, 1879, Rowland, *Jefferson Davis, Constitutionalist*, 7:320; 8:351–52; Hill to Walthall, Oct. 12, 1878, Jefferson Davis, *The Rise and Fall of the Confederate Government*, 2 vols. (New York: Appleton and Company, 1881), 2:561.

141. Benjamin to Davis, Feb. 15, 1879, ibid., 8:356.

142. Hill to Walthall, Oct. 12, 1878, Davis, *Rise and Fall*, 2:561; Seddon to Walthall, Feb. 10, 1879; Reagan to Davis, Feb. 7, 1878; James Lyons to Walthall, July 31, 1878, Rowland, *Jefferson Davis, Constitutionalist*, 8:78, 216, 349.

143. Davis to Bragg, July 14, 1864, *O.R.* 52, pt. 2, 704.

144. Hampton to Johnston (1874), in Johnston, "Opposing Sherman's Advance," 277.

145. Trask journal, July 15, 1864, KMNBP; Bragg to Davis, July 15, *O.R.* 38, pt. 5, 881.

146. Bragg to Davis, July 15, 1864, *O.R.* 39, pt. 2, 712.

147. *O.R.* 33, pt. 5, 881.

148. Davis to Johnston, July 16, 1864, *O.R.* 38, pt. 5, 882.

149. Johnston to Davis, July 16, 1864, ibid., 883.

150. Cooper to Johnston, July 17, 1864, ibid., 885.

151. Richards diary, July 17, 1864, Atlanta History Center.

PART TWO

HOOD STRUGGLES AGAINST THE INEVITABLE; OR, HOW EVEN A STUDENT OF THE "LEE AND JACKSON SCHOOL" COULD NOT PREVENT THE FALL OF ATLANTA

CHAPTER TWELVE

HOW HOOD LEARNED WAR FROM LEE AND JACKSON IN VIRGINIA

No one was more anxious than myself to prevent the
fall of Atlanta; I was not among those who deemed that
result inevitable as soon as the enemy had crossed the
Chattahoochie [*sic*], and I was not willing that it should
be yielded before manly blows had been struck for its
preservation.
—Jefferson Davis to Georgia Senator Herschel V.
Johnson, September 18, 1864

JOHN BELL HOOD sought the command of the Army of Tennessee and
shamelessly joined Bragg, when the latter was in Atlanta, July 13–15,
in deliberately misrepresenting Hardee to the Richmond authorities
so he would be passed over. Hood wanted army command, and as
a professional soldier—commissioned at West Point, veteran of eight
years in the old army, and now a lieutenant general in the Confederate army—he could have viewed his entire career as preparation
for this most desired advancement.

Years after the Civil War, writing his memoirs and attempting
to define his record as a soldier, Hood described himself as a disciple of the "Lee and Jackson school."[1] In doing so, he associated himself with the Confederacy's most illustrious war leaders and implied
that he had learned from them the kind of warfare that had brought
them numerous victories in Virginia. Indeed, Hood was often in the
thick of those victories, significantly contributing to them as well. As
a brigadier general and commander of the "Texas Brigade" at
Gaines's Mill, June 27, 1862, in Lee's Seven Days' Battles against
McClellan, for example, Hood personally led the last desperate
assault of the day that broke the enemy line and brought immediate, decisive Confederate victory. Two months later, at Second Manassas, Hood's Texas Brigade led Longstreet's powerful attack on the
afternoon of August 30 that came as close to crushing a Union army
as any of Lee's battle plans throughout the entire war. In Maryland

just a few weeks later, Hood commanded a small division, his Texans and the brigade of Colonel E. M. Law. At Sharpsburg on the morning of September 17, the ferocious counterattack of Hood's division against Hooker's corps saved the left of Lee's line from almost certain collapse. Here, as at Gaines' Mill, the 31-year-old Hood learned how an aggressive assault could turn the tide of battle. Moreover, Hood was learning the pugnacity, aggressiveness, and preference for attack that characterized the two famed Confederate commanders in Virginia.

At the same time, Hood learned from his mentors their preference for a flanking attack when the opportunity arose. On the second day at Gettysburg, July 2, 1863, when Lee planned to attack the Union left, Hood's division marched in as the extreme Confederate right. Before advancing, Hood sent forward scouts to assess the Union position; they brought back word that there were no enemy troops on Round Top, a big hill at the south end of the Yankees' line that would have dominated their position. Hood repeatedly asked for a change in orders so he could launch, as Harry W. Pfanz terms it, "a detached Jackson-like move." Repeatedly, though, he was refused by General Longstreet, presumably on Lee's authority. Whether Hood's proposal for revised attack would have improved Confederate fortunes that bloody day is speculative. As it happened, Hood himself was severely wounded just as his division engaged the enemy. A shell burst overhead, striking Hood's left arm with several fragments. Bleeding and in shock, he was taken to the rear. "The day's assault had barely begun," Pfanz writes, "and the Army of Northern Virginia's key division commander was already out of the fight."[2]

Despite shell hits in Hood's hand, forearm, elbow, and biceps, Confederate surgeons saved the arm from amputation. But it was limp and useless and would remain so for the rest of Hood's life. It was still in a sling two and one-half months later when Hood, transferred with another of Longstreet's divisions to northwest Georgia, fought at Chickamauga. Here again, on the second day, Hood participated in a massive Confederate assault that sent the Yankees fleeing. This time Hood took a bullet in the right leg. So severe was the wound that surgeons had to amputate at the upper third of the thigh. After spending time in Georgia, in Dalton and Atlanta, Hood was in Richmond by November 17, where he would spend the next three months convalescing among high social circles that included

President Jefferson Davis. Fortunately, Hood's wounds, while phys-
ically incapacitating, seemed to have created no psychological damage. (A cruel aspersion, that Hood habitually used laudanum as pain
medicine, has been dismissed by recent scholars as groundless.)

Even before Hood reached Richmond, Generals Bragg and
Longstreet recommended him for promotion to lieutenant general,
and President Davis promised he would nominate him. Hood's new
rank was confirmed by the Senate on February 11, 1864. A few days
later he left Richmond for Dalton, where on the 25th he assumed his
new position as corps commander in General Johnston's Army of
Tennessee.

In the opening weeks of the Atlanta Campaign, Johnston relied
more on Hood than on even his senior corps commander, Hardee.
Johnston gave Hood responsibility for the main Confederate assault
at Resaca, May 14, and for the proposed attacks at Cassville on the
19th and New Hope Church on the 28th. Only Hood's decision to
bring on a brief, costly fight at Kolb's Farm on June 22, without either
proper reconnaissance or authorization from army headquarters,
marred his otherwise solid, dependable performance as corps commander. Indeed, after the death of Lieutenant General Polk on June
14, Hardee and Hood stood as the Army of Tennessee's preeminent
corps-level leaders, the two men between whom President Davis
deliberated after he had decided to remove Johnston. Davis chose
Hood on July 17—a decision with which even Hardee's biographer
agrees. Hood was promoted to full general effective immediately and
took command of the army on the morning of the 18th.

CHAPTER THIRTEEN

HOOD'S ATTACK AGAINST
THOMAS'S ARMY: PEACHTREE
CREEK, JULY 20, 1864

THE TEST WOULD BE TRYING indeed. Even Bragg, who strongly favored
Hood's appointment, acknowledged on July 15: "Position, numbers,
and morale are now with the enemy, but not to an extent to make

me despair of success." By nightfall of the 17th, before Hood took charge, four of seven corps had crossed the Chattahoochee, and Union forces, particularly those of McPherson's Army of the Tennessee with Kenner Garrard's cavalry, were at Nancy Creek, eight miles north of downtown Atlanta, and marching hard. Hood knew that he was outnumbered by at least 3 to 2. Bragg conservatively estimated on the 15th that the enemy numbered 75,000 effective infantry, cavalry, and artillery, compared with 52,000 effectives of all arms (we know today that Sherman in mid-July had about 90,000 men available for duty). Still, as he reported to Richmond, Bragg judged that there was "but one remedy—offensive action.... We should drive the enemy from this side of the river, follow him down by an attack in flank, and force him to battle, at the same time throwing our cavalry on his communications."[3]

In this manner Bragg established early on the government's expectations of Hood, which were simply that he should try to drive Sherman away from Atlanta by either infantry attack against his armies or cavalry raid into his rear. Either way, Hood clearly understood that he was charged with reversing Johnston's months' long policy of defensive retrograde and with assuming the offensive. Such a plan, as Bragg himself confessed, "would now be assumed under many disadvantages." Hood of course understood the situation and acknowledged it in his confidential letter to Bragg of July 14: "Our present position is a very difficult one"; but with the enemy so near the city, "we should attack him." Secretary of War James A. Seddon reinforced these expectations in a telegram to Hood on the night of the 17th, although he conveyed at the same time his appreciation of Hood's precarious situation, with a superior enemy force bearing down upon him from the north. "It may yet be practicable," Seddon wrote, "to cut the communication of the enemy or find or make an opportunity of equal encounter whether he moves east or west." Cutting communications meant a cavalry raid; "equal encounter" meant bringing on a battle against such part of Sherman's forces as Hood's outnumbered troops might stand a fair expectation of success. By either strategy, Seddon exhorted Hood to "test to the utmost your capacities."[4]

It is not surprising that in its expectation of offensive action the Confederate government deliberately chose a disciple of Lee and Jackson. The Southern people understood the challenge, and the appointment, in those terms as well. After Hood succeeded Johnston in command of the army, editors of the *Atlanta Appeal* declared that the time for skillful retreating had come to an end and that the situation now called for attack, in the manner of Jackson: "It is time perhaps that Stonewall Jacksonism had usurped the place of caution and strategy. There is a limit to prudence. When excessive, our enemies denominate it cowardice. This war must end and the final battle be fought. Why not here, and even now?" The editor of the *Augusta Constitutionalist* was more forthright about the meaning of Hood's assumption of command: "If it means anything it must mean this: *Atlanta will not be given up without a fight.*"[5]

The Georgians and the soldiers of the Army of Tennessee who had wearied of Johnston's tactics received an immediate measure of satisfaction from General Hood when he put an end to General Johnston's policy of giving up territory, largely because there was no more territory to give up. By nightfall of the 18th—which day Hood spent partly in conferring with Johnston and in handling the administrative processes involved in an army's change of commanders—the largest of Sherman's three armies, that of the Cumberland under George Thomas, was approaching Peachtree Creek, barely four miles from the center of the city. Hood at the time had his army in the defensive position he inherited from his predecessor, a line one mile or so south of Peachtree Creek. This line itself was not quite two miles north of Atlanta's main perimeter of fortifications, on which Confederate engineers and slaves had labored for almost a year. Hood's last recourse would be to withdraw back into these works, but beyond that, he had little room for maneuver.

What room he had came as a result of Sherman's movements on the 19th. The plan that the Union commander had announced to Grant as early as April 10—"pass to the left, and act on Atlanta, or on its eastern communications"—was in full tilt. As Thomas's three corps began crossing Peachtree Creek on the 19th, the other two Union armies, McPherson's and Schofield's, swung wide to the southeast, heading for Decatur, a borough six miles east of Atlanta, with the obvious intention of cutting the Georgia Railroad leading eastward to Augusta. The gap being created between Thomas and the rest of Sherman's forces presented Hood with an opportunity to launch an attacking battle—indeed, the battle that his government and the people expected him to fight. Hood called for an assault on

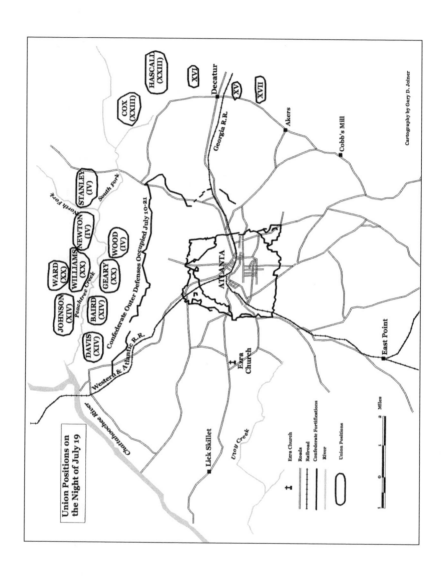

Union Positions on the Night of July 19

HASCALL (XXIII)

COX (XXIII)

XVI

XV

XVII

Decatur

Georgia R.R.

Akers

Cobb's Mill

STANLEY (IV)

South Fork

North Fork

NEWTON (IV)

WILLIAMS (XX)

WARD (XX)

WOOD (IV)

GEARY (XX)

JOHNSON (XIV)

BAIRD (XIV)

Peachtree Creek

DAVIS (XIV)

Confederate Outer Defenses Occupied July 10-21

Western & Atlantic R.R.

Chattahoochee River

ATLANTA

East Point

Lick Skillet

Utoy Creek

Ezra Church

Ezra Church
Roads
Railroad
Confederate Fortifications
River
Union Positions

Miles

0   1   2

Cartography by Gary D. Joiner

Thomas by Hardee's and Stewart's corps the next day, July 20, while
Wheeler's cavalry and Major General Frank Cheatham's corps (formerly Hood's) east of the city guarded against the advance by
McPherson or Schofield. (General Johnston later claimed he was
planning the very same attack when he was relieved, but he left no
documentary evidence; no corps commander ever recollected it; and
Johnston intimated no such plan to the government in his telegram
of July 16.) Hood seems to have accepted that Thomas had moved
his army across Peachtree Creek, or he would have by the time his
attack was launched; his object was "to crush Thomas' army before
he could fortify himself." As Hood explained in his campaign report,
his hope was "to drive the enemy back to the creek, and then toward
the [Chattahoochee] river in the narrow space formed by the river
and creek." General Stewart recalled that even if "the enemy be
found intrenched his works were to be carried, everything on our
side of the creek was to be taken."[6]

That night at his headquarters Hood discussed his plans for the
next day with all three corps commanders, as well as Major General
Gustavus W. Smith, in charge of the several thousand Georgia state
militia then augmenting Hood's army. The attack would begin at
1:00 P.M. on Hardee's right, division by division advancing in eche-
lon, right to left at a distance of 150 to 200 yards. Hood later recorded
that, with all officers looking on, he had carefully asked each commander whether he understood his part of the battle plan. Hood
also sent an afternoon message to Wheeler, asking him to meet as
soon as he could later that evening, when Hood would be back at
his headquarters.

With all this preparation, and his sense that he had caught Sherman in "a serious blunder," Hood clearly believed he had been
"afforded one of the most favorable occasions for complete victory."
The new army commander was therefore openly optimistic, even
excited, on the morning of the 20th. Later, around noon, a Southern
newspaper reporter, Felix G. De Fontaine, chanced to have a few
words with the general at his headquarters. As he leaned on his
crutch and cane in the doorway, Hood impressed De Fontaine with
his full uniform and "his eyes flashing with a strange indescribable
light, which gleams in them only in the hour of battle." Before Hood
and his staff rode off, he told the reporter, "At one I attack the enemy.
He has pressed our lines until he is within a short distance of Atlanta,

and I must fight or evacuate. I am going to fight. The odds are against us, but I leave the issue with the God of Battles."[7]

What the God of Battles was in the classical era, sometimes fickle and almost always inscrutable to mortals, came to be termed the fog of war in the Napoleonic era and the friction of war in the Clause-witzian. Both phenomena were evident in the battle that Hood launched July 20 south of Peachtree Creek. By their insidious work-ings, as so often happens in military history, a battle plan sound in concept began to fall apart almost at the outset. At noon on July 20 Sherman's forces were not where Hood supposed them to be. The Union commander, bristling with his usual determination to keep the pressure on the enemy, had ordered his army leaders to get mov-ing by 5:00 A.M., pressing ever closer on Atlanta. At some point Sher-man expected the Rebels to fight, because on July 19 he had learned from a captured Atlanta newspaper that Hood had succeeded John-ston. Sherman consulted his subordinates on what they thought the change meant. All three, Thomas, McPherson, and Schofield, had known Hood at West Point and agreed that he was aggressive, per-haps to recklessness. With the Rebels now likely to show fight more than at any time previous in the campaign, Sherman instructed his generals to "accept battle on anything like fair terms."[8]

It was McPherson's progress on the morning of the 20th, how-ever, that really threw a hitch in Hood's scheme. Through fault either of Wheeler's cavalry or of his headquarters staff led by Brigadier General Mackall, Hood did not know that McPherson's Army of the Tennessee had already taken Decatur and was advancing at a rate of a mile every three hours, battling Rebel cavalry and destroying the Georgia Railroad as it went. Instead, Hood believed McPher-son's forces were well east of Decatur, as much as another day away. This impression led the Confederate commander to suppose not only that the gap separating Thomas from the rest of Sherman's forces was much wider but, more important, that McPherson so far posed no threat to Atlanta.

Thus was the fog of war, which Hood was not able to penetrate. The friction of war set in after Wheeler informed Hood, mid-morn-ing of the 20th, that his command (2,500 troops and a battery) was being pressed back by McPherson's 25,000 Yankees. The Confeder-ate commander responded by sending Wheeler another 1,000 cav-alry and ordering Cheatham to extend his corps one division front, or roughly one mile, to the south to cover the main Decatur road. Hardee and Stewart were ordered at the same time to extend their line by a half-mile to the right. Even with these previously unplanned movements, Hood saw no reason that his attack should not be launched at one o'clock—hence the "strange indescribable light" of battle ardor in his eyes that reporter De Fontaine observed at noon.

The movement, however, did not proceed as planned. General Cheatham, newly promoted to corps command, moved slowly and too far (eventually up to two miles), forcing Hardee and Stewart to spend more time than Hood had planned in taking their new positions. Thus, when the Confederate attack began the time was closer to 4:00 P.M., and definitely not 1:00. The extra hours allowed Thomas's infantry, which had all reached the south side of Peachtree Creek by noon, to begin rude entrenching or logworking and bringing up divisional artillery. While this delay was certainly hurtful to the Confederates, it was not the critical factor in the battle of Peachtree Creek. If De Fontaine quoted Hood correctly—and the reporter made a point of saying that he stayed behind at headquarters immediately after his interview "to write these hurried words"—the general was not being melodramatic in saying the odds were against him in his attack on Thomas, for they decidedly were. Actually they were the same odds that usually worked against any attacker in the Civil War, and they explain why Hardee and Stewart were repulsed after several hours' hard fighting on the afternoon of the 20th. As it turned out, the two sides were roughly equal in strength, in terms of troops engaged. But Thomas's men enjoyed high ground, rude trench or logworks in places, and some artillery support. Hardee's and Stewart's men, in contrast, had to advance over tangled, wooded terrain without the benefit of any reconnaissance. Still, the Southerners achieved temporary breakthroughs in the enemy line and at some points in Stewart's front even sent the Yankees running in confusion for the rear. By the end of the day, however, Thomas had stabilized his line and the Rebels retired to their outer works. When the casualties were toted up, both sides, literally, were decimated, losing about 10 percent of their engaged forces. As recently tallied by students of the battle, Hardee's and Stewart's corps suffered about 2,500 killed, wounded, and missing; Thomas's approximately 1,900. Regardless of casualties, and even of outcome, the battle of Peachtree Creek demonstrated at once the substance and limitations of John Bell Hood's generalship. Hood showed not only boldness but at least some talent in battle planning. When he caught Thomas's army separated from Schofield's and McPherson's, he determined to strike the Army of the Cumberland before it could fortify, and he hoped to push it back against the creek or the river. Yet in his first battle as army commander Hood also revealed a quite ordinary inability to control events. Like his mentor General Lee, once he had imparted his intentions to his corps commanders, Hood allowed them to handle the work. This style of battle leadership kept the commanding general in the rear and somewhat out of touch with tactical developments. It accordingly reduced his ability to exert any personal strength to overcome the ever-present surprises and hindrances of the battlefield.

On the other side, General Sherman was of course satisfied with the outcome of Peachtree Creek. At the same time, he deserves no credit at all for it. He was at least as removed as Hood from the battlefield, staying throughout the day in Schofield's sector northeast of the city. More to the point, he did not even hear the noise of the fight, nor did he know of it till about midnight, when he received General Thomas's first dispatch, sent near dusk and after the shooting had stopped. Earlier in the day he had even complained of Thomas's slowness in advancing his line. Then, after learning of the battle, Sherman redirected his criticism: inferring that the Rebels east of the city must have weakened their lines, he complained of *McPherson's* slowness. It was an odd attitude for a commander who had just won a significant engagement. Yet it was characteristic of the always aggressive, feisty Cump Sherman.

It was also characteristic of General Sherman that he refused to be bound by the age-old conventions of gentlemanly warfare. Knowing on July 19 that his columns would come within rifled artillery range of Atlanta, he ordered that on the 20th "the place must be cannonaded without the formality of a demand" for the city's surrender. In effect, he was telling his battery commanders to open up a barrage of the city without giving any warning to its civilian populace. Giving a besieged town advance notice of an intended barrage had been a customary practice for centuries; usually the town's defenders were given a couple of days to evacuate the noncombatant women and children. But no: Sherman's cannoneers followed orders and around noon of July 20 dropped at least three shells into the city. In the coming days, with the constricting Union lines drawing ever closer to Atlanta, Federal artillerymen bombarded the Rebel lines and the civilians inside them with increasing intensity. Sherman himself sometimes issued orders for the rate of fire; he intended his bombardment to be just another element of tourniquet-like pressure on Hood to give up the city. As he expressed to Thomas, "My belief is we can approach from the east with certainty of getting within cannon reach of the town, in which case it cannot be held."[9]

Tightening the tourniquet on July 21, Sherman ordered his army commanders to shove their troops closer to Atlanta. He particularly wanted McPherson to push in. "More good results will flow from your pressing hard," he told his friend Mac.[10] Facing McPherson were Joe Wheeler's dismounted cavalrymen, reinforced on the morning of the 21st by Cleburne's division of infantry. The Confederates extended their outer line of entrenchments another three-fourths of a mile south, beyond the Georgia Railroad to an imposing eminence known as Bald Hill. General Frank Blair, commanding the Seventeenth Corps, made up his mind to take the hill, sending Mortimer Leggett's division forward. In a determined charge the Federals drove off Wheeler's troops and took the rise. Bald Hill eventually came to be called Leggett's Hill; upon it Union artillery was soon deployed and firing more shells into Atlanta.

CHAPTER FOURTEEN

HOOD ATTEMPTS ANOTHER CHANCELLORSVILLE, JULY 22

INSIDE THE CONFEDERATE LINES, General Hood remained undaunted: undaunted by his repulse at Peachtree Creek, undaunted by the Yankee bombardment, undaunted by the enemy's tactical successes east of the city. Hood was even confident and full of fight, to the point that he planned yet another attacking battle. This one would be even bolder, more masterfully planned and much more promising of great results than the one on July 20. It was, in fact, Lee-like in its boldness and sweep.

On July 21, Sherman's three armies were still more or less separated. Better yet, Wheeler reported that as McPherson's army
marched in on Atlanta from the east, it had its left flank "in the air"
(Sherman had sent Garrard's cavalry east to wreck the Georgia Railroad). This situation presented Hood with an obvious opportunity
not only for a crushing flank attack, like the one made famous by
Jackson at Chancellorsville, but also for the rout and possible
destruction of the entire Army of the Tennessee, fully a fourth of
Sherman's strength. Besides, McPherson's army, at least, had to be
contained. It was closest to Atlanta, it had broken a key railroad, and,
if it swept southwest, it would be poised to cut Hood's last remaining rail lines. Thus, after sending more infantry support to Wheeler
as he tried to stall McPherson's advance, Hood planned (1) for his
forces in the night of July 21–22 to drop back from their outer lines
into the main fortified perimeter around the city, (2) for Stewart and
Cheatham to hold their newly contracted lines on the 22d so that (3)
Hardee's corps, the most powerful in the army, could march south
through and out of the city in a vigorous night march, swing northeast toward Decatur guided by Wheeler's cavalry, and (4) jump into
McPherson's flank-rear, rolling up the Yankee line as swiftly and
stupendously as Jackson had done, (5) aided by Cheatham's corps,
which would then attack McPherson from the west, while (6)
Wheeler captured McPherson's entire wagon train (known to be
parked in Decatur) and then moved in to help in the piecemeal
destruction of the Army of the Tennessee.

Such was Hood's plan. As with Peachtree Creek we have only
flimsy documentation of it, but all students of the campaign agree
on its outlines and on its ingenuity. A historian of the Army of Tennessee, Stanley Horn, calls it "brilliant in its conception.... There
seems no doubt that the maneuver completely befuddled Sherman."
Alfred H. Burne calls the battle of July 22 "Hood's 'battle of Chancellorsville,'" because the general at Atlanta "believed that the mantle of Stonewall Jackson had descended upon him." John P. Dyer,
Wheeler's biographer, judges that Hood's plan of attack "was a
maneuver similar to Jackson's flank march and attack at Chancellorsville." Albert Castel describes Hood's plan as "worthy of Lee,"
offering prospects for "the most spectacular victory of the war."
Even contemporaries saw in Hood's plan a Jacksonian boldness;
Irving A. Buck, General Pat Cleburne's adjutant, wrote, "General

Hood had conceived a move worthy of Stonewall Jackson, in attempting to strike and crush Sherman's left wing in a flank movement."[11] In his battle of July 22, barely three days into his new role as army commander, General Hood clearly intended to show that he was a disciple of the Lee and Jackson school.

The battle that ensued east of Atlanta (which in most texts is simply named after the city, but which has begun to be called the battle of Bald Hill), though characterized by Hood's bold plan, failed to yield the expected or hoped-for results. To be sure, the hard fighting of Hardee's and Cheatham's soldiers killed General McPherson (the only Union army commander killed in action during the war), inflicted 4,000 casualties (the largest single-battle loss handed Sherman in the entire Georgia campaign), and gave Confederates possession of twelve captured cannon and a division-length of enemy works. Besides its high cost (5,500 killed, wounded, and missing), however, the greatest disappointment to Hood was that his brilliant plan had come unglued. Here again, we see General Hood's inability both to rise above the fog of war and to override its friction.

The Confederates' problems began even before their attack. A late start for perhaps half of Hardee's force, the exhaustion of the men, a hot night, dusty roads, and undisciplined cavalry combined to bring the four assault divisions not nearly far enough into McPherson's rear when Hardee, well behind schedule, decided to deploy. Rough terrain added further delay so that Hood's surprise attack, planned for much earlier in the morning, actually did not begin till shortly after noon. By that time General McPherson, worried all morning about his flank, had begun to shift troops of the Sixteenth Corps toward his left, and against these troops Hardee's attack struck and stopped. Thus, the surprised Confederates, instead of overrunning hospital tents, wagons, and other rearward impedimenta, ran head-on into a division of veteran Union infantry. The extent of the Confederates' difficulties that day east of Atlanta is made clear by a detailed comparison between Hardee's flanking march and Hood's presumed model, that of Lee and Jackson, May 2, 1863, at Chancellorsville, usually viewed as Lee's greatest victory of the war, against Union Major General Joseph Hooker's hugely superior numbers. Such a comparison begins to outline all that can go wrong in implementing a brilliant battle plan—the collective difficulties that Clausewitz called the friction of war. It also elucidates key differences that explain why one flank attack succeeded while another failed.

First, in laying out their plans, Lee and Jackson knew precisely where the enemy flank rested, they had good maps of the march route, and they even had a local resident who confirmed the roads. Hood, however, in planning his flanking march, was much less adequately served by his cavalry and had no topographic intelligence of the kind Lee had. Wheeler and many of his troops, busy during much of the 21st facing and fighting the Seventeenth Corps, were not free to conduct any reconnaissance. As a result, Hood had a far less certain idea of where the Federal left flank lay. This uncertainty doubtlessly contributed to, and may have been the primary cause of, a harmful confusion among the Confederate leadership before the battle.

Second, Lee and Jackson were in perfect agreement on their plan, whereas Hood and Hardee were not. Sometime on the 21st, probably the afternoon, Hood called his three infantry corps commanders together with Wheeler and Smith (as he had done before Peachtree Creek) for a conference at his headquarters. Unsure of the best way to approach the enemy flank, Hood instructed Hardee to bypass it altogether and "to go to or beyond Decatur" in order to get into the enemy's rear, then swing west and begin his assault. Hardee asked for a modification. Because his troops, particularly Cleburne's division, Hardee contended, "had been marching, fighting, and working the night and day previous [and] had little rest for thirty-six hours," he appealed to Hood to shorten the intended march route so he would "strike the enemy in flank." Hood later claimed he never changed his plan; Hardee claimed he did. General Cheatham, present at the conference, wrote after the war: "My distinct recollection is that Genl Hood was very decided that Genl Hardee should move to the rear of Genl McPherson's flank by the way of Decatur; but on account of the lateness of the hour, the distance to be travelled, and the condition of the troops, he finally consented that Genl Hardee should have discretion to make the assault on the flank and rear of McPherson." Perplexed historians have surmised there may have been a second conference later that night, wherein Hardee prevailed in his view, but the issue remains unclear. What is clear, though, is that the army's two senior commanders did not agree on their objective.[12]

Third, Lee and Jackson, aided by their cavalry intelligence and engineers' maps, also benefited from a clearer grasp of the distance involved in their proposed march route, an estimated ten miles, and thus were able more realistically to plan the timing of their attack. As General Hardee set out on his march, July 21, in contrast, he probably had not been able to gauge accurately the distances involved. By the route on which he and Hood agreed, from their works north of the city the corps would proceed through downtown by way of Peachtree, then out the McDonough road, and northeast again to Cobb's Mill and beyond on the Fayetteville and Decatur roads. All officers understood that a wide swing was necessary to maintain the element of surprise. In General Wheeler's words, Hood at his headquarters meeting explained "that the object in going so far south as Cobb's mill was to secrete the movement from the enemy." Yet without adequate cavalry reconnaissance or expert maps on hand, Hood and his officers apparently underestimated the time Hardee's corps would need to get into position against McPherson east of Atlanta. Hood's plan called for Hardee's three divisions north of town and Cleburne's and Wheeler's forces east of it to wait until dark, which meant at least 8:00 P.M. on that summer night, before withdrawing from their works and moving into the city. Then, after marching through the night, Hardee and Wheeler were (as Hood phrased it) "both to attack at daylight, or as soon thereafter as possible."[13]

That timetable, as we see today, was eminently impractical. Well after the war one of Hardee's staff officers, Colonel T. B. Roy, had to write a friend in Atlanta for an estimate of the distance from downtown to Decatur by way of Cobb's Mill; the estimate was fifteen miles. (The distance would be even greater by Hood's original plan, with Hardee turning west from Decatur into McPherson's rear.) As it happened, it was 3:00 A.M. before Hardee's lead division, that of Major General William B. Bate, reached Cobb's Mill, where the worn-out men were allowed to rest. Two hours later, when they should already have been deployed in assault formation, Bate's men were at Grandma Akers's house, more than eleven miles from their point of departure but nowhere near where they should have been for an attack to be made "at daylight, or as soon thereafter as possible."[14]

Fourth, Jackson's men began their march at seven or eight in the morning, refreshed by a night's sleep and breakfast, and they marched on better roads and in pleasant weather. The Confederates' flank march and deployment eventually consumed over ten hours, but it went according to plan, stayed close to schedule, and encountered only minor complication. Not so Hardee's. While Bate's and W. H. T. Walker's divisions withdrew from their lines at nightfall as planned, Cleburne's had much more difficulty disengaging. At 11:00 P.M., with the division still not in motion, Hardee's adjutant issued an order for it to begin marching at one in the morning, already at least five hours behind schedule. Major General George Maney's division, last in line, did not get onto the McDonough road till three in the morning, about the time that Bate's men were reaching Cobb's Mill. Hardee's column was therefore strung out for nearly eight miles. And the men were hardly marching with vigor. The night was hot and humid, and the dry, red dirt road kicked up clouds of choking dust. Some had not slept in two days; hundreds simply fell out and dropped to the ground.

Compounding these difficulties was the general performance of the Confederate cavalry. Whereas the horsemen with Jackson, under General Fitzhugh Lee, operated faultlessly during the march, and Lee personally led Jackson to observe the enemy's position, Wheeler's troops actually impeded Hardee's march. As the Confederate infantry marched through downtown past midnight, Wheeler's undisciplined horsemen broke ranks to loot stores and unoccupied houses. The Southern press later reported that Hood had five of the worst plunderers shot and eighty more arrested, but the damage done downtown that night had the tactical effect of disrupting further a march already slowed and tardy. Anger swelled in Hardee's column when Wheeler's cavalrymen, "their horses literally piled up and almost concealed by the plunder they had on them," according to one disgusted Confederate, got in the way of the infantry as it slogged through the night on the roads south of town. General Wheeler himself seems to have been somewhat confused about his primary mission, that of guiding Hardee. Sometime during the morning of the 22d, he sent back word that Garrard's Yankee cavalry was known to be off toward Covington destroying the railroad and asked whether he should follow. Hardee had to reiterate the obvious: "I cannot spare you or any force to pursue Garrard now. We must attack, as we arranged, with all our force."[15]

Fifth, sometime after 5:00 A.M. on July 22—shortly after day-break, remembered his chief of staff—Hardee conferred with Wheeler and several of his division leaders at William Cobb's house. Wheeler's cavalrymen then left Hardee's infantry behind, riding toward Decatur and their objective, McPherson's wagon train. Hardee was left virtually blind, unable to reconnoiter the exact loca-tion of the enemy line. To this extent, Atlanta historian Wilbur Kurtz is right in observing that Hardee's assault "might have yielded the same results [as Jackson's] if Hardee had known precisely where the Federal lines were placed and how to get in rear of them."[16]

A sixth difference between Hardee's and Jackson's flanking attacks lies in the time taken for deployment. Although Jackson had a larger column (30,000 men, including 27 batteries, ordnance, and ambulance wagons), he spent some two and a half hours massing and arranging his troops before giving the attack order at 5:15 or 5:30 P.M. In contrast, although General Hardee at daybreak sent word back to Hood from the Cobb house that his attack, admittedly delayed, would be launched soon, it would be another seven hours before the Confederate formations were even remotely in place. The men needed rest and took up to two hours at Cobb's Mill, where they slept briefly, got water at Intrenchment Creek, and maybe ate some breakfast. While Bate, at the head of the column, may have resumed march soon after the officers' conference, it would have taken sev-eral more hours for the rest of the column to come up. Then, as the Confederates began to deploy north of the Fayetteville Road, they had to proceed cautiously, almost probing for the enemy as they went. The terrain complicated and hindered every movement. "The ground for the last two miles of the advance," wrote one of Cle-burne's officers, "was covered with such a dense thicket of trees and undergrowth that it was difficult to see 50 yards in any direction, to the front or flanks"; thus, it was "utterly impossible to keep distance or connections, necessitating frequent halts to adjust the alignment." As a result, Bate had to wait an hour or more for units on his left to align. Further complications and delays stemmed from the fact that Hardee's infantry, without cavalry, were walking into the woods vir-tually blind. Walker's division, to Bate's left, became separated when, around eleven o'clock, General Walker encountered a huge mill pond in his front. Already mired in the swampy muck of a creek bed, and finding that a westward jut of the pond would cause even

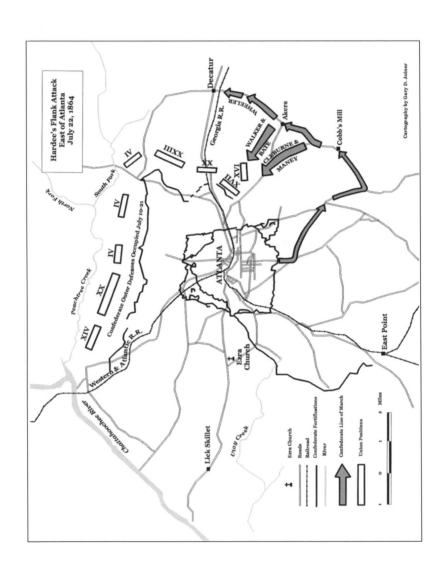

Hardee's Flank Attack
East of Atlanta
July 22, 1864

Cartography by Gary D. Joiner

Decatur

Georgia R.R.

WHEELER

WALKER &
BATE

CLEBURNE &
MANEY

Akers

Cobb's Mill

IV

IIIXX

XX

XVI

XVII
XV

IV

North Fork

South Fork

IV

Confederate Outer Defenses Occupied July 10-21

XX

ATLANTA

Peachtree Creek

XIV

Western & Atlantic R.R.

Ezra
Church

East Point

Chattahoochee River

Lick Skillet

Utoy Creek

Ezra Church
Roads
Railroad
Confederate Fortifications
River

Confederate Line of March

Union Positions

0   1   2   Miles

more delay, Walker got so angry that he threatened to shoot his guide. Pressing on, and riding at the head of his division, General Walker abruptly encountered the Yankee picket line and was shot off his horse, mortally wounded.[17]

By now it was after noon, perhaps 12:30, the approximate time that Hardee's attack finally began. Clearly, a dawn attack had become an afternoon one. Hot weather, dusty roads, nighttime darkness, exhausted men, delayed start, distractions along the way, and inattentive cavalry service, compounded by an overly ambitious, unrealistic timetable set by the commanding general—all combined to vex Hardee's march. The broken-down schedule led to another critical set of differences between Jackson's and Hardee's flank attacks. At Chancellorsville the Yankees were right where Stonewall had planned; better yet, they were not expecting to be attacked. (Early Union picket sightings of Rebels in the Wilderness were discredited by Federal commanders all the way up to Eleventh Corps commander Major General O. O. Howard.) Hardee's troops, however, faced an enemy who was not only alert to attack but at some points even defensively faced against them. Union Major General Blair, holding the extreme left of Sherman's line, was well aware that his flank was in the air. So in the afternoon and evening of the 21st he had extended his lines, ordered his men to entrench, and threw out pickets to watch for an enemy approach. General McPherson, too, was on the alert, warning Blair to expect an attack, perhaps at daybreak. Hardee's delay in attacking that morning allowed McPherson the extra hours he needed to shift elements of Grenville Dodge's Sixteenth Corps to his exposed left. General Dodge then arranged Tom Sweeny's division in a refused line at Blair's flank, just the sort of protection McPherson would have called for against a surprise enemy attack. And the Federals were ready. When General Sweeny received a cavalry vedette's warning of an enemy approach, he sent out more skirmishers, who confirmed the information. Thus, whereas Jackson's carefully arranged formation advanced perpendicular to the Union Eleventh Corps' flank for maximum tactical effect, and thoroughly surprised the unsuspecting Yankees, Bate's and Walker's divisions encountered three enemy brigades, bolstered by artillery, prepared in line of battle facing them.

Finally, there was another factor, too, contributing to the difference between Jackson's and Hardee's attacks: the mettle of the enemy facing the Southerners. Whereas the Eleventh Corps soldiers Jackson faced in the Wilderness were at best mediocre (a third of them had never been in battle; two-thirds of them, Carl Schurz's and Adolph von Steinwehr's hapless German Americans, had never won a victory), the enemy soldiers Hardee faced were tough Union veterans who quickly reacted to the Rebel onslaught.

The initial results on May 2 and July 22 were consequently very different. Howard's Eleventh Corps fled before Jackson's attack; Sweeny's men held their ground and repelled Bate's and Walker's assault in less than an hour. To a certain extent sheer luck played a role in the two different outcomes. "It was surely good fortune for the Confederacy," a recent student of Chancellorsville has written, "that when Stonewall Jackson finally signaled the charge, he was aiming squarely at the ineptly led Eleventh Corps.... Beyond a doubt Dame Fortune was smiling on the South that day." Conversely, Dame Fortune—or the God of Battles, as General Hood might have said—smiled on the North on July 22. Had Dodge's men not been where they were, wrote a Union officer afterward, "there would have been absolutely nothing but the hospital tents and the wagon trains to stop Hardee's command from falling unheralded upon the rear of the Fifteenth and Seventeenth corps in line. Upon what a slight chance, then, hung the fate of Sherman's army that day."[18]

Even though Hood's plan had fallen apart, the battle was far from over. To Walker's left, Cleburne's division advanced into action. Some of Cleburne's men spotted a Union officer and staff riding mistakenly toward them: it was General McPherson, who had mounted up at the first sound of firing and was riding toward the action. The Southerners stood and fired; the volley downed McPherson, killed or mortally wounded (the Federals were later able to recover his body). Cleburne's attack went on to drive the Yankees from part of their trenches, capturing eight field pieces, but it eventually spluttered out against the strong Union position at Leggett's Hill.

At about two o'clock in the afternoon General Hood left his headquarters in town and rode out toward the fighting. At a house near the city cemetery he established an observation post, viewing fighting a mile away to the east. As at Peachtree Creek, his role in the Battle of Bald Hill was minimal. Virtually his only involvement in it the entire afternoon was to order a supporting artillery barrage, at 3:15, and to decide when to send Cheatham's corps into action, around 4:00. Of Cheatham's three attacking divisions, those on the right and left met with repulse. But in the center, John C. Brown's division scored a breakthrough in part of the Fifteenth Corps' line, driving the Federals from their entrenchments. "I never enjoyed a thing better in my life," R. M. Gill of the Forty-first Mississippi wrote. "We had the pleasure of shooting at Yankees as they ran without being shot at much."[19] But even this lodgment was temporary, because Northern counterattacks forced Cheatham's soldiers back to their lines, albeit with a captured four-gun Union battery as their prize. The battle was over.

More than that, it was a failure for the Confederates. To be sure, the engagement of July 22 gave Hood's army claim to at least a partial victory, one that the general himself was quick to claim and that the Confederate press embellished still further. "General Hardee, with his corps, made a night march and attacked the enemy's extreme left at 1 o'clock to-day," Hood wired Richmond that evening; he "drove him from his works, capturing 16 pieces of artillery and 5 stand of colors. Major-General Cheatham attacked . . . at 4 P.M. . . . drove the enemy, capturing 6 pieces of artillery. During the engagements we captured about 2,000 prisoners." Hood later had to adjust these figures (especially the number of guns taken), but this report, telegraphed by the Confederate States Press Association to papers throughout the South, became the basis for such headlines as, "FIGHTING IN ATLANTA. YANKEES DRIVEN FROM THEIR ENTRENCHMENTS. CAPTURE OF PRISONERS AND GUNS. GEN. MCPHERSON KILLED. GEN. HARDEE IN SHERMAN'S REAR," and "GLORIOUS SUCCESS OF OUR ARMS. CAPTURE OF ARTILLERY, PRISONERS, &C." This sort of message, when received in Richmond, "diffused general joy through the community," according to one report. "Everybody is applauding Gen. Hood and his noble army." Hood, however, had reason not to join in the round of celebrating: he had not succeeded in striking McPherson's line in flank and rolling it up, as Jackson had at Chancellorsville. The main reasons for this failure, one is tempted to conclude, lay in luck and in war friction and war fog. But they also involve General Hood. While Hood's daring attacks on July 22 certainly yielded the Confederates their greatest success so far in the Atlanta Campaign, in his timetable, his march orders, and his expectations of success Hood failed to demonstrate one of Clausewitz's indispensable qualities of a good general, "an appreciation of friction's inevitability and everpresence."[20]

Although General Sherman's soldiers won the battle, he, ironically, should receive even lower marks than Hood for his role on July 22. Early that morning, upon reports of the Rebels' evacuation of their outer line of works, he jumped to the conclusion that Hood had evacuated Atlanta and so ordered his army commanders to press forward, seize the city, and pursue the retreating enemy. Later that morning, of course, he had to rescind these directives when it became evident the Rebels very much still held the town. Even then, however, despite McPherson's worries about a flank attack, Sherman dismissed the idea that Hood would launch a battle that day and told McPherson to use Dodge's Sixteenth Corps not in bolstering his left but in destroying the Georgia Railroad more thoroughly. When the battle did start, Sherman kept at his headquarters and did nothing more than direct the firing of artillery. Thus, in the battle east of Atlanta, the credit for victory was certainly not Sherman's. Nor was it McPherson's, killed early on. Major General Logan, named by Sherman as interim commander of the Army of the Tennessee, was therefore left to claim it, but it was rightly due (as in most warfare) to the soldiers themselves. They knew well, as a telegraph operator that night wired Washington, that "Hood fights his graybacks desperately."[21]

CHAPTER FIFTEEN

HOOD'S THIRD SORTIE AGAIN ATTEMPTS A FLANK ATTACK: EZRA CHURCH, JULY 28

HOOD AT LEAST was sticking to his plan, of attacking the enemy in a way Joe Johnston was perfectly incapable of doing. And General Sherman was sticking to his plan, as well, of forcing Rebel evacuation of Atlanta by cutting the railroads feeding into the city. He had known, or had reason to suspect if only from spy reports throughout the spring, that the Rebel fortifications around the city would be strong. On the morning of the 22d he was confirmed, after the withdrawal of the Southerners from their outer line allowed an advance of Thomas's army and a closer look at what lay before him. Both Sherman and his chief engineer, Captain O. M. Poe, agreed: too strong to storm and too extensive to encircle. Hence the need to stick to plan.

On July 24 General Garrard reported on his Covington raid: adding to the damage done by McPherson's infantry, he had wrecked six miles of track on the Georgia Railroad and burned two bridges. Thus, the railway east to Augusta was destroyed. The third line running into Atlanta had also been cut, albeit from afar, by a Union cavalry expedition out of north Alabama that pounced on the road connecting Atlanta with Montgomery. Major General Lovell Rousseau's horsemen destroyed twenty-six miles of track west of Opelika, Alabama, before they made their way toward Sherman's army group. Sherman was delighted, saying on the 23d that the Alabama line looked to be knocked out for a month. These successes fed the nearly always ebullient Federal leader even more. On the 24th Sherman wired General Halleck: "As soon as my cavalry rests, I propose to swing the Army of the Tennessee round by the right rapidly and interpose between Atlanta and Macon, the only line open to the enemy." "I think I will have that soon," he confidently predicted to Grant.[22]

To that end, Sherman sent out orders for the big, coordinated movement aimed at the Macon & Western that would begin early on July 27. He planned to swing the Army of the Tennessee (with Major General Howard acceded to permanent command on the 26th) around behind Thomas's front and extend the Union right toward East Point, a little town four miles southwest of Atlanta where the railways to Macon and Montgomery united to share a line into the city. Complementing this army movement, and doubtless reflecting Sherman's impression from Rousseau's raid that cavalry could severely damage a rail line, would be a two-pronged equestrian strike well south of Atlanta. General Edward McCook would lead 3,000 horsemen southwest, cut the Atlanta & West Point railway, and ride on to Lovejoy's Station, breaking up the Macon & Western as well. As the other point of the pincer, General George Stoneman was to take his 2,150 sabers around the other way: from Decatur south to a presumed junction with McCook. After wrecking track and telegraph, both columns were to ride back to the army group around Atlanta. Before setting out, however, Stoneman asked permission to continue south from Lovejoy's to Macon, free the more than a thousand Union officers held prisoner there, and then ride even farther southwest all the way to Andersonville, where he hoped heroically to free the tens of thousands of Union prisoners languishing and dying at the Rebel prison, Camp Sumter. Sherman consented but stressed that cutting the rails at Lovejoy's remained Stoneman's prime objective. Stoneman's and McCook's cavalrymen rode off at dawn of the 27th. Sherman was hopeful, even confident. But he would experience, compliments of McCook and Stoneman, his worst setback of the entire campaign.

Sherman wanted the swing to the right to catch Hood by surprise. So when the Army of the Tennessee began its march in the early hours of July 27—the Sixteenth Corps first, followed by the Seventeenth and the Fifteenth—the men, wagons, and animals moved as quietly as possible. Even the artillery wheels were sack-wrapped to mute their noise. It really did not matter, for Hood was already alert to the enemy's maneuver. From his cavalry on the left, Hood noticed the day before the Yankees started marching that they "seem desirous of extending their line down the river." At 4:15 A.M. on the 27th, with Howard's movement just a few hours in progress, Hood's headquarters spread the word: "Indications are that the enemy will attack our left." Arriving in Atlanta that day from his inspection tours, General Bragg wired Richmond that the enemy "now seems to be working as if to turn our left. Hood is preparing a move for him which I hope will soon relieve the danger."[23]

General Hood was indeed preparing to counter the enemy's maneuver. On the evening of the 27th he called to headquarters his two junior corps commanders, Peter Stewart and Lieutenant General Stephen D. Lee, who had just arrived from Mississippi to take command of Hood's old corps (Frank Cheatham reverted to division leader). In the meeting Hood laid out his plans. While Hardee's corps and the militia held the defenses, Stewart's and Lee's were to march out and meet the enemy west of the city—Hood had already ordered that sixty rounds of ammunition be issued to each man in both corps. Yet the commanding general did not intend a head-on attack. Although the plan was not written out, and our understanding of it derives from the key officers' reports several months later, historians have assembled its outlines. With the Federals known to be extending their right flank, on the next day, July 28, Lee would march out on the road to Lick Skillet (a crossroads village west of Atlanta) and take up a defensive position to block any further enemy advance. Stewart's corps would follow, passing behind and beyond Lee's position. Then, as General Stewart recalled, "at an early hour next morning [July 29] we were to move out on that road, turn to the right, pass in rear of the enemy, and attack."[24] In short, Hood planned another flanking assault, this time striking the Army of the Tennessee's right as it faced Lee's force on the Lick Skillet road. If flank assaults offered the best chances of success in a Civil War attacking battle—and the Lee and Jackson school in Virginia had demonstrated that they did—once more Hood's battle plan for July 28–29 gave good prospects for the defeat of the second-largest of Sherman's armies, the same one that had been mauled just the week before.

Of note is that General Hood, apparently learning from Hardee's difficulties on the 22d, allowed a very generous timetable for his two corps to get into position—a whole day for Stewart's corps. As it turned out, however, on the 28th, Hood's plan broke down almost from the start. First, the enemy was not where he was expected to be (the same war-fog-induced problem Hood encountered on the 22d). Though General Howard's columns moved slower on the 27th than Sherman wanted (Howard prudently guarded against an attack; Sherman dismissed the possibility), by nightfall his men had extended the Union line southward almost to the Lick Skillet road. On the move at dawn of the 28th, by 11:00 A.M. Howard's army not only had reached the road at Ezra (Methodist) Church but had extended parallel to it in a refused line. The Federals had thus taken the very same position at the important church crossroads that Lee had hoped to assume by Hood's plan. Second, to increase their advantage, the Yankees dug in. In their march that morning the Federals faced sustained opposition from Rebel cavalry, who contested the Union advance with carbine and artillery fire with such vehemence that Howard by 11:30 became convinced he was about to be attacked. He so notified Sherman and halted his troops, who began to intrench. Hood's hoped-for element of surprise, so essential for a flanking maneuver, was thus gone even before Lee brought his troops up.

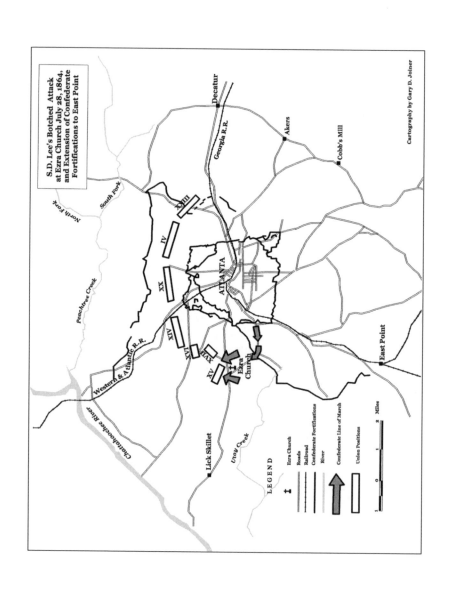

S.D. Lee's Botched Attack
at Ezra Church July 28, 1864,
and Extension of Confederate
Fortifications to East Point

Cartography by Gary D. Joiner

Decatur

Georgia R.R.

Akers

Cobb's Mill

North Fork

South Fork

Peachtree Creek

XXIII

IV

XX

ATLANTA

XIV

Western & Atlantic R.R.

XVI

XV

Ezra
Church

East Point

Chattahoochee River

Lick Skillet

Utoy Creek

LEGEND

Ezra Church
Roads
Railroad
Confederate Fortifications
River
Confederate Line of March
Union Positions

Miles

1   0   1   2

When he did, around noon, he made the worst decision he could have: to begin attacking the enemy position piecemeal, as his divisions arrived. To be sure, the Confederate cavalry officer on hand, Brigadier General William H. ("Red") Jackson, assured Lee that the enemy force in front of him was small. Lee must have judged, too, that the Yankees had barely beaten him to the crossroads and were not yet fortified. Only in this context could his decision to change the commanding general's plan and attack be justified. The battle of Ezra Church thus ensued. Uncoordinated and without reconnaissance, Lee's assault, which Stewart's men joined as they arrived, broke predictably against Howard's fortified defensive line. After a few hours of repeated repulses, the Southerners withdrew from the field, having lost 3,000 men to Howard's just over 600.

Hood clearly had lost control of the situation for several reasons—a speedy enemy march, an opponent alert to the threat of attack, and his own cavalry's peculiarly counterproductive work. Furthermore, General Lee, young (30 years old) and inexperienced (never having before led an infantry corps), acted rashly and without authorization in bringing on the battle. And, finally, Hood was not on the scene and clearly too far away to exercise any authority. He thus lost control of his battle plan and suffered the sharp, costly repulse at Ezra Church.

At their headquarters in town, Hood and his staff, believing that no battle would take place that day, were preoccupied with the Yankee cavalry raids that General Wheeler was already beginning to contest. More than half of the journal entry for July 28 by Hood's new chief of staff, Brigadier General Francis A. Shoup (Mackall, a devotee of Johnston, had left on the 24th), concerns General Wheeler's response to those threats. Through midday and into early afternoon, in fact, Hood and Shoup were unaware of Lee's break with their plan. They nonetheless sent repeated reminders of it, under the assumption that Howard's column was still advancing: "If the enemy should make an assault upon our left the general directs you to strike him in flank" (12:00 noon); "not to attack unless the enemy exposes himself in attacking us" (12:30 P.M.); "hold the enemy in check. The object is to prevent him from gaining the Lick Skillet road" (2:20); "hold the enemy, but not to do more fighting than necessary, unless you should get a decided advantage" (3:25); "not to allow the enemy to gain upon you any more than possible" (4:00).[25]

Only late in the afternoon did the commanding general realize what had happened, when he sent General Hardee to the battlefield to manage the situation. Lee and Stewart had called a halt to the battle by then, anyway.

Hood, surprisingly, seemed to show no anger either at the fickle "God of Battles" or at S. D. Lee for having wrecked his plan for a flanking assault. "Lieutenant-Generals Stewart and Lee were directed to hold the Lick Skillet road for the day with a portion of their commands. About 1:30 a sharp engagement ensued with no decided advantage to either side. We still occupy the Lick Skillet road," Hood told the secretary of war in a telegram that night, with a rather shameful insensitivity to the truth (Confederates did not hold the Lick Skillet road) and to his troops' manful assaults, their sad repulse, and their lopsided casualties. That night Sherman wired Washington that, again, Hood had attacked and, again, had been repulsed: "Our loss is comparatively small, while that of the enemy is represented as heavy." Just as important, Howard's army had worked its way to within two miles of the railroad to East Point. And the cavalry, on which the commanding general pinned such high hopes, had yet to be heard from. "I feel confident they will reach the Macon road," he concluded.[26]

To be sure, the Federal cavalry reached the Macon road but did little beyond that. After crossing the Chattahoochee, McCook's column tore up some track of the Atlanta & West Point Railroad at Palmetto, captured and destroyed a Confederate wagon train, and made its way to Lovejoy's, where they damaged the Macon & Western track in keeping with Sherman's plan. Straying wildly from Sherman's plan, however, was Stoneman's column, which did not aim for a rendezvous with McCook at Lovejoy's at all but instead headed well south toward Macon—General Stoneman had his eyes, apparently, on the glory to be gained from liberating the prisoners at Andersonville. After waiting a while, McCook ordered his troopers back on a return route to the main army. On the way, near Newnan on July 30, McCook was assailed by Wheeler's cavalry and so soundly thrashed that his command was scattered and had to limp piecemeal back to base.

Stoneman fared even worse. After passing over and wrecking a stretch of the Georgia Railroad east of Decatur, he led his horsemen on to Macon, eighty-five miles south of Atlanta. Repulsed there on the 30th by a virtual mob of militia and local citizens, Stoneman gave up his liberating mission and headed back north. On July 31 at a place called Sunshine Church, Confederate cavalry descended upon Stoneman's tired men, fought hard, and hornswoggled them into thinking they were surrounded by superior numbers. Two Federal brigades broke out, but Major General Stoneman surrendered a third. The Yankees soon found themselves ignominiously escorted into Macon as prisoners. The Union cavalrymen who escaped from Sunshine Church were not safe for long, though; Confederate cavalry struck them near Athens and scattered them as effectively as Wheeler had done to McCook.

A disgusted General Sherman, watching his troopers lamely return, singly or in small groups, between July 31 and August 12, concluded that his great attempt at strategic end (cutting Atlanta's last railroad) by cavalry had failed dismally. The two miles or so of the Macon road cut by McCook was repaired in two days, even before the latter's arrival back in Sherman's camps. Supplies continued to flow unabated to Hood's army and the civilian populace of Atlanta (now much reduced to a few thousand, thanks in good measure to the relentless Yankee bombardment). For the moment, at this mid-summer point in 1864, it appeared that Hood had Sherman stymied outside of Atlanta.

Chapter Sixteen

Hood Keeps His Army Together While Enduring Sherman's Semi-Siege

WHEN SHERMAN'S CAVALRY PLAN failed, he returned to his original idea, announced on July 25, of inching his army's right flank south toward the Macon & Western, to strike it somewhere between Atlanta and East Point, perhaps at East Point itself. With the Rebel army safely fortified and apparently impervious to the Federals' artillery shelling, Sherman hoped "to draw the enemy out of Atlanta by threatening the railroad below." "It is our true move," he wrote

General Thomas, one that would force some form of strategic reso-
lution. Who knows, he pondered to Howard, maybe such pressure
on Hood's supply line would "force him to the attack, which is to
be desired."[27]

General Hood was fully aware of the railroad's importance.
Now that Wheeler had defeated McCook's and Stoneman's raiders
and the slight damage to the Macon line had been repaired, Hood
took steps against the gradual extension of Sherman's infantry lines.
Building on positions taken by S. D. Lee's corps the night of July 28,
Hood ordered a line of works (dubbed by Atlantan Wilbur Kurtz the
"railway defense line")[28] constructed southwest of the city's fortified
perimeter across Utoy Creek and on toward East Point. Lee's corps
manned these positions, which Hood reinforced further by posting
Bate's division of Hardee's corps on Lee's left flank.

The Confederates did not have long to wait before their lines
were tested. On August 4 Sherman decided it was time to move forward and seize the railroad to East Point. He ordered Schofield to
advance with his Twenty-third Corps, as well as John Palmer's Fourteenth Corps of Thomas's army, and not stop until he had "absolute
control of that railroad." Sherman emphasized speed: "Every hour's
delay enables the enemy to strengthen." Not much happened that
afternoon, however, in large part because General Palmer balked at
having to take orders from Schofield, his junior in rank. The next day,
August 5, Schofield issued orders directly to Palmer's division commanders but managed to get only one of them, Absalom Baird, to
advance. The Federals succeeded in taking an entrenched skirmish
line and 140 Rebel prisoners, at the cost of 83 killed and wounded.
But that was their only achievement the whole day. An embarrassed
Schofield felt the need to apologize to Sherman that evening for
having "totally failed to make any aggressive movement with the
Fourteenth Corps."[29]

On the 6th, Schofield ordered an assault by his own troops, General Jacob D. Cox's division. By this time, as Sherman had feared,
the Confederates had strengthened their trench line with abatis (the
Federals during the night had heard the felling of trees), and so the
Union attack had little chance of success and was of course repulsed.
The main assaulting force, Colonel James W. Reilly's brigade, lost 76
killed, 199 wounded, and 31 captured, against a mere 15 to 20 casualties in Bate's command. Schofield's other division, Hascall's, had

only slightly better luck as it marched farther west in an attempt to flank Bate's line. Late in the afternoon two Union brigades charged a battery guarding the Rebels' extreme left and suffered several hundred casualties. Mindful of General Sherman's insistence on finding a way to the railroad, Schofield on the next day, August 7, again sent his infantry forward to probe the enemy position. When they found the Rebels strongly fortified and protected by abatis, they dug in themselves. On the 7th the Fourteenth Corps finally went into action as well (General Palmer, relieved at his own request, had turned command over to Brigadier General Richard Johnson). But Johnson's men found the enemy position too strong. The Federals incurred nearly 200 casualties in sallies against the Rebel works.

In the fighting along Utoy Creek, August 5–7, Sherman lost close to a thousand men, whereas Hood's losses were in the hundreds, mainly from skirmishers captured in their rifle pits. These losses made clear to General Sherman that Hood had constructed obstacles and trenches far enough to guard the railroad from Atlanta to East Point. The Federals' grand wheel to the right, begun July 27 with Howard's Army of the Tennessee and followed by Schofield's Army of the Ohio, had been blunted. One Federal officer wrote admiringly albeit with some exaggeration, of the Confederate leader's tenacity and perspicacity: "Hood . . . was watchful to counteract any movement. . . . They . . . continued . . . to confront us at every advance we made on their flank. Hood also seemed perfectly conscious of all our movements, for when we threw a corps with the greatest celerity on their flank, he hurried heavy masses of troops to confront them. Their scouts must have been cleverer than ours, or they were able to fathom our movements through the tangled woods and ravines of the country."[30]

Both Federals and Confederates understood that in keeping open Atlanta's rail line heading south out of the city, Hood was able to keep his army provisioned. Though Sherman personally directed cannon fire against wagon routes and railway facilities in town, the shelling did little to obstruct the Rebels' flow of supplies. One of Hardee's staff officers recorded on July 28 that supplies of bacon and corn meal continued to arrive, although "as low in quantity as they can well get to keep us from downright starvation." Another Confederate officer expressed a cheerier outlook, writing his wife on August 15: "For the last twenty days we have enjoyed . . . tolerable fare . . . and are growing fat." To be sure, scarcity of fresh vegetables was a chronic problem, but it was clear that the Yankees were not going to starve the city into submission. A news correspondent, writing from Atlanta on August 8, recorded: "So far as meal and meat are concerned the fighting men of the army are well fed. Rations of beef and bacon are alternated. . . . It is to be regretted more vegetables have not been forwarded, as they might be. There is plenty in the country, but little reaches here—barely sufficient to supply the hospitals." Sherman was aware of the adequacy of Hood's supplies. He learned, for instance, from a spy, who brought in a report August 18, that the Rebel troops had "plenty of rations and forage from day to day." As late as September 1, the *Augusta Chronicle & Sentinel* published reports out of Atlanta, that Hood's army was "abundantly supplied with provisions of all kinds."[31] Indeed, General Hood and his staff deserve some credit not only for keeping the army fed and armed during the Yankees' semi-siege and shelling in mid-August but also for bringing in enough rations to distribute to the city's neediest civilians. The *Atlanta Intelligencer,* now published in Macon, of August 23 reported that Confederate authorities were distributing 1,500 rations a day to the poor in the city.

Hood and his staff withstood the same hardships of the Yankees' artillery bombardment and quasi-investment of the city as his troops and the civilian populace. General Sherman evidently thought such a shelling, begun on July 20, combined with his armies' front-line pressure, would unnerve Hood and compel him to give up the city. "I doubt if General Hood will stand a bombardment," Sherman wired Halleck on July 21, but he was wrong. The cannonading, which damaged or destroyed numerous buildings and killed or wounded scores of civilians and soldiers, failed to shake Hood's resolve or hasten a Confederate evacuation. Hood actually expressed little concern over the bombardment. After the Federal batteries opened fire, Hood telegraphed Richmond that the enemy were "occasionally throwing shell into the city," but he took no further official notice. It is worth noting that Hood never petitioned Sherman to stop the cannonading. During the bombardment a civilian who fled into Union lines told a correspondent of the *New York Times* that Mayor James Calhoun had beseeched Hood to take action to spare the city but that the general had refused. This refusal became something of a point of pride with Hood, and, after Atlanta fell, in a bitter exchange of letters with Sherman, Hood reminded the Federal commander, "I made no complaint of your firing into Atlanta."[32]

Hood did not buckle under the pressure of the Union bombardment even when his personal headquarters came under shellfire. After the Confederates withdrew from their outer line into the city's main defensive works on the night of July 21–22, Hood moved his headquarters to a new site, the downtown home on Whitehall Street of John S. Thrasher. Here he came under the fire of Sherman's batteries. "While I was at General Hood's," wrote a Confederate officer, Thomas J. Key, in his diary on the 29th, "shells were exploding near his headquarters."[33] Sherman soon learned where Hood was staying; the "scout" Milton Glass reported August 3 that the Rebel headquarters were on Whitehall Street near a tannery five blocks southwest of the downtown train depot.

On August 7, aware that the Rebel army and its fortifications blocked extension of his lines to the right, Sherman decided against any further movement, at least for a while. He remained confident of his ability eventually to drive the Rebels from Atlanta, if only because of his continued numerical advantage. Though he had lost about 9,000 men in the hard July fighting, after additional subtractions because of disease and discharges, Sherman's army group on August 1 still mustered 85,000 effectives. (Through reinforcements, the Army of the Ohio was actually stronger than at the start of the campaign.) Satisfied that he could wait out the game, if that was what it took, General Sherman determined to intensify the bombardment of the Rebel city. He wanted his artillery to "reach the heart of Atlanta and reduce it to ruins"; part of his purpose was to disrupt the flow of wagon supply trains into town. More generally, he felt that continuous, severe shelling could weaken the enemy's resolve. He thus announced his intent, in a telegram of August 7 to Washington, to "make the inside of Atlanta too hot to be endured." To that end he had brought down from Chattanooga eight huge 4.5-inch rifled siege guns, which began to be positioned on the 8th and 9th. On the 9th he ordered all his batteries within reach of the city to fire fifty rounds per gun. His newly arrived siege cannon were to fire "with great precision, making all parts of the town unsafe." "One thing is certain," he wrote General Halleck, "whether we get inside of Atlanta or not, it will be a used-up community by the time we are done with it."[34]

On August 9, Union batteries threw some three thousand shells into the city. General Thomas, aware of Hood's whereabouts on Whitehall, may have directed his artillery to enfilade the Rebels' headquarters. On the 9th Hood's chief of staff, Brigadier General Shoup, noted in his journal that a "great many" enemy shells fell "immediately around General Hood's headquarters." That same day Episcopal bishop Henry C. Lay visited Hood and recorded in his diary, "Shells are exploding all around Head Qrs (at Thrasher's House) and it is proposed to remove them." A chaplain accompanying the bishop later wrote, "I thought the locality seemed very unhealthy, but . . . the General and his staff did not seem in the least disturbed." Though no official memorandum exists to suggest it, Hood seems to have moved his headquarters, possibly that evening, a half-mile farther out from downtown, to a Whitehall Street residence owned by the attorney Windsor Smith. The informer Glass reported to Federal officers on August 12 that Hood's headquarters were "near where White Hall street intersects Faith's alley" and that on the 10th "shells passed over General Hood's headquarters and struck 300 or 400 yards beyond." Hood seems to have occupied the Smith house for the rest of the semi-siege, relatively safe from enemy gunfire. Indeed, a Confederate telegraph officer felt relief when his post was transferred from a downtown hotel to "out on Whitehall Street, opposite General Hood's headquarters," so as to evade the heaviest Yankee shelling.[35]

Even under the duress of Sherman's bombardment of the city, Hood managed his army capably in the first three weeks of August. A particular achievement, not generally recognized, was the commander's stringent effort to strengthen his ranks. The chief task was to make good his battle losses from the three engagements of July 20–28. Army medical officers tallied the killed and wounded alone during July 18–31 as 8,319. This number did not include deserters and the captured and missing, whose number on the army rolls rose almost 4,000 from July 10 to August 20. Instead of asking Richmond for reinforcements from other departments, Hood and his staff strained to bring every available man present in the army to the front ranks as an effective on the firing lines. Special scrutiny was given the thousands of patients languishing in the army hospitals. Hospital surgeons-in-charge were hounded to send forward all convalescents able to resume duty. Because of such efforts, military hospitals serving the Army of Tennessee returned over 9,800 soldiers in July, 43 percent of their total admissions for the month. A Macon newspaper in late August observed with satisfaction "a decline in the number of sick and wounded in the hospitals of this city" that was due at least partly to "the stringent orders of Gen. Hood to forward every man able for duty." Medical officers stood firm against malingerers who hoped by feigning illness to stay out of the trenches. The *Macon Telegraph* ran a story about a Confederate surgeon in the city who went through a line of sick-leave applicants on August 14, dismissing the complaints of most, if not all. To a man with a weak back, for instance, the doctor pointed out that he, too, got a weak back when he stayed at home too long. "Therefore, going to the country a little while, and perchance killing a Yankee will do you more good than anything else. Fall in."[36]

Within the army itself soldiers detailed in noncombat positions were reassigned to the trenches. An order went out reducing the number of clerks for the commissary and other departments to one man for each department. According to Captain Thomas Key, this measure alone "returned many men to the ranks." A correspondent for the *Griffin Rebel,* formerly a Chattanooga newspaper, saw this order as "evidence of Gen. Hood's determination to increase the strength and efficiency of the army." Heads of departments were to do their own clerical work; if they had to have a clerk, he was to be a man unfit for field duty. Because this order was directed "not only to Quartermasters, Commissaries, Commandants of Post, Provost Marshals, and Surgeons, but also to Generals," the reporter speculated that it would free "several thousand" men for active service. Hospital employees, if able to shoulder a musket, were ordered to the front. A Union officer, exchanged and released from confinement in Macon, brought home stories of ward stewards who were pressed into the ranks, their places taken by female volunteers from the town. Hood also strictly limited the number of couriers that corps, division, and brigade headquarters would be allowed. An order dated August 3 directed all men in excess of that number to return to their commands and hand over their horses. Orderlies, cooks, and teamsters were also directed to the front lines, their places to be taken by hired slaves. "In Clayton's division alone," wrote a correspondent for the *Columbus (Georgia) Enquirer,* "the number of new men returned from the cooking detachments reached 300, which at this time is considered a good regiment." A correspondent for the *Augusta Chronicle & Sentinel,* writing from Atlanta on August 5, observed: "Our army has been strengthened to a considerable extent of late. . . . The old fighting material has been increased by putting guns into the hands of the working details," for which slaves were being substituted.[37]

The same correspondent, "Rover," wrote that Hood had also launched an effort to secure blacks as wagon drivers, "which, if it succeeds, will add three thousand more to the ranks." Soldiers in the ranks were particularly impressed by the commanding general's arming of teamsters. "Among the many steps Gen. Hood has made towards the reformation and the increase of the army," wrote a member of the Twenty-ninth Georgia to the *Savannah Republican* on August 19, "none deserves the commendation of his friends more than his efforts to replace the white teamsters with negroes. The uninitiated can form no idea of the large force it requires to supply an army with drivers." Procuring enough slaves to do this work was in itself a task. Military officials placed advertisements in newspapers across the state, calling for at least 1,500 blacks to work as teamsters. Typical was this announcement, signed by Hood's transportation chief, that appeared prominently on the front page of the *Macon Telegraph* on August 11: "The General Commanding wants in the front *every man* able to handle a musket, and has called upon me to procure two thousand negroes to supply the places of soldiers at present used as teamsters, who can be placed in the trenches by the side of their comrades now struggling on the bloody field." Slaves offered for this service would be fed and clothed; owners would be paid twenty-five dollars a month and compensated "in case of the loss of the slave by the casualties of war." Editors of the *Telegraph* called attention to the advertisement and added their endorsement: "Georgians, take a wise, liberal, and patriotic course in this matter. The time has come when every sinew must be strained to its highest tension to save anything you have left. Let the enemy overrun your State and nothing is left worth saving." The implication was clear: better to give up one's property in the hope of saving the institution than to hold back and lose both one's slaves and slavery itself. Hood also sent out officers across Georgia to hire blacks; slaveholders evidently cooperated. To a Confederate army officer visiting the Milledgeville area in late August, seeking black workers for Hood's army, several planters advised simply asking for volunteers among the slaves. In a few days, some 300 had so offered themselves for work in the army.[38]

General Bragg, traveling between Montgomery and Atlanta in the third week of July, also attempted to help Hood. On July 22 he sent word that he expected soon to send forward 2,000 reinforcements. Many were from among the detailed men whom Hood and his staff had also targeted. The *Atlanta Appeal* lauded Bragg for having "inaugurated the policy of sending to the front the thousands of detailed men, post officials, contractors, purchasing agents, and other parties who have long been filling easy, safe and remunerative positions. The number of these was legion, and thousands of them have been driven from their bomb-proofs and sent to the front." At times, though, Bragg's zeal in finding replacements raised controversy. When he ordered to the front men who were assigned to the Macon arsenal and other munitions facilities, ordnance officers protested. Some of the men nevertheless went forward as front-line infantry. A battalion of government mechanics from the Columbus armory and shoe factory reported in Atlanta and were assigned on the 26th to Edward C. Walthall's division. About 150 strong, though perfectly innocent of combat experience, they were thrown into battle at Ezra Church. Some ran from the field; most, however, acquitted themselves well. Apparently because of their greater usefulness in the factories, however, the workers were soon sent back. During July 29–31 Hood's headquarters staff sent out reassurances as far as Richmond that the armorers and shoemakers would be returned immediately; the *Columbus Times* reported their arrival on August 3 "in rather a dingy condition, but quite buoyant in spirits." In general, despite certain missteps, Bragg received widespread compliments for his zeal in sending detailed men to the front. One soldier in Hood's army wrote in a Columbus paper, "This of itself, if he never does anything more, should endear him to the soldiers of this army." Another of Hood's men wrote his hometown paper, saying that Bragg should go even further and conscript the able-bodied men who worked around the state as government agents, postmasters, and other "petty clerkships." Such individuals, he pointed out, "are looked upon as mere skulkers"; their jobs could be done by wounded or disabled soldiers.[39]

When Hood called for one man from every artillery gun crew to come forth, however, and receive an infantryman's musket, there was "considerable fluttering among the battery boys," according to a newspaper report. The correspondent justified the measure, though, for leaving gunners 1–6, the ones absolutely necessary to serve each field piece, and for yielding up hundreds of soldiers for riflemen's duty in the trenches. Besides, the reporter noted, "many of them take the thing quite easy, perfectly willing to serve the country at this critical juncture in any capacity that will aid in the overthrow of Sherman and his 'Hessians.'"[40]

General Bragg, in Atlanta on July 27, reported to President Davis, albeit in a rather self-congratulatory glow, the new commander's success in strengthening his army. The number of men "on extra duty, all able bodied, . . . will in a few days be reduced at least half." Bragg guessed that the "arrival of extra duty men and convalescents, &c. is about 5,000; more are coming in daily." Moreover, Hood did not confine himself to his own department; he asked Adjutant General Cooper in Richmond August 2 whether all his troops then in the Trans-Mississippi who were absent without leave could be summoned to "rejoin their commands on this side of the river" by a promise of pardon for desertion. "I am informed that many men can thus be had," he added. Later, upon his return to Richmond, General Bragg continued to assist Hood by organizing details to go across the Mississippi in search of absentees. Hood also sought replacements nearer, as when he informed Major General Dabney Maury, commanding at Mobile, that he had heard that soldiers from his army were in Maury's department. "I am in need of every man I can get," Hood wrote.[41]

On August 2 Hood tried another tack when he asked his friend John Thrasher, superintendent of the Confederate States Press Association in Atlanta (which fed daily telegraphic news reports to subscribing newspapers across the South): "Cannot the papers assist us by appealing to absent soldiers to return to their colors? If you think so, please give them the cue." Thrasher apparently did, and newspapers across Georgia, which routinely printed Governor Brown's frequent appeals for manpower, added words of their own. "Every man capable of pulling a trigger should be at the front. No excuse can be deemed valid. The decisive hour is fast approaching," warned the *Atlanta Appeal*. The *Macon Telegraph* on August 4 trumpeted:

"Absentees to the front!" The exhortation of he *Augusta Chronicle & Sentinel* of August 5 was entitled, "Appeal to Soldiers Absent from their Commands." Another such call, by the *Columbus Times* on August 6, was addressed to "all who are absent with or without leave—to every man of whatever position whose name is on the roll of the country's defenders." Columbus's other paper, the *Enquirer*, that same day addressed a column to "The Absentees in Hood's Army." "Loiterer in the rear!" it began, "It is not to your absent comrades alone, but to *you*, that this appeal is made by Gen. Hood, by your immediate superior officers, and by your toiling and weary fellow-soldiers at the front. Neglect it not another day, or you may have to mourn through life a lost opportunity to participate in a conflict forever memorable and honorable as the battle that won victory and nationality for a great people."[42]

These appeals to patriotism carried the backing of conscription officers and military provosts. The *Telegraph* noted on August 5 that "armed men have been patrolling our streets for several days, examining the passes of all parties, whether attired as citizens or soldiers." By such measures, "quite a number of men subject to perform duty have been arrested and sent to camp, where they will be armed and dispatched to Atlanta." "The General commanding at Atlanta wants them, needs them," proclaimed the *Augusta Constitutionalist* about convalescents and soldiers on leave. "To the friends and relatives of soldiers on furlough, we say, it is your duty to urge forward the gallant men now absent from the Atlanta front. The Commanders of Posts, at this juncture of the campaign, should see that every man goes forward who is able for duty, and Surgeons, above all men, should not hesitate to return men at once, and critically examine all convalescents."[43]

All of these efforts took effect. Bragg reported in late July that "stragglers who left despondent are returning with revived confidence," to such a degree that Hood was even having trouble finding arms for the returnees. (Ordnance officers in Richmond sent a rushed shipment.) "The return of the 1st of August will show a gratifying state of affairs," Bragg predicted, and indeed it did. According to staff reports, the army's effective strength, about 51,000 on July 10, stood at a respectable 44,500 on the 31st, even after the three big battles of the month. In the returns of August 10, effective strength even increased slightly. Within the army some units waxed disproportionately. Company G of the 36th Alabama, for instance, which had only 14 effectives at Kennesaw Mountain in late June, numbered 34 muskets as of August 13, according to its captain; 12 men had been received since July 22 alone. Its captain, J. B. Jordan, boldly told Federal interrogators after his capture in mid-August that he guessed Hood's "re-enforcements . . . [from] militia and . . . from convalescent camps and hospitals . . . including cooks, teamsters, and other detailed men, will reach 15,000 men." In a column entitled "Hood Vacates the Bomb-Proofs," the *Augusta Constitutionalist* on August 20 set the additions to the Army of Tennessee as "8,500 men to wit 4000 ex-cooks, 3000 artillerymen, and 1,500 teamsters."[44]

Included in Captain Jordan's estimate were the old men and boys of the Georgia militia. At the time of Hood's assumption of command, militiamen serving at Atlanta numbered some 2,000. To be sure, these extras, largely untrained and comically armed with flintlocks and shotguns, were clearly not effective in open combat. But Hood prudently recognized their worth in manning his defensive lines, which extended for nine miles around the city, exclusive of the "railway defense line" to East Point. Hood accordingly called for more militia. He wrote Governor Brown on July 24: "I need all the aid Georgia can furnish." Brown had already issued calls for troops, designating Macon their rendezvous point. From there they entrained for Atlanta. The *Appeal* of the 20th stated that "a considerable number of the reserve State force arrived in the city yesterday, and will, we presume, continue to arrive from day to day, until the army is very considerably recruited from this source." The *Macon Telegraph* of July 21 noticed that two trainloads of militia left the city on the previous day, "and the movement has only just fairly begun." The *Confederate* of that city reported on July 24 that militiamen were "pouring into Macon on every train." Another Macon paper, the *Telegraph,* noted that 1,600 militia left for Atlanta on the 26th and that more would be leaving in the next few days. A Federal spy in Atlanta reported on August 3 that 3,000 state troops had just arrived; Hood on the 11th announced to Richmond that the Georgia militia "furnish now about 5,000 muskets in the trenches here." The commanding general did not stop there, though, and on August 14 he wired Governor Brown: "Can you send me any more Militia." Hood even sought the 500 state militia serving with other reservists as guards for the Confederate prison camp at Andersonville. By such strenuous efforts, supplies and reinforcements came into Atlanta during late July and early August. Thus, with good reason General Hood reported on August 4 that "at present everything here looks well" and reasserted, "I have no intention of abandoning this place."[45]

CHAPTER SEVENTEEN

HOOD DOES WHAT JOE JOHNSTON ONLY DREAMED ABOUT: HE SENDS HIS CAVALRY OFF TO CUT SHERMAN'S RAIL LINES, AUGUST 10

"THE ENEMY CAN build parapets faster than we can march," Sherman confessed on August 10, "and it would be the same thing by extending the right or left." Thus, as he told General Thomas, he was content to let his big 4.5-inchers and Parrott rifles "hammer away, and I will think of the next move." General Hood had already thought of his next move. With Sherman's advances against his railroad stalled for the moment, but with the enemy too strongly positioned to be attacked, Hood determined to take the initiative in the only other way left to him. On July 30, with the enemy's cavalry raid defeated, or about to be, Hood announced to Richmond his intent "in a few days to send Wheeler, with his cavalry, to break Sherman's communications." If successful, the raid would force the enemy either "to fight me in position or to retreat." President Davis readily approved the plan, based on his hope that Sherman's army "can be forced to retreat for want of supplies."[46]

Indeed, Sherman's railway support system seemed long and vulnerable to attack. The single-track Western & Atlantic stretched for a hundred miles back to Chattanooga. Beyond it were the Nashville & Chattanooga and Nashville & Decatur Railroads. Earlier in the campaign Wheeler's scouts had penetrated enemy lines and brought back information about trestle bridges and other burn-able targets along these railways. There also lay the tempting prospect of tunnel destruction. North of Dalton at Tunnel Hill was a fourteen-hundred-foot rail underpass, perhaps the Western & Atlantic's most vulnerable stretch. To be sure, tunnel destruction required a large quantity of blasting powder, drilling equipment, and even miners' knowledge, none of which Civil War cavalrymen were likely to carry with them. Nevertheless, Confederate raiders had succeeded at least once in destroying a rail tunnel. In August 1862 General John H. Morgan's command wrecked an eight-hundred-foot tunnel on the Louisville & Nashville Railroad north of Gallatin, Tennessee, by building a cross-tie fire inside, then crash-ing a locomotive into the flaming barrier. The boiler explosion ignited the roof supports, and the slate rock overhead crashed down. It took Federal engineers over three months to rebuild the tunnel.

There were several key tunnels in Tennessee, but both sides clearly recognized the importance of Tunnel Hill in north Georgia. Sherman himself included in his memoirs an anecdote about a Rebel soldier who predicted that when "General Wheeler had blown up *the tunnel* near Dalton, . . . the Yanks would have to retreat, because they could get no more rations." With some reasonable expectation of success, therefore, Hood authorized a cavalry raid into the enemy rear. Wheeler's orders, in his own words, were "to move upon the enemy's line of communications, destroy them at various points between Marietta and Chattanooga; then cross the Tennessee River, break the line of communication on the two roads running from Nashville to the army; to then leave 1,200 men to continue these operations on those roads; to then return again striking the railroad south of Chattanooga, and join the main army."[47] On August 3, a week before Wheeler set out, Hood's headquarters wired ordnance officers in Macon to send up three hundred pounds of blasting pow-der. The Augusta Arsenal was also asked for blasting powder and soon sent a thousand pounds to General Wheeler—clear indication of his intent to destroy bridges, culverts, perhaps tunnels along Sherman's supply lines.

Wheeler left Covington, east of Atlanta, on August 10 with some 4,500–5,500 horsemen, half of Hood's horse—certainly a force suffi-cient to inflict considerable damage. Once the raid began, however, the commanding general had very little information about its progress. Wheeler sent back a message on August 16 from near Dalton, reporting on railroad damage done to date, but there is no indication of when the courier brought it to headquarters. (A dispatch sent back on the 19th did not reach Hood in Atlanta till the 28th.) Similarly, after some of his troops captured a herd of cattle near Calhoun on the 13th, Wheeler sent them back to Atlanta, but they did not arrive until the 26th. Hood's first information about whether Wheeler had cut Sherman's supply line therefore came from what Yankee prisoners said or from random scouting reports.

This initial news that reached Hood's headquarters was quite favorable. "Wheeler reported to have torn up ten miles of railroad at Acworth and captured large drove of cattle," General Shoup recorded in his journal on August 16. The next day a civilian who sneaked through the lines reported that the Yankees were beginning to grumble about short rations. "Railroad in enemy's rear reported to be badly torn up," Shoup noted. If enemy troops were going hungry, they could be expected to forage more energetically; Hood therefore on the 17th ordered his cavalry to take special efforts to prevent them from gathering hogs and other food supplies. A Southern spy's report on the 18th related that one of Sherman's officers, General Jacob D. Cox, when asked by a civilian for food, said he had none: "I have been living on short rations for seven days, and now your people have torn up our railroad and stolen our beef-cattle, we must live a damned sight shorter." This report, according to General Hardee, reinforced Hood's impression that the Federals might have to retreat back across the Chattahoochee. At the same time, the enemy seemed to be constructing earthworks on the north bank of the river—another signal of a possible Union withdrawal. Shoup also recorded on the 18th that "prisoners report the tunnel blown up by Wheeler, captured Dalton and Resaca, burned Etowah bridge, and are going up the railroad." "Enemy continue to complain of short rations," Shoup noted on August 20; "they have not had meat for ten days" and were reportedly down to quarter-rations of just hardtack and coffee. The enemy's horses and mules were also suffering, according to prisoners on the 22d. Confederate scouts two days later confirmed that no supply train had come into Sherman's lines in six or seven days. To tighten the pinch Hood again on the 25th ordered his cavalry to prevent the enemy from gathering in

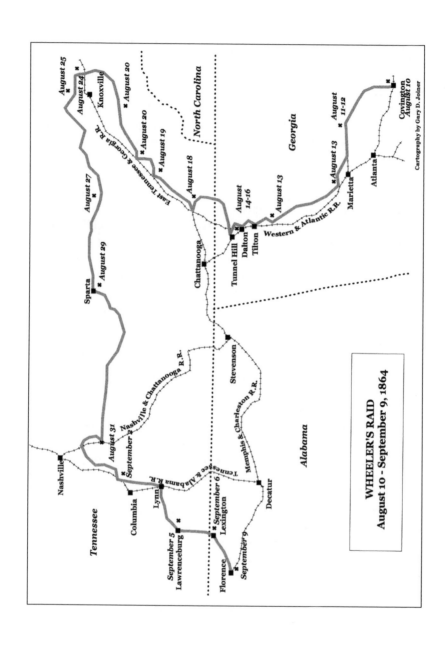

WHEELER'S RAID
August 10 - September 9, 1864

Cartography by Gary D. Joiner

North Carolina

Georgia

Tennessee

Alabama

East Tennessee & Georgia R.R.

Western & Atlantic R.R.

Nashville & Chattanooga R.R.

Memphis & Charleston R.R.

Tennessee & Alabama R.R.

August 25
August 24
Knoxville
August 20
August 20
August 19
August 18
August 27
August 29
Sparta
August 31
Nashville
Columbia
Lynn
September 2
September 5
Lawrenceburg
September 6
Lexington
September 9
Florence
Decatur
Stevenson
Chattanooga
Tunnel Hill
Dalton
August 14-16
Tilton
August 13
August 13
Marietta
August 11-12
August
Atlanta
Covington
August 10

any civilians' hogs or cattle. He was determined to starve Sherman's army, and it looked as if he were succeeding.[48]

Actually, though, no such thing was happening. Wheeler's cavalrymen failed in their mission for several reasons. For one, Sherman knew they were coming; on August 1, he telegraphed his garrison commander at Nashville to begin assembling all the cavalry he could, "as the enemy will surely be on our railroad very soon."[49] All spring Union engineers had busily constructed blockhouses to protect bridges along the rail lines to Nashville; twenty-two of these little forts guarded river crossings between Atlanta and Chattanooga. In addition to this static defense of key points was the initiative of Sherman's rearward garrison commanders who hounded Wheeler's column. Four days into the expedition, the Confederates were sixty miles behind enemy lines, having wrecked track of the Western & Atlantic for several miles at three separate points. They managed to capture a blockhouse below Dalton, August 14, and tear up some track, but the approach of Yankee infantry on trains from Chattanooga drove Wheeler away from Dalton after he captured some stores and 200 prisoners. The same enemy infantry prevented any serious attempt against Tunnel Hill and then forced the Southerners to withdraw after wrecking a mere half-mile of track south of Chattanooga on the 16th, the complete extent of Wheeler's damage to the Western & Atlantic. It was all repaired by the 18th.

Unable to cross the rain-swollen Tennessee above Chattanooga, Wheeler led his troops northeast toward Knoxville. Sherman was delighted at this news. "Wheeler cannot disturb Knoxville or Loudon," he wrote on the 17th; "He may hurt some of the minor points, but, on the whole, East Tennessee is a good place for him to break down his horses, and a poor place to steal new ones."[50] After circumventing Knoxville, the Confederate cavalry headed west, over the Cumberland Mountains and into middle Tennessee. Not until August 30 did Wheeler's men strike the Nashville & Chattanooga Railroad. The next day they burned a bridge north of Murfreesboro and destroyed some thirteen miles of track toward Nashville, but this damage had no real consequence. On August 31 below Atlanta Sherman's armies cut Hood's railroad with much more force and impact; this action proved to be the decisive event of the campaign. Wheeler's railroad raid had no such effect.

Sherman's anticipation of a cavalry strike, Federal fortification of railway bridges, energetic pursuit by ample Union reserves, untoward weather or high rivers, Wheeler's deviation from his planned route, along with the Northerners' very efficient railroad-repair operations—all of these factors contributed to the failure of the raid. General Hood eventually came under criticism for having sent Wheeler off in the first place. Several months later, in his official report, he responded by crediting Wheeler with having "succeeded in partially interrupting the enemy's communications by railroad"—a very generous assessment—and by emphasizing that Wheeler's departure "still left sufficient cavalry to meet the necessities of the army." Years later in his reminiscences he still felt compelled to defend himself against charges of "having committed a serious blunder by sending off the cavalry."[51] In dealing with these contentions, Hood stood unprotected by the mantle of the "Lee and Jackson school," for cavalry raids on enemy communications were a product of the Civil War's western theater. In Virginia, Union supply lines were either too short or too well supported by river traffic to allow General Lee any opportunity of launching the kind of raid that characterized the Confederate cavalry in Tennessee and Kentucky in 1862–63.

At the same time, it is worth noting that in launching Wheeler's raid in mid-August, Hood was not only fulfilling his government's expectations of him as army commander but also complying with the desires and hopes of the Southern people at large. Georgia governor Joseph E. Brown had already warned Davis on July 5 that unless the he ordered a cavalry strike on Sherman's line of communications and thus compelled him to fall back, the mistake could "result in the loss of Atlanta," a "blow . . . fatal to our cause." In much more subtle manner, an Atlanta newspaper in early July spoke of the need for bold action from the cavalry. The paper paid compliment to the Army of Tennessee's "brave, gallant corps of Cavalry" but judged that in view of its want of activity against Sherman's communications, "there seems to be something lacking." Indeed, General Wheeler himself wanted to launch such a raid and had so written Bragg on July 1. Then, at the time of Hood's appointment, both General Bragg and Secretary Seddon had urged the cavalry strike; upon Hood's suggestion of it President Davis had personally given his approval. One may assume also that the soldiers of the Army of Tennessee and citizenry as a whole would have favored the launching of a raid. Writing for the Augusta *Chronicle & Sentinel* on August 10, "Rover" related: "The *on dit* throughout the army and city today is that a body of our cavalry has reached the enemy's rear, and captured and burned the enemy's stores at Marietta. . . . I may not mention army movements explicitly, but this much I can say—something of the kind *should* have taken place ere this."[52] Thus, given these expectations, if Hood had *not* attempted to cut Sherman's rail line, he would have been culpable of imitating General Johnston's practice of objecting to and not complying with the administration's wishes. Like his mentor Lee in Virginia, who took great pains to cooperate with the president in Richmond, Hood was very much a team player, as much as Sherman was with Grant. His decision to dispatch Wheeler showed it.

Chapter Eighteen

Hood Is Unable to Parry Sherman's "Movement Round Atlanta by the South," August 25–September 1

CONCLUDING THAT HIS continuous artillery barrage of the city was apparently not pressuring the Rebels to give it up, General Sherman returned to his notion, held all along, that cutting the last railroad into Atlanta was the only way to take it: "I have broken the West Point road good, and will try the Macon road, without which Hood cannot feed his army." Mere gradual extension of his right, as Schofield had tried to do along Utoy Creek, had failed and would probably fail again. So he determined on a far bolder move, one that "will bring things to a crisis." As he wrote it out to Halleck on August 13, he would leave one of his seven corps near the Chattahoochee, guarding the army's surplus wagon trains, and with the rest of his forces, "60,000 men, reduced to fighting trim," march widely around to the south of Atlanta on a fifteen- or twenty-mile route, heading for the Macon road.[53]

Wheeler's raid off to the rear, however, caused Sherman to put this plan on hold. Having been chastened by the poor, indeed disastrous, results of the McCook-Stoneman raid, Sherman nevertheless decided to make one last effort at a cavalry raid against the Macon & Western. He had several reasons to do so. First, he was emboldened by Hood's dispatch of Wheeler's horsemen on August 10, of which he soon learned. "If we cannot use [our] cavalry now, at this moment, when can we?" he asked Thomas. "Wheeler is out of the way, and when shall we use cavalry, if not now? If we wait till Wheeler returns, of course an opportunity is lost, which never is repeated in war." He also reckoned that Wheeler's departure with a strong force (which Sherman estimated as 3,000–6,000 troops, "the very flower of his cavalry") had left behind a far weaker contingent of Rebel horsemen to contend with a new Federal raid. Finally, the idea of a cavalry raid swap appealed to the gutsy Cump. He did not really think Wheeler could do much damage to his own logistical lines, but, he said, even if Wheeler did, "we can surely cut off those of Hood, and see who can stand it best."[54]

For all these reasons, Sherman dispatched the cavalry leader he had now judged his most audacious: Brigadier General Judson Kilpatrick, the "Kill Cavalry" officer now returned to the service after recovering from a wound at Resaca. Kilpatrick followed his orders, setting out early on the morning of August 18 with 4,000 troopers. Striking the railroad to West Point after midnight on the 19th, they tossed only a half-mile of rails (not their main target), then hit the Macon & Western before noon that day and tore up one and a half miles of track before rain extinguished the tie-setting fires and Confederate cavalry extinguished their ardor and drove them back to camp. Kilpatrick exaggerated this destruction in his report to General Sherman, predicting that the enemy railroad would be disabled for ten days. It was actually out of operation for only two, as Sherman discovered when signal officers spotted a train entering Atlanta from Macon even before Kilpatrick had returned to headquarters on the afternoon of August 22.

Unhappy, then, with the results of Kilpatrick's raid and aware that his shelling of the city would not drive the Rebels out of Atlanta, Sherman returned to his earlier-announced plan to move against the Macon & Western with virtually his entire army and "to swing across to that road in force to make the matter certain." Orders for the grand movement by the right flank went out on the 23d: sick and wounded men and unnecessary wagons went back across the Chattahoochee; nine days' rations were distributed to the troops; and everyone was expected to be ready to march early on the 26th.[55]

At the time, Union lines hugged the Rebel defenses north and west of the city. Thomas's three corps were the first to withdraw on the night of August 25–26. The Fourth Corps, on Thomas's left, northwest of the city, started marching. The Twentieth Corps pulled back to the Chattahoochee, guarding the bridgehead and army trains. The next night, the Fourteenth Corps and Howard's Army of the Tennessee, west of the city, also withdrew and began marching south. Schofield's Twenty-third Corps, positioned along Utoy Creek, would serve as the army group's pivot, the last to pull out of position (at noon on the 28th) and join the other five corps in Sherman's wide swing, what he called his "movement round Atlanta by the south."[56]

Inside the city, General Hood and his staff settled down to the task of interpreting the news on the morning of the 26th that pickets had found the Yankee trenches north of the city empty. (Already, curiosity had been raised when the Federals' bombardment of the city ceased.) For a short while that day the Confederates relished the idea that maybe Wheeler's raiders, now two weeks into the enemy's rear, had pinched their supply lines so hard as to compel them to retreat. Within hours of Thomas's withdrawal, however, W. L. Trask, one of General Hardee's staff officers, recorded in his diary, "We learn that Wheeler has gone into Middle Tennessee without doing Sherman's rear much harm. So his raid, too, has turned out a failure." Perhaps more significant, Hood's soldiers, wandering into the enemy's evacuated trenches, brought back intelligence that the Yanks had certainly not been scrimping for food the past few weeks. "Several Sutler stores were left full of nice things," Captain Trask wrote on the 26th, "and to-day our troops are feasting on sardines and lobsters, canned fruit of every kind, candies, cake and raisins, besides many other good things their stomachs had long been strangers to."[57]

If Sherman was not hungry and retreating, what was he doing? Henry Watterson, writing as "Shadow" for the *Mobile Advertiser and Register*, aptly described the possibilities. The Yankees' sudden disappearance "cannot have been occasioned by the operations of

Wheeler in rear of the Chattahoochee; for he is understood to be at Athens in East Tennessee, having only temporarily injured the State road and burned the supply depot at Cleveland. It cannot be a dearth of food; for quantities of flour, bacon and meal have been found in the abandoned camps. What can be the meaning of it? There are any variety of opinions. It is a plan of assault. It is a preparation for retreat. It is a flank. It is merely a pause. It means everything, it means nothing. In short, you can hear all sorts of expression upon the unexpected event."[58]

It was one thing to take in and assemble the various dispatches and bits of news from the front, and another to deduce from them the enemy's intentions—and still another to move and deploy one's own troops in anticipation of any enemy advance. Generals Hood and Shoup applied themselves to all three tasks, straining for all the information they could get from infantry pickets, cavalry vedettes, and scouting expeditions. By 8:00 A.M. on the 26th Confederate headquarters knew that the enemy had disappeared from Stevenson's and Maney's division fronts, north of the city and east of the Western & Atlantic Railroad. In the next hour Hood ordered his cavalry out on both flanks—down Peachtree Creek on his right, and on his left as well "to ascertain what is going on." To Cleburne, at East Point, went the order at 9:00 A.M. to "push out your scouts and ascertain what the enemy is doing." Northwest of the city, skirmishers from Stewart's corps advanced and located the enemy's infantry lines. Hood soon had a fix on Sherman's new position. "His left now rests on the Dalton railroad. He has not extended his right at all," the general accurately reported to Richmond. Sometime on August 26, probably that night, Hood consequently freed up his two rightmost infantry divisions, Stevenson's and Maney's, for movement farther to the left, as the situation developed; their sector would be occupied by the state militia.[59]

Enemy movements the next day, August 27, complicated the situation. By dawn, pickets along both Stewart's and Lee's corps fronts reported the enemy gone (Howard's army, we know; Hood did not}, but there were still a few brigades of Yankees facing Hardee (Schofield). Thus, although the Federals had abandoned virtually their whole line west of the city, they still held their right-most positions toward East Point. Then a reconnaissance in force by French's division toward the Chattahoochee established that the enemy held bridgeheads at both Turner's Ferry and the Western & Atlantic railroad bridge three miles upriver. From prisoners French learned these troops were the Twentieth Corps; he reported this intelligence to headquarters. Sometime after noon, too, news came in from more than six miles southwest of East Point, north of the Atlanta & West Point Railroad, where cavalry brigadier Sul Ross reported an enemy column of unknown strength marching south on the roads from Sandtown to Fairburn; another was south of Mt. Gilead. By midafternoon the Confederate cavalry reported this infantry fortifying south of Camp Creek.

So far Hood had a reasonably accurate picture of where the Federals were, but he had no reports on their strength. He knew only that one corps was at the Chattahoochee. Most important, he had no way of knowing their intent. Sherman was clearly moving his forces south; Hood inferred that their objective might be East Point, which he had established as key to his defense ("To hold Atlanta I have to hold East Point," he had told President Davis earlier). To forewarn of such a possible strike, Hood at 4:30 P.M. directed Frank Armstrong's cavalry brigade to "oppose stoutly" any enemy advance along the road from their mid-afternoon position toward East Point. Confederate headquarters still did not know what enemy corps were on the move; at 5:45 P.M. Chief of Staff Shoup told Jackson, "Genl thinks it important that you should find out to night what infantry force it is reported to be in front of Ross & Armstrong." Hood further called Jackson, his interim cavalry chief, to headquarters that evening, presumably to hear personally all available intelligence. Without further dire callings, Hood felt no need to move his infantry. "The general commanding has disposed of his troops so as to be prepared for any emergency," Shoup recorded that night in his journal. These precautions included ordering Maney's division to be held "in readiness to move at a moment's notice."[60]

With the action obviously shifting beyond the fortified perimeter of Atlanta, early on the 28th Hood called for officers in Macon to send forward more militia to protect the city defenses against enemy assault. He also prepared that day to swing more troops toward the south. Brown's division (formerly Bate's—Grits had been wounded August 10), already southwest of Atlanta, was directed to march to East Point; its trench lines were to be manned by Stevenson's division, now freed from duty north of the city.

On the morning of the 28th Hood also had to contend with the possibility that Sherman might unleash another cavalry raid against the railroad at points south. "Do you think Cavalry starting on raid?" Hood asked Armstrong at 10:00 A.M. Around noon headquarters wired the post commanders at Jonesboro, Griffin, and Macon, "Look out for raid." That afternoon most of Brown's division was sent to Rough and Ready, another three and one-half miles down the line from East Point. Farther still, two brigades of infantry and a regiment of cavalry were sent to Jonesboro, all intended, as Shoup wrote, "to co-operate with General Armstrong in repelling raids." But by nightfall the threat of a Yankee equestrian strike seemed to have abated. At the same time, Confederate cavalry reported that a large enemy infantry force had reached the Atlanta & West Point Railroad and had halted. "No immediate danger of raid," Hood wired a subordinate on the night of August 28. "Yankees have not left West Point railroad." Yet at 9:00 P.M. with the enemy forces understood to be arced all the way from the Chattahoochee crossings to near the railroad north of Fairburn (as Hood reported that night to Secretary Seddon), they could strike anywhere. Hood accordingly had stretched his forces some twenty-five miles from the city fortifications on the Western & Atlantic down to Jonesboro, in order to meet all contingencies. At the close of the 28th, Shoup recorded, "Every precaution has been taken by the commanding general to keep our line of communication from being cut by the enemy."[61]

He used the singular form, "line," because the Confederates had, since the wrecking of the Montgomery-to-Atlanta railway by Rousseau, McCook, and Kilpatrick, come to rely on the Macon-to-Atlanta line, the Macon & Western, as the army's lifeline. The irrelevance of the Montgomery-Atlanta line did not seem to matter to General Sherman, who had by now developed a virtual fetish about the wrecking of rail. After Howard's troops struck the Atlanta & West Point line around noon of the 28th, they began tearing up the track according to the explicit instructions issued by General Sherman himself. Soon they were joined by the Fourth and Fourteenth Corps. For the rest of the day and into the 29th, the Northerners worked on the Rebel road thoroughly and extensively. "Let the destruction be so thorough," Sherman had decreed, "that not a rail or tie can be used again." They were so thorough and worked so long, in fact, that the Yankee front remained unchanged August 29;

the only marching was done by Schofield's Twenty-third Corps, catching up with the rest of the army group.[62]

Hood was kept apprised of this activity by Red Jackson's cavalry, which skirmished with Federals at the railroad. But once they were done with their rail-wrecking, where would they go? Hood on the 29th directed Hardee and Lee to do what they could to ascertain the enemy's intentions; he traveled by train to Hardee's headquarters at East Point to confer and size up the situation. Jackson and Armstrong were further instructed on the need to bring in all intelligence. They did so and apparently quite well. Called to Hood's headquarters in Atlanta that evening, Hardee learned the latest, which he related to his wife: "We know that five certainly, perhaps six Corps are on the West Point R. Road," which was indeed true. In the meantime Shoup recorded the prevalent feeling at headquarters: "The enemy are still moving to our left and appear to have a large force of cavalry, artillery, and infantry, moving in the direction of Jonesborough and Rough and Ready, on the Macon railroad." The next morning, in his letter home, Hardee wrote rather confidently: "We have made some dispositions to meet the exigency." And while Hardee noted that the Federals seemed headed toward Rough and Ready, Sherman's objective remained unclear. "I suppose by tonight," wrote Hardee, "we shall know more of his designs."[63]

Armchair historians, drawing on the huge literature of how wars happened and making use of the luxury of hindsight, have criticized General Hood for his actions during these several crucial days of the Atlanta Campaign. Some commentators have charged that the Confederate commander for several days simply lost contact with the enemy forces and was ignorant of their movements (presumably because he had blunderingly sent off his cavalry chief with half the army's mounted troops). The truth is, the Confederate cavalry brigades that were not riding with Wheeler served industriously, feeding Hood with regular and accurate information on the enemy positions. But there is a vast difference between knowing where the enemy is and what he intends to do. Hood figured Sherman was heading for the railroad, but he did not know precisely where. That latter knowledge belonged only to General Sherman himself. "I don't think the enemy yet understand our movement," he wrote on August 28. "They have made no effort to stop us, only cavalry holding the road."[64]

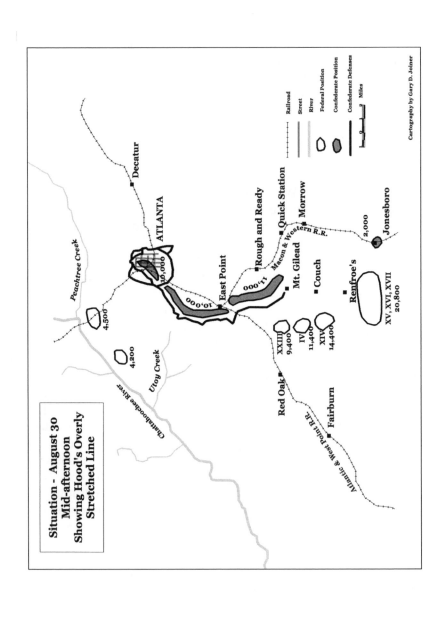

Situation - August 30
Mid-afternoon
Showing Hood's Overly
Stretched Line

Peachtree Creek

Chattahoochee River

Utoy Creek

Decatur

ATLANTA

10,000

4,500

4,200

East Point

10,000

Rough and Ready

Quick Station

Morrow

11,000

Mt. Gilead

Macon & Western R.R.

Couch

Jonesboro

2,000

Renfroe's

XV, XVI, XVII
20,800

Red Oak

XXIII
9,400

IV
11,400

XIV
14,400

Fairburn

Atlantic & West Point R.R.

Railroad
Street
River
Federal Position
Confederate Position
Confederate Defenses

0   1   2   Miles

Cartography by Gary D. Joiner

August 30 was to be the critical day of the campaign, for both sides. Satisfied with the destruction of the West Point road—having personally inspected the twelve and a half miles of twisted rails, burned ties, and embankment cuts filled with logs, rocks, and artillery shells rigged as booby traps—General Sherman ordered his six corps on the move by 7:00 A.M., generally east toward the Macon railroad. From Red Oak, Schofield was to march toward Morrow's Mill and Mt. Gilead Church; Thomas's Fourth and Fourteenth Corps would leave Red Oak and head toward the Couch place, a couple miles south of Morrow's; Howard's three corps, aiming for Jonesboro, were to get as far as Renfroe's.

Trying to deduce where on the Macon & Western Sherman would thrust his infantry, General Hood challenged his cavalry leaders to keep close to the foe and hinder their advance as much as possible. He told Red Jackson, as early as 8:00 A.M., that he "must detain them as long as possible." From these cavalry bodies the news started to come in, confirming that the Yankees seemed to be marching on a wide front. Armstrong's and Ross's brigades stayed before a "very heavy column of infantry" seemingly headed for Jonesboro. Rebel skirmishers, termed obstinate by the Federals, contested another column to the north, apparently aimed for Morrow's Station, three and one-half miles closer to Atlanta. Hood's headquarters continued to worry not just about Yankee infantry but also about detached cavalry striking the railroad. Frank Armstrong at 11:00 A.M. thought the enemy was about to launch a raid toward Griffin, another 20 miles south of Jonesboro. (Accordingly, Shoup asked Brigadier General Joseph Lewis, commanding one of the two infantry brigades at Jonesboro, to begin finding horses for his men, should they have to mount up "at any moment.") Much farther up, Hood seemed anxious about East Point and asked General Jackson to send a "dashing" colonel with a regiment to reconnoiter west of East Point toward the Chattahoochee. There was, after all, the Twentieth Corps north of Atlanta; would it continue to stay idle?[65]

Clearly, though, the main enemy thrust would be against the Macon & Western somewhere between East Point and Jonesboro. In the early afternoon of the 30th, therefore, Hood extended Hardee's entrenched lines by pushing Cleburne's division some three miles farther south. On its left the three brigades of Brown's division formed the army's extreme left flank southwest of Rough and Ready.

To General Hardee, who moved his headquarters from East Point to Rough and Ready after 1:00 P.M., this support was not enough; he wanted more troops sent to Jonesboro. Hood, however, declined. "General Hood does not think the necessity will arise to send any more troops to Jonesborough to-day," Shoup wired Hardee at 1:00 P.M. At the same time, Hood brought a brigade from Stewart's corps, Scott's, to East Point and shifted Lee's corps to the left. Anderson's division was moved to the trench works near East Point, there to be close to the railroad should further movement be necessary; Lee himself was instructed to transfer his headquarters to East Point. All this movement extended the Confederate "railway defense line" to Mt. Gilead Church, more than ten miles beyond Atlanta's fortified perimeter. Hardee wanted it extended even farther and asked that Anderson's division be moved to his left, not his right at East Point. Hood at first ordered the move, then changed his mind; he evidently believed that East Point remained a possible enemy objective and that its defense required adequate strength in his center. For this reason he took the bold step of second guessing intelligence reports that came in early afternoon, indicating that the Federals were moving on Jonesboro; Hood considered them a secondary force, perhaps a feint. "General Hood does not think there can be a large force advancing upon Jonesborough," Shoup wrote General Jackson at 1:20. Twenty-five minutes later, though, Hood advised Hardee: "It may become necessary for you to send another brigade and battery to Jonesborough."

The commanding general was weighing all the possibilities of enemy attack on the railroad but by early afternoon of the 30th could still not ascertain Sherman's main target. Hardee was accordingly instructed "to take whatever measures you may think necessary" to guard Jonesboro and Rough and Ready, Shoup advised, so that Hood "may make other dispositions tonight," redeploying his divisions against the enemy. In the meantime, Shoup added, "he does not think they will attack Jonesborough to-day." An obviously nervous Hardee sent out his own reconnaissance, led by staff officer Colonel William D. Pickett. Pickett's news—enemy movements toward Rough and Ready and Jonesboro—added emphasis to what headquarters already knew but apparently convinced Hood of the need to shift more strength to Jonesboro. "Had anticipated it before your dispatch was received," Hood wired back at 3:15. Thus by 3:00

or 3:15 Hood had decided that the main enemy thrust was indeed aimed at Jonesboro and that he would have to shift considerable infantry to his left. To plan the troop movement, Hood announced that he would send a train for Hardee, Lee, and Red Jackson to bring them to his headquarters on Whitehall Street for a conference after dark. Each of the two corps commanders was told to "have your command under arms at sunset," while the cavalry leader was instructed to have his horsemen saddled up. A night march was clearly in store. At the same time, the Confederate commanding general had to keep the prize itself well guarded: he held Stewart's Corps and the militia inside Atlanta's fortifications, against any sudden lunge by the Twentieth Corps at the river.[66]

The situation on the afternoon of August 30 changed faster, however, than Hood anticipated. Southern cavalry, battling Kilpatrick's, contested Howard's advance throughout the day. Delayed for a while in the mid-afternoon by enemy cavalry at Renfroe's plantation, Howard decided to press on toward Jonesboro, four miles to the southeast, largely because his thirsty men needed watering at the Flint River, which runs north-south a mile or so west of the railroad. Hood ordered his infantry at Jonesboro, fewer than 2,000 men under General Lewis, to join Armstrong's cavalry "in preventing the enemy crossing Flint River to-night." That was at 5:15. The Confederates could not do so. By 6:00 the Yankees, estimated at a full corps, were across the Flint and pushing the defenders before them. Armstrong wired that the enemy could strike the railroad during the night. Hood immediately telegraphed Hardee to prepare to move his infantry to Jonesboro that night; to Lewis, Hood could only say: "Help is ordered to you." On its own, though, Lewis's force either "easily repulsed" the enemy outside Jonesboro, as Shoup recorded in his diary, or (more likely) the hot and footsore Federals simply halted their advance, content that by nightfall they had entrenched within a half-mile of the Macon & Western. Hood had by that time found that two, maybe three, enemy corps were near Jonesboro. Clearly, the Yankees had to be dislodged; when Hardee and Lee arrived at Hood's headquarters around 9:00 that night, the generals planned their night march and next day's attack.[67]

The situation had changed drastically in five hours, as indicated by two of Hood's messages to Hardee that afternoon—from an assurance that no troop movement to Jonesboro would be likely that day (1:00 P.M.) to "your corps will move to Jonesborough to-night" (6:10 P.M.). It had taken at least that long to convince Hood that he had been wrong in telling Jackson, as he did at 1:20, that there could be no "large force advancing upon Jonesborough." By nightfall, headquarters realized that three enemy corps (the Fifteenth, Sixteenth, and Seventeenth of Howard's army) were entrenching precariously near the Macon & Western at Jonesboro. But where was the rest of Sherman's army? Two corps (the Fourth and the Twenty-third), as well as part of the Fourteenth, were marching east all day; General Hood, of course, did not know the composition of these forces, nor even their strength. Although Confederate cavalry had resisted their advance and sent dispatches to headquarters on the Federals' progress, Hood and Shoup were compelled to give secondary attention to this railroad threat, given the unexpectedly fast crossing of the Flint by Howard's army. Ironically, if Logan's Fifteenth Corps, in the advance, had followed Sherman's instructions for its march on August 30, Hood would have been correct in holding back strength from his extreme left to protect his center. Told to halt at Renfroe's for the day, the men of Logan's corps, hot and thirsty, had found no water on the plantation, and so in mid-afternoon General Howard authorized them to keep going, toward the Flint River two and one-half miles ahead. Once across, they advanced another half-mile by dusk. According to Sherman's plan, they should have been camping miles to the rear.[68]

There was irony, too, in Hood's rapid troop movement to his left (Hardee's and Lee's corps' night march), brought about by his need to attack at Jonesboro in order to save the railroad there, for the movement actually opened the Macon & Western to enemy interdiction at the center of his "line." Thus it happened that on the 31st Union infantry finally fell upon Atlanta's last railroad. This campaign-deciding triumph did not occur at Jonesboro, though; it happened well to the north. Completing the irony, General Sherman himself believed that the Rebels' last road would be cut by Howard at Jonesboro. He issued orders to this effect for the 31st; Thomas was to advance as support on Howard's left; Schofield would continue marching toward the railway, too. While General Howard knew that Logan's men had entrenched eight hundred yards from Jonesboro's train depot and that his artillery could easily shell any passing train, he was also well aware (as he reported to Sherman) that the Rebels were "shoving troops down here with great rapidity." Howard therefore expected to be attacked the next day.[69]

He was. In the Confederate generals' night conference, Hood told Hardee and Lee to take their corps, attack the Yankees at Jonesboro, and drive them into the Flint River. Hardee's men had already started marching to Jonesboro at 4:00 that afternoon, but Lee's men did not get moving till just before midnight. Because of the lack of train cars, the infantry had to march that hot, dusty night. Hardee's lead division did not reach Jonesboro until sunrise on the 31st. Most of Lee's troops arrived by 10:00 A.M., but some units were still marching into position after 1:00 P.M. It was not until 3:00, therefore, that Hardee's and Lee's attack began. The Southerners knew it would be rough going. "The yanks have made good use of the past 18 hours," noted one Rebel soldier, who could see that the enemy were well entrenched on high ground. In between was generally open field, another bad omen. Doomed from the start, the Confederate attack thus fell apart under heavy Union musketry and cannonade. The men's exhaustion from night marching added to their difficulties; even the Federals noticed, as one put it, that the Rebels did not attack that day with their "usual impetuosity."[70] By 4:30, their charges repulsed, the Southerners all along the line were withdrawing to their jump-off positions. The casualties, however, were not heavy, some 2,200 between both Confederate corps. In the Army of the Tennessee, 179 killed and wounded attested to the one-sidedness of the battle at Jonesboro, August 31.

Farther up the Macon & Western, Cox's division of the Twenty-third Corps reached Mt. Gilead, formerly Hardee's extreme left, about eighteen hours after the Rebels had abandoned their entrenchments there (Cox's men actually passed through the Rebels' abandoned earthworks at Mt. Gilead on their way to the railroad). At 3:00 P.M. (about the time the Confederates opened their attack against Howard), the Federals reached the railway a mile and a half below Rough and Ready, just above Quick Station. "The advance was sharply resisted by the enemy's cavalry," General Cox reported, "but no infantry force was found"—the Rebel infantry had gone to Jonesboro. In another hour two more divisions of the Fourth Corps came up; the Federals began digging in, intent upon securing their lodgment on the railroad. As Cox's troops were driving off the Rebel cavalry, two southbound trains came in sight, stopped, and reversed.

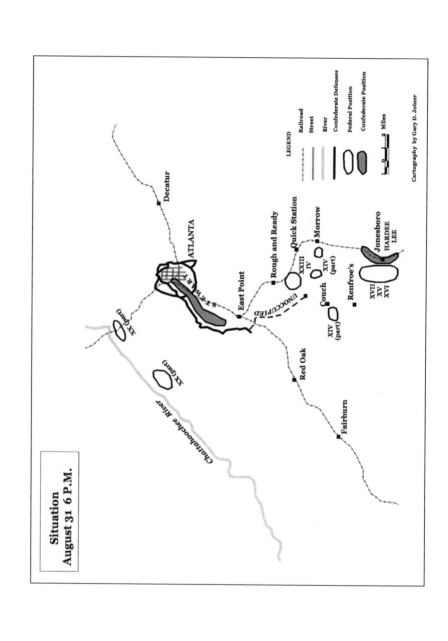

Situation
August 31 6 P.M.

LEGEND

Railroad
Street
River
Confederate Defenses
Federal Position
Confederate Position

0   1   2   Miles

Cartography by Gary D. Joiner

Chattahoochee River

Decatur

ATLANTA

S. F. & W. R. R.

XX (part)

XX (part)

East Point

Red Oak

Fairburn

Rough and Ready

UNOCCUPIED

XIV (part)

Couch

Renfroe's

Quick Station

XXIII
IV

Morrow

XIV (part)

XVII
XV
XVI

Jonesboro
HARDEE
LEE

Their return to East Point, along with the receipt of dispatches from the Confederate cavalry fighting Cox, prompted the commander at East Point, Brigadier General John T. Morgan, to notify headquarters. By 5:00 P.M. on the 31st Hood knew that the railroad and telegraph had been cut below Rough and Ready. All he could do was to tell Morgan to "make the best resistance you can" if attacked, and "retire fighting" back on Atlanta.[71] Hood had no reinforcements to send; his thin line had stretched to the breaking point. Actually, it was already broken. Hood sent courier messages to Hardee and Lee alerting them that their two corps were now detached from the rest of the army.

The enemy lodgment at Quick Station and Hood's inability to counter it had rendered the outcome of the Confederate attack at Jonesboro virtually inconsequential. Almost as inconsequential, as if Sherman needed another interdiction of the Macon & Western, was the breach made at 6:00 P.M. by several regiments of the Fourteenth Corps at Morrow's Station, five miles north of Jonesboro. One thing was certain: Atlanta's last rail line had been cut.

Hood's difficulties in predicting where the enemy would strike the railroad and in deploying his troops to meet every contingency are strikingly similar to the difficulties faced by his mentor, the other Confederate army commander, Robert E. Lee, just two and a half months earlier. The two situations, Lee's in mid-June and Hood's in late August, were themselves quite alike in three respects. After the battle of Cold Harbor, June 3, General Lee's Army of Northern Virginia held defensive positions northeast of Richmond, stalemating General Ulysses S. Grant's operations, much as Hood's Army of Tennessee held defensive positions west and southwest of Atlanta in mid-August, stalemating Sherman. Grant sent his cavalry off on a raid June 7, at least partly to force Lee to send off the bulk of his cavalry. When he did so, Lee diminished his capacity for cavalry intelligence, much as General Hood is criticized for having done in sending off half of his cavalry on Wheeler's raid August 10. To break the deadlock, Grant determined upon a sudden swift and secret march by his left flank south, across the James River, aimed at breaking Lee's vital railway supply system by capturing Petersburg. Sherman's purposes were the same. To break his deadlock along the railway defense line, he planned his grand movement by the right flank, aimed at cutting Hood's railroad far below East Point.

Lee and Hood, both without their ordinary capacity for cavalry intelligence, responded to the enemy initiatives in much the same way—extremely cautiously. Unwilling to expose Richmond to a surprise enemy strike, Lee kept much of his army on the north side of the James, just as Hood had to keep a corps plus state troops in the Atlanta defenses, watching against the Twentieth Corps. Lee had to deal with the increasingly frantic telegrams from the Confederate commander at Petersburg, General P. G. T. Beauregard, who warned that Union forces in his front were gathering strength. Lee gradually ordered divisions south of the James as the threat seemed to develop; but he remained concerned for the safety of the capital and felt he could not shift farther to the south until he knew whether Grant was just feinting to Petersburg. "I do not know the position of Grant's army, and cannot strip north bank of James River," Lee wired Beauregard mid-morning of the 16th. "Have you not force sufficient?"[72]

Virtually the same message could have been sent by Hood to Hardee on August 30, for Hood had to worry for the safety of Atlanta even as Hardee called for more troops to be shifted toward Jonesboro. We can see that four or five days after the enemy's initial disappearance, Lee and Hood faced the same crisis of intelligence. Indeed, Lee's June 16—a day the commanding general spent "in a furious passion. . . . He was mad because he could not find out what Grant was doing," as one Confederate officer observed—was Hood's August 30, when he could not find out what Sherman was doing.[73]

Clearly, Grant had outmaneuvered Lee, just as Sherman had outmaneuvered Hood. Lee at the James River is usually seen as a temporary victim of the fog of war, whose potentially disastrous deployments can be understood, if not forgiven, as the exceedingly cautious response of a wise commander. Not so Hood at Jonesboro. His exceedingly cautious response to Sherman's movements August 26–30 has not been viewed with nearly so much compassion. Instead of seeing Hood as disciple of the "Lee and Jackson school" straining to conform his positions to available intelligence, writers in their blunter passages have in fact portrayed the Confederate commander at Atlanta as befuddled, deluded, or asleep: "Hood had apparently been completely bewildered by Sherman" (Horn, 1941); "it was August 30 before Hood . . . realized Sherman was attacking, not retreating" (McDonough, 1972); "Hood woke up to the truth a day too late" (McPherson, 1988). In coarser hands still Hood is even turned into a moron. According to Mark Coburn, Hood had been "badly fooled by Sherman's move. . . . 'I let my opponent make a flaring ass of me' is not a line often found in military memoirs. Still, one wonders what Hood might have done had Sherman left behind a huge wooden horse."[74]

In the end, there are four important distinctions to make between Lee at the James and Hood at Jonesboro, in explaining why the Confederates succeeded in holding onto their rail base in Virginia but failed to do so in Georgia. First, when Sherman began his stealthy march Hood did not have a base of strength at Jonesboro. The place was an undefended railway station; what troops Hood eventually had there were extensions of his army pushed toward the south August 28–29. But in Virginia before Grant set out, Beauregard, commander of his own department on the Southside, had a division of infantry nearby at Bermuda Hundred, in addition to at least a few thousand local defense troops in Petersburg; another division soon joined these forces June 15–16. Second, the Confederates at Petersburg had a well-constructed line of works, the Dimmock line, already in place before Grant began moving south of the river. Thus, Beauregard and Lee enjoyed an immense defensive advantage when the Federals launched attacks June 16, 17, and 18 (during which Lee moved the rest of his army to the threatened sector). Hood had no such advantage south of Atlanta. Not only was the key position for stopping Howard's advance on the afternoon of the 30th, the Flint River, unfortified but Confederate cavalry even failed to destroy the river bridge, allowing its use by the Fifteenth Corps. Federals were able to get so close to the railroad that evening that Hood was forced to attack them the next day. This third difference reversed the odds that Confederates enjoyed at Petersburg. There, Southerners were on the entrenched defensive; at Jonesboro on August 31, the Federals were. Therein lay the virtually predictable outcome of the two battles, June 16–18 in Virginia and August 31 in Georgia. Finally, Grant's and Butler's forces had only one target, made obvious by the convergence of three railroads at Petersburg and the contours of the James and Appomattox Rivers. Sherman's forces, in contrast, were spread out in a six-mile front on the afternoon of August 30, aiming in at least two if not three directions, with their only objective to hit the Macon & Western somewhere south of East Point. Sherman's

wide fan and open target made Hood's task of deployment that
much harder. To repeat, while Hardee and Lee attacked Howard's
army, elements of the larger Union force (the Fourth, Fourteenth, and
Twenty-third Corps) reached the rail line near Rough and Ready, a
half-day's march north of Jonesboro, against far less opposition—
cavalry and no infantry, largely because Hood had no more infantry
to throw in their front.

These circumstances have not been explored or even laid out in
the literature of Hood at Jonesboro. As a result, only a very few
scholars have attempted to defend General Hood against the pre-
vailing charges of befuddlement during Sherman's movement in
late August. Thomas Lawrence Connelly is the first military historian to have come vigorously to Hood's defense. To him, accusing
Hood of "being blind toward the danger on the Macon Road on
August 30 seems incredible. By then Hood already had shifted
Hardee's corps to Rough and Ready, and Lee's corps to East Point,
both within ten miles of Jonesboro. Why should Hood have thrown
most of his force to Jonesboro, as Hardee by hindsight argued that
he should have done? The sparse cavalry intelligence Hood had
received on August 29 and on 30 did not pinpoint Sherman's
advance squarely on Jonesboro, but on Rough and Ready as well.
To stretch three slim corps the entire distance from Atlanta to Jonesboro would have been impossible. Hood did the next best thing by
placing two-thirds of his infantry on the left flank at East Point and
Rough and Ready. In short, Hood seemed to do all that he possibly
could do by August 30." Richard McMurry, the general's principal
biographer, concurs; the charge that Hood was "thoroughly befuddled by Sherman's brilliant maneuvers" at Jonesboro is "unwar-
ranted." Albert Castel agrees that Hood after August 26 was "far
from being deluded" and managed his response as well as he could,
under the limitations of intelligence at hand.[75]

Nonetheless, it cannot be denied: just as Lee was outgeneraled
at the James, so was Hood at Jonesboro. The real difference between
the two generals' performances, though, lay in their outcomes. Beauregard's defense force, reinforced steadily by Lee's troops June 16–18,
repelled Union attacks at Petersburg and saved the railroad. Lee sur-
vived the fog of war and Grant's surprise crossing of the James to
carry on the campaign for months more. The situation was different
for Hood. To be sure, Hardee's and Lee's corps, 20,000 strong,

marched industriously through the night; their arrival and deployment at Jonesboro after noon on the 31st caused Sherman momentarily to think he had been outsmarted. As he told Howard: "The enemy is too smart for us. . . . It may be that some accident will happen, of which we can take advantage."[76] Actually, it was no accident at all but part of Sherman's plan that the Macon & Western was cut well north of Jonesboro that afternoon by Cox's division. It had proven impossible for Hood to stretch his outnumbered army twenty-five miles from the northwest Atlanta defenses to Jonesboro, to predict where Sherman intended to strike and to move.

The Federals' breaking of the railroad, rather than the failure of Hardee's and Lee's assault, meant that Atlanta was lost. Learning of the repulse after midnight of August 31–September 1, Hood ordered his troops to evacuate the city on the next day. S. D. Lee was already marching back toward Atlanta for a junction with the rest of the army, Stewart and the militia would march south, and Hardee, still holding defensive positions at Jonesboro, would have to join as best he could. Sherman realized Hardee's precarious position and ordered an attack against the Rebels on the afternoon of the 1st. In this second day of the battle of Jonesboro, the Federals succeeded in breaking Hardee's line, taking 900 prisoners and two batteries, but the Confederates held and withdrew that night.

In the next two days Hood was able to reassemble his army, while General Sherman was content to have his soldiers occupy Atlanta, which they did on the 2d. Sherman later came in for criticism for having allowed Hood's beaten army to get away, when for a while the opportunity for its piecemeal destruction presented itself. Sherman, though, had won the prize: "So Atlanta is ours," he telegraphed Washington, "and fairly won."[77]

NOTES TO PART TWO

1. J. B. Hood, *Advance and Retreat: Personal Experiences in the United States and Confederate States Armies* (New Orleans: Published for the Hood Orphan Memorial Fund, 1880), 130.

2. Harry W. Pfanz, *Gettysburg: The Second Day* (Chapel Hill: University of North Carolina Press, 1987), 166, 173.

3. Bragg to Davis, July 15, 1864, U.S. War Department, *The War of the Rebellion: A Compilation of the Official Records of the Union and Confederate*

Armies, 128 vols. (Washington: Government Printing Office, 1880–1901), 39, pt. 2, 713. All references to the *Official Record (O.R.)* are to series 1.

    4. Hood to Bragg, July 14, 1864; Seddon to Hood, July 17, *O.R.* 38, pt. 5, 880, 885.

    5. *Atlanta Appeal,* undated [probably July 19 or 20], 1864, quoted in *New York Times,* July 29; "The Army of Tennessee," *Augusta Constitutionalist,* July 20.

    6. Sherman to Grant, April 10, 1864; Hood's report, Feb. 15, 1865, and of Gen. Alexander P. Stewart, Jan. 12, 1865, *O.R.* 32, pt. 3, 314; 38, pt. 3, 630, 871.

    7. Hood, *Advance and Retreat,* 165–66; "Personne" [De Fontaine], "From the Army of Tennessee. Severe Fighting Around Atlanta. Behind the Chattahoochee. July 20, 1864," *Savannah Republican,* July 25, 1864.

    8. Special Field Orders No. 39, July 19, 1864, *O.R.* 38, pt. 5, 193.

    9. Ibid.; Sherman to Thomas, July 19, 1864, *O.R.* 38, pt. 5, 185.

    10. Sherman to McPherson, July 20, 1864, ibid., 208.

    11. Stanley F. Horn, *The Army of Tennessee* (Indianapolis: Bobbs-Merrill, 1941), 304; Alfred H. Burne, *Lee, Grant, and Sherman: A Study of Leadership in the 1864–65 Campaign* (New York: Charles Scribner's Sons, 1939), 105–6; John P. Dyer, *"Fightin' Joe" Wheeler* (Baton Rouge: Louisiana State University Press, 1941), 178; Albert Castel, *Decision in the West: The Atlanta Campaign of 1864* (Lawrence: University Press of Kansas, 1992), 379; Irving A. Buck, *Cleburne and His Command* (Jackson: McCowat-Mercer Press, 1959), 234.

    12. Hood's report, Feb. 15, 1864; Hardee's report, Apr. 5, 1865, *O.R.* 38, pt. 3, 631, 699; Cheatham to T. B. Roy, quoted in Nathaniel Cheairs Hughes Jr., *General William J. Hardee: Old Reliable* (Baton Rouge: Louisiana State University Press, 1965), 226.

    13. Wheeler, quoted in T. B. Roy, "General Hardee and the Military Operations Around Atlanta," *Southern Historical Society Papers* 8, no. 8–9 (Aug.–Sept. 1880): 355; Hood's report, Feb. 15, 1865, *O.R.* 38, pt. 3, 631.

    14. Hood's report, Feb. 15, 1865, *O.R.* 38, pt. 3, 631.

    15. F. Jay Taylor, ed., *Reluctant Rebel: The Secret Diary of Robert Patrick, 1861–1865* (Baton Rouge: Louisiana State University Press, 1959), 200; Hardee to Wheeler, July 22, *O.R.* 38, pt. 5, 901.

    16. Wilbur G. Kurtz, "The Death of Major General W. H. T. Walker, July 22, 1864," *Civil War History* 6, no. 2 (June 1960): 175–76.

    17. Buck, *Cleburne and His Command,* 235.

    18. Stephen W. Sears, *Chancellorsville* (New York: Houghton Mifflin, 1996), 271; W. H. Chamberlin, "Hood's Second Sortie at Atlanta," in Robert Underwood Johnson and Clarence Clough Buel, eds., *Battles and Leaders of the Civil War,* 4 vols. (New York: Century, 1888), 4:326.

    19. Gill to his wife, July 23, 1864, quoted in Bell I. Wiley, "A Story of Three Southern Officers," *Civil War Times Illustrated* 3, no. 1 (April 1964): 33.

    20. "Telegraphic Reports of the Press Association" and "The News from Atlanta. How It Was Received in Richmond," *Augusta Chronicle & Sentinel,* July 24, 1864; Hugo von Freytag-Loringhoven, *The Power of Personality in War,* trans. Oliver L. Spaulding, in *Roots of Strategy: Three Military Classics, Book 3* (Harrisburg, Pa.: Stackpole Books, 1991), 240.

21. J. C. Van Duzer to Maj. Thomas T. Eckert, July 22, 1864, *O.R.* 38, pt. 5, 232, 900.

22. Sherman to Halleck, July 24, 1864; to Grant, July 25, *O.R.* 38, pt. 5, 240, 247.

23. Brig. Gen. L. S. Ross to Brig. Gen. William H. Jackson, July 26, 1864; John S. Smith to Wheeler, July 27, ibid., 911, 913; Bragg to Davis, July 27, *O.R. 52*, pt. 2, 714.

24. Stewart's report, *O.R.* 38, pt. 3, 872.

25. Shoup to Lee, Stewart, and Hardee, July 28, 1864, *O.R.* 38, pt. 5, 919–20.

26. Hood to Seddon; Sherman to Halleck, July 28, 1864, ibid., 917, 919–20.

27. Sherman to Thomas, July 29, 31, 1864; to Howard, July 29, *O.R.* 38, pt. 5, 291, 297.

28. Wilbur G. Kurtz, "Dugout Home in Atlanta," *Atlanta Journal Sunday Magazine,* July 10, 1932, 3.

29. Special Field Orders No. 51, Aug. 4, 1864; Schofield to Sherman, Aug. 5, *O.R.* 38, pt. 5, 364, 380; Wilbur G. Kurtz, "Dugout Home in Atlanta," *Atlanta Journal Sunday Magazine,* July 10, 1932, 3.

30. David P. Conyngham, *Sherman's March Through the South with Sketches and Incidents of the Campaign* (New York: Sheldon and Company, 1865), 201.

31. W. L. Trask, journal typescript, entry of July 28, 1864, Kennesaw Mountain Battlefield Park; Capt. William L. Nugent to "My dear Nellie," in William M. Cash and Lucy Somerville Nugent, eds., *My Dear Nellie: The Civil War Letters of William L. Nugent to Eleanor Smith Nugent* (Jackson: University Press of Mississippi, 1977), 200; *Augusta Chronicle & Sentinel,* Aug. 12, Sept. 1, 1864; "Statement of J. Milton Glass [scout]," Aug. 18, *O.R.* 38, pt. 5, 580.

32. Sherman to Halleck, July 21, 1864; Hood to Seddon, July 23; Hood to Sherman, Sept. 12, *O.R.* 38, pt. 5, 211, 903; 39, pt. 2, 420.

33. Key diary, July 29, in Wirt Armistead Cate, ed., *Two Soldiers: The Campaign Diaries of Thomas J. Key, C.S.A., December 7, 1863–May 17, 1865, and Robert J. Campbell, U.S.A., January 1, 1864–July 21, 1864* (Chapel Hill: University of North Carolina Press, 1938), 105.

34. Sherman to Howard, Aug. 8, 1864; to Halleck, Aug. 7; to Thomas, Aug. 9, *O.R.* 38, pt. 5, 408–9, 429, 436.

35. Shoup journal, Aug. 9, 1864, *O.R.* 38, pt. 3, 690; Bishop Lay diary, May 1863–Dec. 1865, Henry Champlin Lay Papers, Southern Historical Collection, University of North Carolina at Chapel Hill (entry of Aug. 9, 1864); Arthur Howard Noll, ed., *Doctor Quintard Chaplain C.S.A ... His Story of the War (1861–1865)* (Sewanee: University Press of Sewanee Tennessee, 1905), 100; Glass statement, Aug. 12, *O.R.* 38, pt. 5, 477; Charles W. Hubner, "Some Recollections of Atlanta During 1864," *Atlanta Historical Bulletin* 1, no. 2 (Jan. 1928): 6.

36. *Macon Confederate,* quoted in *Richmond Enquirer,* Aug. 27, 1864; "Going to the Front," *Macon Telegraph,* Aug. 16.

37. Key diary, July 26, 1864, 102; *Griffin Rebel,* quoted in *Augusta Chronicle & Sentinel,* July 29; "J.T.G.," in *Columbus (Georgia) Enquirer,* Aug. 2,

reprinted as "Gen. Hood Increases His Army," *Atlanta Intelligencer,* Aug. 10; "Rover," in *Augusta Chronicle & Sentinel,* Aug. 9.

38. "Rover," in *Augusta Chronicle & Sentinel,* Aug. 9, 1864; Letter from "B.," Aug. 19, *Savannah Republican,* Aug. 21; "To the People of Georgia" and "Negroes for Teamsters," *Macon Telegraph,* Aug. 11.

39. "A Good Work," *Atlanta Appeal,* Aug. 1, 1864, reprinted in *Macon Telegraph,* Aug. 4; *Columbus Times,* Aug. 4; "Confederate," *Columbus Sun,* July 30; "Detailed Men," *Augusta Constitutionalist,* Aug. 10.

40. "Gen. Hood Increases His Army."

41. Bragg to Davis, July 27, 1864; Hood to Cooper, Aug. 2, *O.R.* 52, pt. 2, 713–14; 38, pt. 5, 940; [Hood] to Maury, Aug. 15, Telegrams Book No. III, Hood Papers, National Archives, Washington, D.C.

42. Hood to J. S. Thrasher, Aug. 2, 1864, Telegrams Book No. III; "Rallying," *Atlanta Appeal,* quoted in *Augusta Chronicle & Sentinel,* Aug. 6; *Macon Telegraph,* Aug. 4; "Appeal to Soldiers Absent from their Commands," *Augusta Chronicle & Sentinel,* Aug. 5; *Columbus Times,* Aug. 6; "The Absentees from Hood's Army," *Columbus Enquirer,* Aug. 6.

43. *Macon Telegraph,* Aug. 5, 1864; "To the Front," *Augusta Constitutionalist,* Aug. 5.

44. Bragg to Davis, July 27, 1864; statement of Capt. J. B. Jordan, Aug. 14, *O.R.* 52, pt. 2, 714; 38, pt. 5, 494; "Hood Vacates the Bomb-Proofs," *Augusta Constitutionalist,* Aug. 20.

45. [Hood] to Gov. Joseph E. Brown, July 24, 1864, Cipher Dispatches to Richmond 1864, Hood Papers; *Atlanta Appeal,* July 20, and *Macon Telegraph,* July 21, quoted in *Columbus Sun,* July 24; "The Militia," *Augusta Constitutionalist,* July 26 (quoting the *Macon Confederate* of July 24); "Off for the Front," *Macon Telegraph,* July 27; Hood to Seddon, Aug. 11, *O.R.* 38, pt. 5, 955; Hood to Brown, Aug. 14, Telegrams Book No. III, Hood Papers; Hood to Bragg, Aug. 4, *O.R.* 52, pt. 2, 718.

46. Sherman to Thomas, Aug. 10, 1864; Hood to Seddon, July 30; Hood to Davis, Aug. 2; Davis to Hood, Aug. 5, *O.R.* 38, pt. 5, 448, 930, 940, 946.

47. Sherman, *Memoirs,* 2:151; Wheeler's report, Oct. 9, 1864, *O.R.* 38, pt. 3, 957.

48. Shoup journal, Aug. 16–18, 20, 1864, *O.R.* 38, pt. 3, 691–92; Jacob D. Cox, *Atlanta* (New York: C. Scribner's Sons, 1882), 197–98.

49. Sherman to Gen. Joseph D. Webster, Aug. 1, 1864, *O.R.* 38, pt. 5, 321.

50. Sherman to Halleck, Aug. 17, 1864, ibid., 547.

51. Hood's report, *O.R.* 38, pt. 3, 632; Hood, *Advance and Retreat,* 201.

52. Brown to Davis, July 5, 1864, in Rowland, *Jefferson Davis Constitutionalist,* 6:280; *Atlanta Southern Confederacy,* quoted in Evans, *Sherman's Horsemen,* 243; "From the Georgia Front," *Augusta Chronicle & Sentinel,* Aug. 14.

53. Sherman to Brig. Gen John E. Smith, Aug. 16, 1864; to Brig. Gen. William Vandever, Aug. 15; to Halleck, Aug. 13, *O.R.* 38, pt. 5, 482, 517, 540.

54. Sherman to Thomas, Aug. 16–17, 1864, ibid., 526, 528, 548.

55. Sherman to Halleck, Aug. 22, 1864, *O.R.* 38, pt. 5, 628.

56. Ibid., Aug. 24, 1864, 649.

57. Trask war journal, typescript (entry for Aug. 26, 1864).

58. "Shadow," "Letter from Atlanta," Aug. 26, 1864 (7:00 P.M.), *Mobile Advertiser and Register*, Aug. 30.

59. Shoup to Jackson (9:00 A.M.), Aug. 26, 1864, *O.R.* 38, pt. 5, 992; [Hood] to Maj. Gen. Patrick R. Cleburne, Aug. 26 (9:00 A.M.), Telegrams Book No. III, Hood Papers; Hood to Seddon, Aug. 26, *O.R.* 38, pt. 5, 990.

60. Hood to Davis, Aug. 9, 1864; to Jackson, Aug. 27 (4:30 P.M.), *O.R.* 38, pt. 5, 951, 994; [Shoup] to Jackson, Aug. 27 (5:45 P.M.), Telegrams Book No. III, Hood Papers; Shoup journal, Aug. 27, *O.R.* 38, pt. 3, 693.

61. [Hood] to Armstrong, Aug. 28, 1864 (10:00 A.M.); to "Cmg Officers Jonesboro, Griffin, Macon," Aug. 28 (12:15 P.M.), Telegrams Book No. III, Hood Papers; Shoup journal, Aug. 28; Hood to Brig. Gen. M. J. Wright, Aug. 28 (9:40 P.M.), *O.R.* 38, pt. 3, 693–94; pt. 5, 999.

62. Sherman to Thomas, Aug. 28, 1864, *O.R.* 38, pt. 5, 688.

63. Gen. William J. Hardee to his wife, Aug. 30, 1864, Hardee Papers, Alabama Department of Archives and History, Montgomery; Shoup journal, Aug. 29, *O.R.* 38, pt. 3, 694.

64. Sherman to Howard, Aug. 28, 1864, *O.R.* 38, pt. 5, 694–95.

65. Hood to Jackson, Aug. 30, 1864 (8 A.M.); Armstrong to Brig. Gen. Joseph H. Lewis (11:00 A.M.); Shoup to Lewis (noon); Hood to Jackson, Aug. 30 (10:30 A.M.), *O.R.* 38, pt. 5, 1004, 1005; 52, pt. 2, 727.

66. Shoup to Hardee, Aug. 30 (1:00 and 2:00 P.M.); Hood to Hardee (1:45, 3:15, and 3:20 P.M.); Shoup to Jackson (1:20), *O.R.* 38, pt. 5, 1000–1001, 1004.

67. Hood to Lewis, Aug. 30, 1864 (5:15 and 6:35 P.M.); Shoup journal, Aug. 30, *O.R.* 38, pt. 5, 1004; pt. 3, 694.

68. Hood to Hardee, Aug. 30, 1864 (6:10 P.M.); Shoup to Jackson, Aug. 30 (1:20 P.M.), *O.R.* 38, pt. 5, 1001, 1005.

69. Howard to Sherman, Aug. 31, 1864 (9:10 A.M.), ibid., 726.

70. A. D. Kirwan, ed., *Johnny Green of the Orphan Brigade: The Journal of a Confederate Soldier* (Lexington: University of Kentucky Press, 1956), 154; Brig. Gen. William Harrow's report, Sept. 9, *O.R.* 38, pt. 3, 283.

71. Report of Brig. Gen. Jacob D. Cox, Sept. 10, 1864; Hood to Brig. Gen. John T. Morgan, Aug. 31 (8:30 P.M.), *O.R.* 38, pt. 2, 692; pt. 5, 1009.

72. Lee to Beauregard, June 16, 1864 (10:30 A.M.), *O.R.* 40, pt. 2, 659.

73. Brig. Gen. Eppa Hunton, quoted in Thomas J. Howe, *The Petersburg Campaign: Wasted Valor June 15–18, 1864* (Lynchburg, Va.: H. E. Howard, 1988), 58.

74. Horn, *Army of Tennessee*, 367; James L. McDonough, *Schofield: Union General in the Civil War and Reconstruction* (Tallahassee: Florida State University Press, 1972), 95; James M. McPherson, *Battle Cry of Freedom: The Civil War Era* (New York: Oxford University Press, 1988), 774; Mark Coburn, *Terrible Innocence: General Sherman at War* (New York: Hippocrene Books, 1993), 108–9.

75. Connelly, *Autumn of Glory*, 460–61; McMurry, *Hood*, 149; Castel, *Decision in the West*, 487.

76. Sherman to Howard, Aug. 31, 1864 (12:30 P.M.), *O.R.* 38, pt. 5, 726.

77. Sherman to Halleck, Sept. 3, 1864, ibid., 777.

CONCLUSION

Historical inevitability is a troublesome concept, evoking contentious notions of predestination and equally arguable theories of human causality and consequence. "Inevitability" is helpful, though, in suggesting a more plausible, useful line of thinking in historical study. Framed for the Atlanta Campaign, the question is this: after their rout from Missionary Ridge in late 1863, what could the Confederates have done to save Atlanta? Given the events of December 1863–May 1864, the answer, determined well before the campaign began, is *nothing*.

Nothing, for the three reasons in the subtitle of this book—Sherman, Joe Johnston, and the Yankee heavy battalions—which all came together to decide the outcome of that Atlanta Campaign. It is possible that just one, even two working together, might have led to a different outcome. But all three combined doomed Atlanta with the certainty of a mandate from the Greek gods. Simply put, General Johnston was appointed to command the Army of Tennessee; Major General Sherman succeeded Grant as commander of the Military Division of the Mississippi; and Sherman brought together his group of three armies that gave him a dominating numerical strength.

First, the Yankees had the heavy battalions. During the campaign, Sherman's numerical advantage, which had begun as a comfortable 2-to-1 edge, remained very favorable (even after Johnston's reinforcement in late May), at 10 to 6; the arrival of Blair's corps the next month roughly restored the ratio (both sides having lost, *hors de combat* and *de mal*, about the same percentage of effective strength). Although both Johnston and Sherman were accurately informed of the other's strength, General Sherman used this knowledge to feed his confidence, which never wavered, whereas General Johnston used this knowledge to reinforce his self-doubt, expressed even before the campaign opened, that he had not the strength even to hold his Dalton lines, let alone attack the enemy and force him back.

Second, Joe Johnston commanded the Southern army. Well before 1864, he had shown President Davis and uncounted other observers his several unhappy characteristics as army leader: passivity, overcaution, fear of failure, uncommunicativeness. Because of these qualities, Johnston had (fairly or unfairly, and even to this day) been branded as a retreater. Truth to tell, he did very little to rub out this unfortunate reputation. The general's visit to inspect Atlanta's fortifications in March, two months before the campaign even opened, says as much about his predisposition to retreat as does his unimpressive performance on the Peninsula, east of Richmond, in spring 1862, when he showed no fight till the enemy was at the gates of the prize city. One might add to his list of unflattering attributes a determination to pin on others (especially those in civil authority) the blame for the military reverses that he felt himself powerless to avert. His frequent calls for cavalry strikes against Sherman's rearward rail lines, when he refused to send his own superior mounted forces, formed a trail of posturing exercises that proved so strident that even others (such as Governor Brown) picked it up as their own cause for shrill complaint against the beleaguered Confederate president.

The third reason was General Sherman himself. His careful, meticulous, and disciplined preparations before the campaign to ensure that his army would be well supplied (even if Rebel cavalry swooped in on his rail lines) shows abundantly his drive to succeed. Considering this drive coupled with Sherman's knowledge of his armies' numerical strength and the experience of his having stared Joe Johnston down once before at Jackson in July 1863, it is no wonder Sherman overbrimmed confidence throughout the campaign. He knew from the start how he would try to take Atlanta and, what was more, knew he *would* take it. Then, through north Georgia, his savvy combination of pressure against enemy lines even while he was flanking them fed his confidence further; more than once did he think the Rebels would flee when they ended up next morning standing their ground.

Such was the inevitable feel he had, shared probably by many of his men throughout the campaign: they would have Atlanta, at some time or other. Many Southerners feared they would, too, beginning as early as late May with such commentators as "Shadow" Watterson, when the contours of the campaign—Sherman's smart, scrappy generalship, Johnston's cowed and passive attitude, and the Yankees' supremely huge numbers—began to show themselves in repeated form. When the Southern defending forces found themselves outside of Atlanta, and with Johnston evincing no greater confidence than at the start of the show, President Davis was sternly logical enough to figure that Old Joe would give up the city. (He may have, as he later claimed, really been planning a battle at the gates of the city like that at Seven Pines, as he had done in May 1862, but no one before his removal noted it, not even he.) Thus, to try to avoid the inevitable, Davis made the decision so stark and bold as to be rarely made by commanders in chief in wartime: fire an army commander and replace him.

This switch of commanders may have caused Sherman to think a while, but it did not cause him to change his planned tactics. The succession of General Hood to army command on July 18, however, very much brought about a change in Confederate tactics. Hood gave up no more ground; he attacked (even devising some masterful Lee-like battle strokes); and he threw his cavalry into Sherman's rear. Then, when the enemy launched his campaign-deciding maneuver, he responded as well as his outnumbered and outstretched army could. He did, in short, all he could to avert the inevitability of the campaign's outcome he had been handed when he took command, when the South's prospects appeared so dim.

General Bragg, well a supporter of Hood, had expressed the opinion just before the switch of commanders that numbers, position (Yankee armies just a few miles outside of Atlanta), and morale favored the enemy. This combination, he hinted, would make it hard to hold Atlanta, but something had to be done if the Confederacy were going to try at least to hold its second-most important city. President Davis retrospectively said the same thing: he feared that in mid-July the city's fall was inevitable, but he was determined that it should not fall without a manly struggle.

This fierce, manly struggle General Hood gave Davis and the Confederacy, as well as the Yankees themselves. In this way, Hood lived up to the country's expectations. Thus, in his test of merit, he served the South admirably. By this view, Hood should not be blamed for the outcome of the campaign (the fall of Atlanta); he had accepted the chances of the city's fall on July 18 and he struggled to prevent it. He did everything in his power to prevent it and in doing so acted very heroically. By this view, too, the Confederate general who lost the campaign (Hood) should nonetheless get reasonably high marks for performance.

So, too, should General Sherman, who, faced after July 18 with a more dogged resistance than he had heretofore faced, kept up by sheer persistence and self-confidence an array of combative tactics through which at some time he felt he would win. (At times, though, he felt more stymied by Hood than he had ever felt when faced by Johnston; even on the campaign's last day, August 31, he confessed he thought he had been outgeneraled.) But throughout late July and August he tried everything he thought would work: he sent behind the enemy lines his cavalry (McCook, Stoneman, and Kilpatrick) with the same failed results that Hood encountered with Wheeler; he ordered a continuous battering of the enemy lines with cannonading and skirmishing (which brought forth, by the end of the campaign in both commanders' views, as many casualties as an open-field battle); finally, he ordered an undignified (by the old usages of war) artillery barrage of the city and of the civilian occupants themselves—which Cump mistakenly thought would of itself drive Hood to give up the city. All these things did not work. Only the final, massive flanking drive to Jonesboro, with more men than Hood had in his entire army, succeeded in achieving the climactic result.

Because of this evaluation, General Johnston, whose performance in December 1863–July 1864 brought it all about, should in all the grading get the lowest marks. Johnston's sad record as commanding general in the two and one-half months of his campaign, whose start offered the South its sunniest hopes for a successful defense of north Georgia, effectively doomed Atlanta to its eventual fall. It is he, not Hood, who should get the blame for the Confederacy's disastrous campaign failure. But not just he: for he was faced not only with the faults and frailties of Joe Johnston but with the Yankees' inexorably superior numbers, and Sherman's confident, unrelenting use of his strength to bring about the penultimate collapse of the Confederacy. "Atlanta will fall," one Southerner had said earlier on; many others knew it; and so it happened.

A NOTE ON THE
MAJOR AUTHORITIES

Scholarly Resources' American Crisis series happily spares readers from the excessive annotation that sometimes typifies academic writing. True to the design of the series—and to avoid the emperor's famed criticism of Mozart's music ("too many notes")—I have restricted my endnotes to documenting sources of directly quoted material. A scan of these notes will disclose my major research sources. Here I wish to reaffirm them, add a few more, and place all in context.

Volume 38 of the U.S. War Department's *The War of the Rebellion: A Compilation of the Official Records of the Union and Confederate Armies,* 128 vols. (Washington: Government Printing Office, 1880–1901), is the starting point; the officers' Correspondence (parts 3–5) in itself tells much about how the Atlanta Campaign turned out as it did. Other titles add to the contemporary literature: Joseph E. Johnston, *Narrative of Military Operations* (New York: D. Appleton, 1874), William T. Sherman, *Memoirs of General William T. Sherman,* 2 vols. (New York: D. Appleton and Company, 1875), and J. B. Hood, *Advance and Retreat: Personal Experiences in the United States and Confederate State Armies* (New Orleans: Published for the Hood Orphan Memorial Fund, 1880), join Robert Underwood Johnson and Clarence Clough Buel, eds., *Battles and Leaders of the Civil War,* 4 vols. (New York: Century, 1888) as the key generals' major writings. Reflecting Atlanta's importance to the Confederacy in 1864, President Jefferson Davis was much more involved than his Federal counterpart in the progress of the campaign. In reconstructing the probable discussions of the Cabinet meeting (which I think took place July 14) I have relied on Dunbar Rowland's edition of the president's papers (*Jefferson Davis, Constitutionalist: His Letters, Papers, and Speeches,* 10 vols. [Jackson: Mississippi Department of Archives and History, 1923]), which, happily, has begun to be supplanted by the far more comprehensive series *The Papers of Jefferson Davis* (Baton Rouge: Louisiana State University, 1971–; 10 vols. to date).

Among unpublished sources I found the most important by far to be the journal of Confederate Lieutenant Thomas B. Mackall, who served on General Johnston's staff. I am indebted to my good friend Richard McMurry for lending me his typescript of Mackall's writings, which repose at the Earl Greg Swem Library of the College of William and Mary, Williamsburg, Virginia. General Hood's Papers in the National Archives in Washington, D.C., thoroughly raked through by previous scholars, nonetheless offered me some new documentation of how strenuously Hood labored in August to build the strength of his army as it endured the summer's trench warfare.

I also cite two specific manuscripts, previously unused in the literature of the Atlanta Campaign. Among the Lemuel P. Grant Papers in the Library and Archives of the Atlanta History Center is the message to Captain Lemuel P. Grant, the Confederate engineer who supervised construction of Atlanta's fortifications, from Johnston's headquarters on March 14, 1864, ordering Grant to give Johnston a tour of the defenses. Why is this message important? As I say in the text, with the campaign not even started, already the Confederates' commanding general was looking to his rear, anticipating retreat, and eyeing his last-stand stronghold. Just as damning to General Johnston are the manuscript maps belonging to Confederate Brigadier General Henry D. Clayton, in the Alabama Department of Archives and History, Montgomery, which would have been given him by army headquarters. One particular map I found shows clearly the gap by which Major General James B. McPherson flanked Johnston at Dalton. This map confirms that Confederate topographical engineers recorded the gap and that Johnston therefore knew of it. Most important of all, the map indicts Johnston for negligence in not guarding his flank. No longer can he be excused (as he has been for so long) for not knowing of Snake Creek Gap; henceforth he should be condemned for a severe strategic blunder.

Confederate newspapers tell us much about how Southerners, both in the army and among the citizenry, viewed the unfolding events. Henry Watterson's prediction, voiced in his "Shadow" column of May 24, 1864, in the *Mobile Advertiser and Register,* gives this book its title. Georgia papers in late summer 1864 show how Hood kept up his army's strength after the three bloody battles of July 20–28. I emphasize them in Part Two in large part because they have heretofore not been heeded by previous writers on the campaign. In the main, I have used the microfilm holdings of Emory University and the University of Georgia to get at these newspaper files.

The recent biographers of Generals Sherman, Johnston, and Hood—John Marszalek, Craig Symonds, and Richard McMurry—contribute to the literature through diligent plumbing of original sources and acute analysis. I wish to emphasize an important conclusion in McMurry's *John Bell Hood and the War for Southern Independence* (Lexington: University Press of Kentucky, 1982), McMurry's implied admission that he has found no evidence of General Hood's use of opiate derivatives for his long-assumed post-amputative pain. This stupid, baseless derogation has dogged Hood for too long; I bury it in my essay, "John Bell Hood's 'Addictions' in Civil War Literature," *Blue & Gray* 16, no. 1 (October 1998): 28–31.

I am obliged to the major studies of the Atlanta Campaign that precede mine: Albert Castel's *Decision in the West: The Atlanta Campaign of 1864* (Lawrence: University Press of Kansas, 1992) is now the sine qua non of our topic. Richard McMurry's recent *Atlanta 1864: Last Chance for the Confederacy* (Lincoln: University of Nebraska Press, 2000) offers benefits that my own slight book will not afford. Lee Kennett's *Marching Through Georgia: The Story of Soldiers and Civilians During Sherman's Campaign* (New York: HarperCollins, 1995) has not been accorded its due for the depth of the author's research and facile writing. A few older studies also bear mention. Overlooked because of its unfortunate withdrawal from sales is James Lee McDonough and James Pickett Jones, *War So Terrible: Sherman and Atlanta* (New York: W. W. Norton, 1987). Thomas Lawrence Connelly's *Autumn of Glory: The Army of Tennessee, 1862–1865* (Baton Rouge: Louisiana State University Press, 1971) still offers keen insights.

Finally, a bit of digression. Though they are uncited in my text, and possibly transcended by more modern scholarship, I observe the value of my college mentor's famous works, *The Life of Johnny Reb* and *The Life of Billy Yank* (Indianapolis: Bobbs-Merrill, 1943 and 1951, respectively) as a way of paying tribute to my memory of Bell Irvin Wiley—a great friend and professor, in the finest sense of both.

INDEX

Page numbers followed by *f* indicate illustrations.

Hooker, Joseph: at Cassville, 56–57; at Chancellorsville, 139–40; at Chattahoochee, 102; at Dallas-New Hope, 61, 63; at Gilgal Church, 78–79; at Kennesaw Mountain, 82; at Resaca, 49; and retreat from Resaca, 53; at Rocky Face Ridge, 41, 44; at Sharpsburg, 128

Horn, Stanley, 138

Howard, O. O.: assault on Macon railway, 175, 176, 183, 184–85; at Cassville, 56–57; at Chancellorsville, 145; at Chattahoochee, 98; at Dallas-New Hope, 63–64; at Ezra Church, 151, 153, 154; at Resaca, 49; at Rocky Face Ridge, 44; and siege of Atlanta, 149

Hubner, Charles W., 117

Intelligence, Confederate: and assault on Macon railway, 176–77, 179; at Bald Hill, 140, 141; and cavalry raids, 76; at Chancellorsville, 140, 141; at Chattahoochee, 101; at Dallas-New Hope, 63, 64; at Kennesaw Mountain, 82, 92; at Lost and Pine Mountains, 75; prior to Atlanta campaign, 26, 30, 31, 33; in retreat to Chattahoochee River, 93; at Rocky Face Ridge, 36–37, 42; in siege of Atlanta, 169, 175–76; at Utoy Creek, 157

Intelligence, Union, 78; at Chattahoochee, 84, 98; and Confederate raids, 77; at Dallas-New Hope, 61, 63, 64; at Kennesaw Mountain, 82; prior to Atlanta campaign, 23; at Rocky Face Ridge, 40; in siege of Atlanta, 134, 148–49, 158, 159, 160, 166

Intelligencer, 68–69, 84, 97, 100, 106, 107

Jackman, John, 66

Jackson (Mississippi), siege of, 4–7

Jackson, Thomas J. (Stonewall), 9; at Chancellorsville, 140, 141–42, 143, 145–46; as Hood mentor, 127–28

Jackson, William H. (Red), 58; and assault on Macon railway, 179, 181, 183; cavalry raids, 76; at Dallas-New Hope, 61; and defense of Atlanta, 153; at Gilgal Church, 79

Johnson, Herschel V., 127

Johnson, Richard, 157

Johnston, Albert Sidney, 16

Johnston, Joseph E.: at Allatoona Pass, 60, 61, 65, 70; Benjamin on, 110; and Bragg, 71, 73–75, 81, 88, 112; career, 7–18; and cavalry support, 66–67, 76–77, 85, 88–89, 91–92, 99, 100, 102, 103; character and outlook, 8–9, 24–25, 71, 72, 76, 85; at Chattahoochee, 98, 99; and command of Army of the Tennessee, 17–18, 103–5, 107–8, 110–12; at Dallas-New Hope, 61, 64, 66; and Davis (Jefferson), 9–10, 15, 16, 17, 28–29, 33, 52, 58, 60, 75, 99, 103–4, 114–15; defense of Atlanta, 32–34, 102, 103, 108, 114, 133; defense of Richmond, 11–15; and Department of the West, 16, 17; engagements *vs.* Sherman, 4–7; and evacuation of Atlanta, 97–98; evaluation of, 83, 197–99, 200; at Gilgal Church, 79; at Harper's Ferry, 8; Hood on, 83; at Kennesaw Mountain, 84, 88, 89–91; at Lost and Pine Mountains, 73–75, 76; at Manassas, 8; and morale, 25–26; in Northern Virginia, 9–10; officers' opinions of, 105; passivity of, 60; Peninsula campaign, 10–15; preparations for defense of Atlanta, 24–27; public opinion of, 84–85, 100, 106–7; relief from command, 116–17, 199; at Resaca, 46, 47, 49, 50, 51;

About the Author

Stephen Davis of Atlanta has been a Civil War enthusiast since the fourth grade. At Emory University, he studied under Bell Wiley, going on to earn his Master's from Chapel Hill and doctorate from Emory. Longtime Book Review Editor for *Blue & Gray* magazine, he has also published on a wide range of war topics in buffs' and scholarly publications. At his day job he is Medical Relations Manager for MAG Mutual Insurance Company.

ISBN 0-8420-2787-4

9 780842 027878

90000 >